THE NATIONS AT WAR

THE WORLD'S GREATEST SEA FIGHT

The naval battle off Jutland on the afternoon of May 31, 1916.   Though the losses were heavy on both sides the British control of the sea was not broken

THE NATIONS AT WAR

BY
WILLIS J. ABBOT

AUTHOR OF
"PANAMA AND THE CANAL," "THE STORY OF
OUR NAVY," "THE STORY OF OUR ARMY"

WITH NUMEROUS ILLUSTRATIONS FROM DRAWINGS
BY THE FOREMOST WAR ARTISTS AND PHOTOGRAPHS
TAKEN IN THE FIELD BY EXPERTS OF EVERY NATION

THE 1917 EDITION

LESLIE-JUDGE CO.
PUBLISHERS   NEW YORK

Copyright, 1917,
DOUBLEDAY, PAGE & COMPANY

—

All Rights Reserved

INTRODUCTION

FOR YEARS wise men had said that there could be no general European war. Despite the menace of rival armaments they thought that the financial ties which bound all nations together were stronger than the political differences which tended to bring them into conflict. The tremendous power of international capital and credit exerted in every land and operating as a unit would certainly check any wasteful war. The bankers controlling the money and credit of the world would suppress the war-like ambitions of the crowned heads by locking up their strong-boxes.

So the wise men thought. But the event showed the bankers bowing low to the will of Kaiser, King, Emperor, and President. Not only did they lend more than twenty billions to the belligerents in the first two years of the war, but stood ready to lend more and more—for a price.

The world thought public opinion would check the war at the outset. Nobody wanted war—except those in high place who alone had the power to make or to avert it. But before public opinion could be expressed the invading columns were on the march, the guns were thundering and the heavy hand of military authority stilled any sound of public protest.

Men thought there would be no war because International Socialism would reduce the belligerent governments to impotence. For years the world had been told that the cause of labor was international, that the workingman's struggle against capitalism was the same in France as in Germany, in Italy as in Austria. With this greater warfare in progress, involving the well-being of the workingmen of all the world, no working man would be deluded into taking up arms against his fellows who happened to speak a different tongue or render fealty to a foreign state.

But at the test the internationalism of labor vanished as had the internationalism of capital.

A long war was impossible, we were told, because the greater destructiveness of modern weapons would make it impossible for human beings to sustain the shock of conflict. Every inventor of a new and peculiarly effective device for wholesale murder, for long time past, had been assuring the world that his first thought in inventing it had been to make war so horrible, so ruinous, that it would be abandoned in horror.

War, thereupon, responded to this theory by stimulating the invention of, and eagerly using asphyxiating gas, liquid fire, lachrymal bombs, armored tractors that crushed the wounded in their path while mowing down platoons of men with their perfectly protected machine guns. Aircraft were perfected—mainly that they might rain bombs upon inoffensive civilians;

INTRODUCTION

hospitals and schools being favorite targets. The submarine was developed to a point that outdid the imagination of Jules Verne and was employed largely to sink helpless merchantmen, often with utter disregard for the lives of their passengers whether belligerent or neutral.

One by one the forces which the world had relied upon to avert the calamity of a general war were swept away. The ties of finance, of commerce, of mutual interest, of common humanity, even of a common religion were broken. One War Lord, most vociferous of all in the claim that God was especially enlisted under his eagles, did not scruple to ally his Christian nation with the Turk, and exerted every influence to stir up all Islam to waging a Holy War on the Christian peoples of the world.

The lessons of this war should be political, not military. The world should learn not how to make perfect the art of devastating countries and slaughtering enemies but how to prevent the need, or the excuse for either.

Decades will be required even to partially obliterate the scars of conflict from ravaged Belgium, France, and Poland. Centuries will not lift from the shoulders of the people the burden of taxation this frenzied outbreak has laid upon them. But the scars might be made honorable memorials of a march upward to a higher international ideal, the debt be gloried in as a burden incurred in a struggle for the ultimate good of the human race, if out of this war could come an effective movement to end all future wars.

Only by a league of all civilized nations can such an end be attained. Without the participation of the United States such an association would be incomplete and impotent. But, it is urged, the entrance of the United States upon such an alliance would be to abandon the historic policy of the nation, thus first enunciated by George Washington: "It is our policy to steer clear of permanent alliances with any portion of the foreign world."

But the world has changed since Washington's day. The old isolation of the United States is ended. Oceans have become highways instead of barriers. The interests of all nations are inextricably interwoven. While a few of our people have profited by supplying food and munitions to the allies, the great mass has suffered by the enormous increase in the cost of living due to the war. Our interest in a long and enduring peace to come is a very real and positive one.

In the remaining months of the war—and may they be few!—the thoughts of the American people should be concentrated upon the best method of preventing any recurrence in future time of so calamitous a conflict. They must grapple with new conditions in a new way. If concerted and permanent action on the part of all, or a considerable group of nations, promises such a result America must not, by too great loyalty to an outworn creed, be lacking to it. Of all nations of the world we are not the one to "attempt the future's portal with the past's blood rusted key."

WILLIS J. ABBOT.

New York, Oct., 1916.

THE NATIONS AT WAR

THE NATIONS AT WAR

CHAPTER I

ASSASSINATION OF ARCHDUKE FERDINAND—DIPLOMACY PRECEDING
THE WAR—POSITION AND RELATIVE STRENGTH OF THE POWERS

IN JULY, 1914, the turbulent waters of the English Channel presented a most impressive spectacle. All the way from the Needles to the Hook of Holland the estuary was crowded with ships of war all flying the white ensign of Great Britain. At one point a line of destroyers was drawn up, at a distance of perhaps a hundred yards apart, extending across the straits from England to France. Their noses facing the rushing tide, their screws were kept turning just sufficiently to maintain their position unchanged. A monster surveyor's tape, if drawn across the tossing waters, would have touched the stem of each ship, so accurately were they aligned. Squadrons of super-dreadnoughts, fleets of battle cruisers, covies of submarines dashing about with decks awash were to be seen on every side from the deck of the Holland-American liner on which was the writer bound to Rotterdam. The holiday crowd that thronged the decks of that liner looked on the thrilling exhibition of Great Britain's sea power as a mere playtime pageant. They were told that it was the season of the King's birthday and that Winston Churchill, First Lord of the Admiralty, had ordered the mobilization of the home fleet to lend éclat to the celebration. Content with that the voyagers, most of whom were Americans little used to wars and rumors of wars, went about their pleasure trips little dreaming that they were steaming into the vortex of the bloodiest war the world had ever known.

For as a matter of fact the review of the British fleet was far from being a mere festivity. It was one card in a desperate diplomatic game which all Europe had been playing for nearly a month. It was intended to recall vividly to the minds of foreign chancelleries the overpowering measure of Great Britain's supremacy upon the sea, and to impress them with the mighty force that would be unloosed should they rush into war heedless of Britain's attitude. But the warning unhappily was without effect.

War was in the air. Ever since the Archduke Francis Ferdinand, heir to the Imperial Crown of Austria-Hungary had been shot dead on the 28th of the preceding June at Sarajevo, Bosnia, hell-broth had been brewing in the cauldron of the Balkans. The assassination, Austria-Hungary's offended sovereignty, were but pretexts for the war which the ruling powers of Germany were determined to force.

Briefly summarized these rival ambitions were as follows:

3

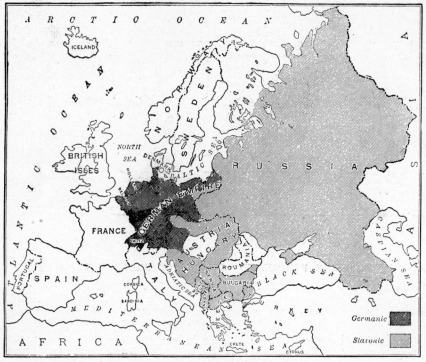

The Germans and Slavs whose racial antipathies and conflicting territorial and commercial ambitions were largely responsible for the war. It will be noticed that the Slavic peoples far overlap the political boundaries even in Eastern Germany

The Archduke Francis Ferdinand, heir apparent to the throne of Austria-Hungary, whose murder was the starting-point of the war

Under the masterful rule of William II the governing class in Germany had come to aspire to dominance over all of central Europe. They aimed at an extension of the German Empire proper to the English Channel, absorbing by steps more or less gradual Belgium, Holland, and Denmark. With this outlet to the sea they determined to challenge Great Britain's maritime supremacy both by the creation of a naval fleet that would equal that of the British and by building up a merchant marine that might challenge the primacy of British merchant shipping. To the southward, utilizing the close alliance of the houses of Hohenzollern and the Austrian ruling house of Hapsburg, they planned to extend German influence to the Mediterranean by the gradual absorption of the western Balkan states and Turkey. This plan of empire contemplated immediately this extension of the empire of Austria-Hungary and its domination by the methods of German diplomacy. But that the far-seeing eye and active imagination of William II unquestionably looked forward to the time when the diminishing house of Hapsburg should finally disappear, and the southern half of this Teutonic alliance should become wholly German, indeed Prussian, in its government, is undoubted.

Naturally this plan of expansion, worthy of Frederick the Great or of Napoleon, instantly aroused the suspicion and antagonism of Great Britain, Russia, and France. For years, therefore, indeed ever since the end of the Franco-Prussian war of 1870-1, these powers had been opposing the Germanic pretensions by every device of diplomacy, and had steadily prepared themselves for this conflict by building up those prodigious armaments afloat and ashore which had made Europe an armed camp.

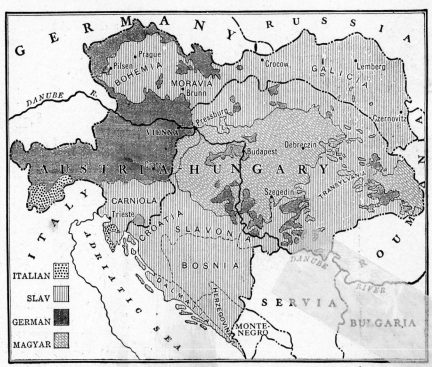

The intricate racial distribution in the Austro-Hungarian monarchy

England, which was in fact last to enter upon this conflict, was the one most gravely menaced by the German program. For that empire with its nucleus and governing centre in the British Isles is scattered over the four quarters of the globe. It is dependent for its coherence, even for its very life, upon its absolute control of the sea. The people of England and Scotland in time of actual war could live scarcely a week upon the food supplies in their possession should the carriage of foodstuffs from other lands to their shores be interrupted by a hostile fleet superior to their own. Moreover, their rule in India and in Australasia would be seriously menaced by the presence at the eastern end of the Mediterranean of so militant a power as Germany. The growing evidence of the character of the German menace had been apparent to Great Britain for two decades or more. The actual, overt act which compelled the British entrance upon the war was, however, the advance of the Germans through Belgium to a threatening position on the coast.

France, which at the date of this writing has suffered more than any nation involved in the war, save little Belgium, had less interest in the conflict than any of the Allies. True, any growth in power of her implacable enemy was a menace. But her sentimental desire, cherished ever since 1871, for the recovery of her lost provinces of Alsace-Lorraine was obviously dying out. Mainly loyalty to her alliance with Russia, coupled with a dread of the further enhancement of German power on the Continent, drew her into the struggle in which of all the allied nations she won the brightest laurels.

More than any other the Russians' ambitions clashed with the German and Austrian advance to the south. With her northern ports on the Baltic and Arctic Ocean locked by ice for a large portion of the year and her southern borders opening only on the Black

Emperor Francis Joseph, whose long rule over the dual monarchy was a welcome one to his people

Belgium's most flourishing business. There is a world of pathos in the sign, "Mourning Complete in 12 Hours."

Sea blocked by Turkish cannon at the Dardanelles, this mighty empire has for centuries been striving to secure an outlet to navigable waters open the year around. It sought this path to the Mediterranean by way of the Balkan states. The Slavs of Servia, Bosnia, Roumania, Bulgaria, were kin by blood and allied by customs to the Russian people. Russian ascendancy in their politics gave assurance of their ultimate complete domination by some future Czar. Could they jointly throw off the Turkish yoke and expel the Turks from Europe the Russian way to the Mediterranean would be clear. In 1912 this ambition bade fair to be gratified. For the Balkan states declared war upon Turkey and won a swift victory, carrying their armies to the very doors of Constantinople. At this juncture the Germanic powers intervened. The Turkish armies had been trained and officered by Germans. English influence at Constantinople, which had been dominant for a century, had been shattered by the diplomats of the Kaiser. At the critical moment Austria backed by German power intervened, robbing the Balkan states of the fruits of their victory, and particularly denying to Servia the right of access to the Adriatic Sea. To block this route the Teutonic powers insisted on the creation of the state of Albania under a German prince. Thereupon the Balkan states fell to fighting among themselves, and the greater states of Europe, foreseeing that out of this situation would grow a general war, began their preparations for it.

It is significant that immediately after her interference in the Balkans Germany passed a new army law so increasing her military establishment as to give it a preponderance of 30 per

French troops respond to cheering crowds. In every village the crowds gathered around the railway station to cheer and applaud the men who were on their way to die for "La Belle France"

cent. over the trained forces in France. France with a far smaller population and all available men already under arms met this by increasing her term of military service from two years to three. Great Britain continued to place her reliance solely on her fleet, neglecting any development of her army, a course which she had bitter cause to regret in the early years of the great war.

It was therefore the resentment of Servia at having been balked of the fruit of its victories in the Balkan war that caused the assassination which brought on the later general conflict. A large part of the subjects of the empire of Austria-Hungary, those in the southern half bordering on Servia, are themselves Slavs eager to throw off the Hapsburg yoke and sympathetic with the aspirations of their Servian neighbors. The house of Hapsburg had become concentrated in the persons of the Emperor Francis Joseph, already approaching the senility of advanced years, and his heir the Archduke Ferdinand. All Europe had long believed that the death of the old Emperor would be the signal for a general war. The Servian plotters conceived the idea that if the only apparent successor to the Emperor were killed this war would be assured, and out of the general breakup of states they might pluck their own independence, unite with the Slavs of Hungary, and regain their outlet to the Adriatic. Out of this hope sprang the assassination of the Archduke.

Austria incensed at the murder of its heir apparent made demands upon Servia for redress. For a month these demands were pressed greatly to the disquiet of the chancelleries of all Europe, but not so openly, nor yet so strenuously, as to cause public apprehension of a menace to the general peace of Europe. It has been shown since

Better than being captured. About 20,000 Belgian soldiers got across the border into Holland when Antwerp was evacuated, and were there disarmed by the Dutch army and placed in camps

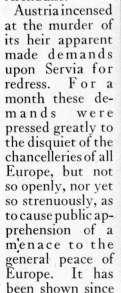

English infantry. The enthusiasm that is transformed into grim determination under fire

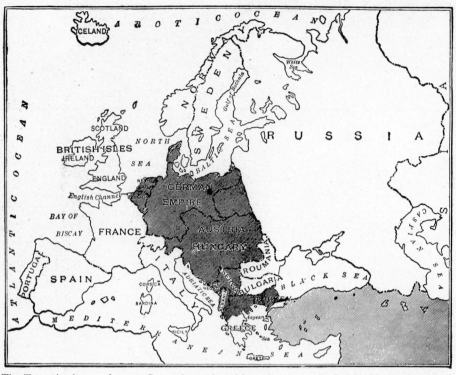

The Teutonic dream of a pan-Germanic empire with outlets upon the Baltic, North, and Mediterranean seas

ponse to this demand, and although the Servian government conceded nine-tenths of the points at issue, Austria, backed by Germany, swept aside all the efforts of the other powers of Europe to intervene in behalf of peace and declared war upon Servia on the 27th of July. Russia thereupon, having already declared that it would not permit war to be made upon Servia on "a mere pretext," declared war upon Austria.

Thereafter every effort to stay the spread of the conflagration was in vain. At every point German influence blocked negotiations for peace. Austria, indeed when she found that Russia could not be kept out of the con-

that the thirty days occupied in secret and underground diplomacy was also utilized by the two Teutonic powers to make hurried preparations for the war which they unquestionably intended to force. On the 28th of June the assassination was committed. On the 23d of July the government at Vienna sent to the government at Belgrade an ultimatum of a sort hitherto unknown to civilized diplomacy. It practically demanded the surrender of Servian sovereignty and the installation of Austrian magistrates in Servian courts to try and condemn Servian subjects and officers at the pleasure of the Austrian government. Forty-eight hours only was allowed for a res-

British reservists arriving at the equipment station to secure their uniforms and arms

flict, expressed herself as willing to take up negotiations with Petrograd although the guns were already roaring along the Servian border. But this chance of peace was blocked by Germany, which presented on the very next day an ultimatum to Russia and to France. Sir Edward Grey, the English Foreign Secretary, tried until the last moment to secure an international conference for the maintenance of peace, but was blocked by the entrance of the German forces into the Duchy of Luxemburg, the neutrality of which had been guaranteed by all the powers of Europe, including Germany herself. After this it was a matter of hours only before all Europe was at war.

Russia's conflicting dream of empire, including the Slav and Scandinavian peoples

England, last of the embattled powers to go into the fight, might possibly have been held neutral save for the German invasion of Belgium. That state, together with the Netherlands to the north of it, had been created and maintained as "buffer" states by a general agreement of European powers. Its neutrality was guaranteed. So far as solemn engagements on the part of sovereign powers could secure it Belgium was to be held free from all danger of invasion, to be kept sheltered from the shock of war. To this agreement Prussia, prior to the formation of the German empire, had been a party, and as the ruling member of that group of states was still bound by it. None

German officers lunching on the spoils of Liége

Czar Nicholas and King George V., royal cousins with a long-standing colonial rivalry and divergent political beliefs, drawn together in an unexpected alliance

Motor trucks proved invaluable in drawing heavy siege guns and supplies more rapidly than it would have been possible with horses

the less the advantage of rushing upon France through an almost powerless state and attacking the greater nation on a frontier that had been left unfortified was too much for the German sense of honor. That part of the French frontier which faced Germany was a line of powerful fortresses. Verdun, Toul, Epinal, and Belfort reared sinister fronts in the face of a German invader. We know now that the superiority of the German artillery at the opening of the war would have enabled them at that time to demolish these fortresses

A British ammunition train halted on the road for lunch

The celebration in Berlin when captured Russian, Belgian, and French guns were brou

hrough the Brandenburg Gate down Unter Den Linden to the Imperial Residence

William II of Germany, who forged that nation's magnificent fighting machine and directed the campaign which astonished the world by its power and swift movement

as easily as they did those at Liége and at Namur. But at the moment the Germans, with cynical indifference to their treaty obligations, chose what they thought was the easier way. It proved in the end to be the harder way. For except for the invasion of Belgium it is possible, even probable, that England might not have entered the war. "You surely would not fight for a mere scrap of paper?" said the German Ambassador to Sir Edward Grey, but England did fight and for that concrete reason, though it

Roads in Belgium filled with homeless wanderers

Going to war in motor busses. When the order for mobilization was issued the French government seized all the automobiles, horses and motor busses it could lay its hands on, to assist in the transport of troops

Cossacks, respected and feared in the eastern theatre of war as the Uhlans are in the western field

is entirely probable that more selfish considerations, having to do with German ambitions for high standing on the sea and for a foothold on the North Sea and Mediterranean shores were also influential factors in forming the British conclusions.

So in a few days Austria had declared war upon Servia, Russia upon Austria, Germany upon Russia and France, France upon Germany and Austria, and England upon the two Teutonic powers. The whole structure of European government went down like a row of card houses and into the general turmoil far-off Japan, England's ally in Asiatic waters, cast her defiance of German power, and the guns were roaring on the borders of the German colony of Kiaochau, almost as soon as they were on the borders of Belgium.

Almost had the German Emperor paralleled in this twentieth century the situation created nearly two hundred years earlier by his famous progenitor Frederick

The French aeroplane in its automobile conveyance. Of all the warring nations, France was best supplied with aërial craft

British field artillery, brought to a high point of efficiency through lessons learned in the South African War

the Great and described by Macaulay in this famous passage:

"On the head of Frederic is all the blood which was shed in a war raged during many years and in every quarter of the globe—the blood of the column of Fontenoy, the blood of the mountaineers who were slaught-ered at Culloden. The evils produced by his wickedness were felt in lands where the name of Prussia was unknown; and, in order that he might rob a neighbor whom he had promised to defend, black men fought on the coast of Coromandel, and red men scalped each other by the Great Lakes of North America."

French troops before Altkirch. The French invasion of German territory at the opening of the war was not successful, but it roused great enthusiasm in France. Altkirch, in Alsace, was one of the first towns taken

Boy scouts at work. The French Boy Scouts were useful in a thousand ways in the early days of the war

It is significant of the deference which belligerent governments pay to the wide-spread sentiment for peace, and particularly to public opinion in neutral lands, that for months after the outbreak of the war each country engaged in it was eagerly protesting that the conflict had been forced upon it and that it could not be charged with being the aggressor. The presses of all Europe were busied with putting out "White Books," "Red Books," "Orange Books," and other diplomatic documents named by the public in accordance with the colors of their covers and each intended to demonstrate the innocence of the nation issuing it. Germany, upon which neutral condemnation rested most heavily, because the marvelous swiftness with which it struck suggested perfect preparation and early determination for war, was particularly insistent that the war had been forced upon it and was fought in self-defense only. But this position the German diplomats were never able to establish to the satisfaction of neutral public opinion. Later developments, however, made it appear that Germany had not expected up to the very last moment that England would fight. In the last inter-

Belgian cavalry bringing straw to sleep on in the trenches

view between the German Ambassador and Sir Edward Grey, the British Minister of Foreign Affairs, the former was told that if Belgian territory was violated England MIGHT enter the war. It seems possible that had the British statesman stated bluntly that in such event England WOULD enter the war Germany might have receded from her truculent position and the frightful conflict would have been averted. For the final declaration of war was received by the German government with every indication that it was wholly unexpected.

It seemed at the outset that the odds were overwhelmingly against the Teutonic allies. The mere statement of the problem looks wholly one-sided. Against Germany and Austria-Hungary, at the outset, were arrayed Russia, France, Great Britain, Belgium, Japan, and Servia. Against a population of 114,900,000 were arrayed nations numbering 322,500,000. In the estimate of the latter are not included the teeming millions of British India though they furnished the allied forces with tens of thousands of gallant soldiers.

Against the German and Austrian navy was pitted the British navy, vastly superior to both combined, as well as the

England collects horses. The great necessity for horses for the British Army resulted in the war department taking them wherever found. They were, of course, paid for, but the owners had no option about selling

Belgian infantry defending a village near Liége

British lines swept by searchlights and shrapnel. In the fighting in the Arras region, during the last days of August, the British lines were under almost continuous fire day and night

The little soldier at salute

The hour of farewell.   British soldier saying good-bye to his wife and child

floating forces of Russia, France, and Japan, which combined might be fairly held superior to those of Germany.

In military force the disparity between the two groups of belligerents was at the outset less apparent. Germany was admittedly the foremost military nation of the world. Her equipment for war was unequalled by any nation or group of nations. Every endeavor of an inventive and an efficient people had been bent to the task of making the German army the most magnificent fighting machine known to history. In the newer devices of Zeppelins, aeroplanes, military motors, new and prodigious types of field artillery, the German superiority was incalculable.

In the mere number of soldiers trained to arms the two belligerent bodies were nearly matched. The comparative figures as they stood at the opening of the war may be put in round numbers as follows:

King George inspecting a portion of the British expeditionary force

The battle of Tirlemont.   This drawing was developed from a sketch made on the spot.   It shows the Belgians defending trenches hastily thrown up in the harvest fields

THE TEUTONIC ALLIES

Germany, Standing Army	. . .	800,000
War Footing	. . .	4,000,000
Austria-Hungary, Standing Army		472,000
War footing	.	1,360,000
Maximum war strength		4,320,000

ENTENTE ALLIES

Great Britain, Standing Army	.	125,000
First Reserve	:	206,000
Second Reserve	.	463,000
Total trained men	. .	794,000
France, Standing Army	. . .	750,000
First Reserve	. .	700,000
Second Reserve	. . .	700,000
Total trained men	. .	2,150,000
Russia, Standing Army	. . .	1,073,000
First Reserve	. . .	1,838,500
Second Reserve	. .	2,488,500
Total trained men	. .	5,400,000

To the allied force should be added the Servian army which on a peace footing numbered 160,000, and on a war footing 380,000. As a result of the almost constant war in the Balkans these troops were practically all veterans. With them, too, are to be counted the Belgian army with a peace strength of about 50,000 men and a war strength of 340,000. The Belgian troops were well armed, but by their heroic effort to stop the invasion of their neutral country they sacrificed at the very outset practically the whole of their army on a peace footing to the overwhelming strength of the German invaders. Furthermore, the swiftness with which the Germans overran and subdued the greater part of Belgian territory made it impossible to call to the colors all of the men constituting the army on a war footing.

As the war progressed, and as the result of diplomatic plots and counter plots, Turkey and Bulgaria, both nations of notable military strength with armies well trained

A pontoon bridge destroyed by British shell fire while German Uhlans were crossing

under German officers and made up of natural fighters of notorious ferocity, cast their lot with the Teutonic allies, while Italy, Roumania and Portugal joined forces with the *entente allies*, as the British, French, and Russian forces were termed. In the case of Portugal the declaration of war upon Germany was purely formal as her forces took no part in the struggle until late in the war.

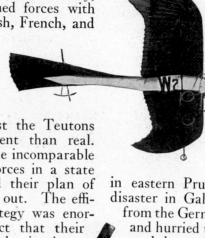

The apparent odds against the Teutons were, however, more apparent than real. They had at the beginning the incomparable advantage of having their forces in a state of complete preparation and their plan of campaign thoroughly worked out. The efficiency of their military strategy was enormously increased by the fact that their armies were under a single dominating mind, for leadership was early conceded by the Austrians to the German military authority. It may be noted here that during the first two years of the war whenever the Austrians alone were left to combat the Russian advance they were beaten. It was only when German troops were hastily withdrawn from the western theatre of war and sent to the Austrian aid that the progress of Russia was blocked. This German domination of all the Teutonic forces was obviously an advantage when contrasted with the almost complete independence of the Russian military authority from any domination by, or even association with, the British and French allies.

Geographical conditions were even more advantageous for the Teutons. Their territory was contiguous, compact. Where it took weeks for the British and French to get into actual physical contact with their allies the Russians, the Germans and Austrians were in actual contact at

Firing from the shoulder. Although the Lewis gun weighs over 26 pounds a strong man can use it like an ordinary rifle

all times. If the allied line was menaced in Flanders it was a matter of utter impossibility to bring to its assistance any reënforcement from the enormous armies of Russia. Indeed it was not until near the end of the second year of the war that Russian troops figured at all in the struggle in western Europe.

But if the Germans were menaced by Russian troops in eastern Prussia or the Austrians facing disaster in Galicia, troops could be drawn from the German lines in Belgium or France and hurried to the point of peril by a day's travel along railroads wholly within protected German territory. The situation was not unlike that presented in our own Civil War, during its earlier years, when the Confederates could easily rush troops from Virginia to Tennessee or back again as need arose without any possible interference on the part of the Union generals. This advantage of a shorter line and interior communications is recognized by strategists as of the highest value to the belligerent enjoying it.

In any consideration of the comparative strength of the rival belligerent forces the fact of Great Britain's enormous reserve force must be considered. At the outset England had to oppose to the resistless force of the German armies a scant 125,000 regular troops, and the record of that gallant handful doomed to early extinction is glorious enough to make a story of its own. But by the end of the second year of the war England had put into the field more than 4,500,000 men, though the greater part of these had then just become available for service. Delay in enlistment, the time necessary to turn raw recruits into skilled soldiers, the herculean task of gathering the units of its force from Canada, New Zealand, Australia, and India, and above all the difficulty of securing arms and munitions, which British factories were utterly inadequate to supply, made the British entry upon actual land hostilities seem to be both grudging and dilatory. It was the failure, as we shall see, of the Germans to press their first drive into France to the point of actual victory, before the prodigious latent strength of Great Britain could be

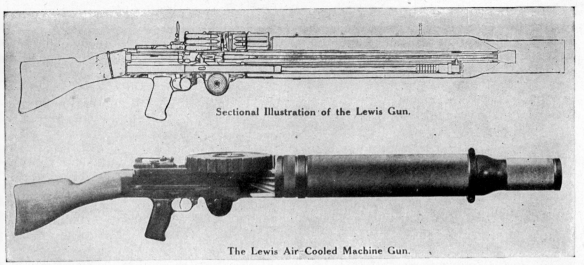

Sectional Illustration of the Lewis Gun.

The Lewis Air-Cooled Machine Gun.

The "Belgian rattlesnake." This name was given the Lewis gun because of its spiteful whir when firing at high speed

brought into action, that determined the final outcome of the war.

The difficulty which the British found in raising and equipping an army adequate to meet the situation forced upon them should be most instructive to the people of the United States. Like our own government, Great Britain is a democracy. It has the forms of monarchy but is in some respects even more democratic than the United States. The ultimate consent of the people is necessary to any such military establishment as the crisis of 1914 demanded. For centuries the English people had relied upon their navy as a complete defence against any menace from without. This, too, has been the attitude of the people of the United States who are accustomed to regard the broad oceans that separate us from any possible enemy as obstacles to possible invasion. As a matter of fact to-day the ocean is a highway across which troops can be more readily transported than they could across one-fifth the distance ashore.

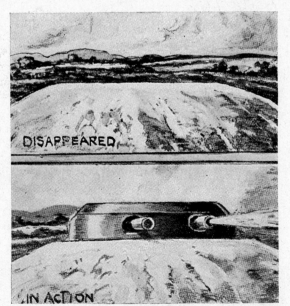

The forts at Liége. The fortifications at Liége were planned by the Belgian engineer General Brialmont. One of their most effective features was the disappearing turrets, in which the guns were mounted

Like the people of the United States the British people have always been jealous of a great standing army. The troops they had at the outbreak of the storm in 1914 were only enough to man the military posts in their widely scattered colonial dependencies. They were good troops, none better. In the first six months of the war practically every man of them was killed or otherwise put out of action. When the French sprang nobly to arms, a united nation in the field, Great Britain could send as its share of the line which blocked the German advance only 125,000 men. The first and most serious task which confronted the government was to add to this little fighting force an army which should rank with the 3,500,000 of France and the more than 4,000,000 of Germany.

To accomplish this task Lord Kitchener, the victor of Khartoum, was summoned from retirement to become Minister of War. It took eight months for him to raise and equip the first 750,000 men which the English called Kitchener's army, and the Germans, "Kitchener's mob." In a way it was a mob, for its component parts were drawn from all the widely scattered outposts of British power. Canada in particular was magnificent in its contribu-

African colonies were all represented in this first army of volunteers.

But even that army was inadequate to the need of the nation. As the other nations had given all their citizens to the defence of the common cause it was asked why Great Britain gave only the few who were willing to volunteer. A cry for conscription and universal service was raised. It was opposed, honestly enough, by labor unions who in every country complain that it is the workingman who fights and the capitalist who reaps all the profit. It also incurred the hostility of those who dreaded lest with the abandonment of the long-time volunteer system England should fall a prey to the militarism which had proved such a burden to continental Europe. Lord Derby made a magnificent attempt by systematic recruiting endeavors to meet the needs of the situation, but finally theory had to give way

The German army in Belgium. The armed hosts of the Kaiser poured into Belgium during the harvest, when the wheat had been cut but was still in the fields

tions of men for the defence of the empire, and among the troops it sent was an "American Legion" composed of citizens of the United States who had enlisted, of course, without the knowledge or consent of their own government. Australia and New Zealand, the multitudinous tribes of India, residents of the British

to the desperate menace of the situation and a qualified system of conscription was put into effect. By this method the British were able to put into the field, by the middle of 1916, an army that totaled about 4,000,000.

To arm and equip this force was more than the manufacturing facilities of Great

Britain were equal to. Like France and Russia the British found it necessary to buy huge quantities of arms and munitions in the United States. Their orders were gladly accepted and filled. But the fact that the British controlled the sea made it impossible for the Teutonic allies to get like assistance on this side of the water. German orders would have been as gladly filled, but no cargo of munitions for the German army could ever have succeeded in reaching a German port. Out of this situation grew a natural but unjust resentment on the part of the German people against the United States.

But if the British were slow in getting into action by land, their fleet from the first day of the war exerted a controlling force on its destinies. It was 100 per cent. efficient in preventing Germany from drawing at all upon the United States for munitions of war. Unhappily its success in maintaining a lawful blockade and preventing contraband of war from reaching German ports led the British to go far beyond any regulation of international trade hitherto justified by international law. The legitimate business of American citizens was wantonly interfered with, the foreign mails of this country delayed and rifled, and our ships held up sometimes for weeks. The resentment of Germany against America for supplying her enemies with arms came in time to be almost paralleled by the indignation which

Panic stricken mobs escaping from Antwerp. The congestion was terrific around the end of the bridge that furnished the only means of escape from the beleaguered Antwerp

the United States felt because of the aggressions of the British.

This, however, has nothing to do with the record of the efficiency of the British fleet as compared with the early inefficiency of the British army. In later chapters will be told the story of the naval operations of the war.

SARAJEVO, WHERE THE ARCHDUKE FRANCIS FERDINAND WAS ASSASSINATED

Emperor Francis Joseph and the Archduke Francis Ferdinand, whose assassination in Sarajevo lighted the great European conflagration

Enough here to say that at the very outset German commerce was swept from the seas, the German fleet bottled up in Kiel, whence it could make only sporadic raids without material bearing on the fortunes of the war, and a blockade established that deprived the Teutonic allies of any supplies of munitions of war from neutral countries and speedily made the question of food supplies for their people one of the greatest gravity.

The Imperial Guard passing in review before Emperor William.   At the left of the Kaiser is General Lowenfeldt and at the extreme right General von Buelow.   The latter was the first general to fall

Defending the Belgian swamps. Every ditch and canal was used as a line of desperate resistance

CHRONOLOGY OF THE DIPLOMACY THAT LED TO WAR—1914

e 28. Assassination of the Archduke Francis Ferdinand, eir to the throne of Austria.

y 23. Austria's ultimatum to Servia.

y 24. Russia asks Austria for delay. Austria refuses.

y 25. Servia concedes all Austrian demands, save that ustrian officials shall be allowed to participate in the nquiry by Servians into the assassination.

y 27. Russia notifies Austria that it will not permit in-asion of Servian territory—Semiofficially Germany inti-ates that no one shall interfere in the controversy between ustria and Servia—Sir Edward Grey proposes mediation etween the two countries embroiled by a conference of mbassadors in London—France and Italy accept; Ger-nany and Austria decline.

y 28. Austria announces a state of war with Servia.

y 29. Russia calls all reservists to the colors. Germany nsists that Austria-Hungary shall negotiate further with Russia. Nothing comes of the suggestion.

y 30. Germany asks Russia to stop mobilization within twenty-four hours. England notifies Germany that if eneral conflict should occur it will not remain neutral.

'y 31. Russia ignores German ultimatum and declares that t will not allow Servia to be crushed.

gust 1. Germany declares war upon Russia. The French overnment orders general mobilization.

gust 2. Germany begins the invasion of France through he neutral Duchy of Luxemburg. England asks Germany f she will respect the neutrality of Belgium. Germany eclines to answer.

August 3. Germany sends ultimatum to Belgium demanding free passage for her troops. Belgium refuses. Demands that Germany respect her neutrality, and proclaims martial law. King Albert of Belgium asks England's diplomatic intervention to safeguard Belgian neutrality. The German Ambassador to London promises that if England will remain neutral Germany will not attack the northern and western coasts of France. Italy proclaims neutrality. German Emperor gives the Russian Ambassador his passports. France declares that war with Germany began automatically with invasion of her territory.

August 4. English ultimatum to Germany demands satis-factory assurance on the neutrality of Belgium. King George orders the mobilization of the British army. At midnight, no reply to ultimatum having been received from Germany, war is declared.

August 5. Germans attacked Liége, Belgium.

August 6. Austria-Hungary declares war on Russia.

August 8. Portugal announced its decision to support Great Britain (while technically Portugal thus assumed a position of hostility to Germany she did not participate in actual hostilities during the first two years of the war).

August 9. Servia declares war against Germany.

August 10. France declares war on Austria.

August 13. Austria and Great Britain each declare war on the other.

August 23. Japan declares war on Germany.

CHAPTER II

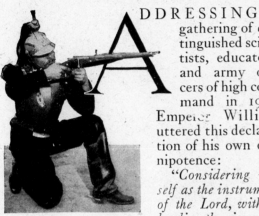

A French cuirassier

ADDRESSING a gathering of distinguished scientists, educators, and army officers of high command in 1910, Emperor William uttered this declaration of his own omnipotence:

"Considering myself as the instrument of the Lord, without heeding the views and opinions of the day, I go my way."

Accepting this as the rule of conduct of a monarch, vested with almost irresponsible and unfettered command over the lives of millions of men, and all the resources of a great nation, we can understand better the early events of the great war. For the first act of the German Emperor was to brush aside every treaty right or obligation which hampered his freedom of action, or for a moment put in jeopardy his plan of conquest.

This plan was in brief to dash into France, seize Paris, and subdue the French people in the first sixty days of the war. The Germans estimated that the great inert mass of the Russian fighting forces could not be mobilized and brought into effective action on the eastern frontier of Germany in less time than this, so they would be able to crush France and return to their own eastern frontier in time to save it from the horrors of a Russian invasion. Long before the declaration of war the German troops planning this invasion of France were massed along the frontier. The French should have recognized, and perhaps did recognize, that it was

not along the French frontier, extending from the neutral Duchy of Luxemburg to the neutral territory of Switzerland that the heaviest German divisions were arrayed. Instead it was along the line that separates Germany from Luxemburg and from Belgium. The reason for this was promptly shown upon the declaration of war. Going his way, heedless of the views and opinions of the day, and equally of the treaties to which his government was a party, the Kaiser instantly filled the Duchy of Luxemburg with his troops. The reigning Duchess protested mildly and went into retirement. Her country had no force adequate to check the torrent of two hundred thousand or more of armed Germans which overwhelmed it. The invasion was lawless, how lawless the Chancelor of the German Empire at once confessed when in a speech to the Reichstag he said:

"We are now in a state of necessity, and necessity knows no law! . . . We were compelled to override the just protest of the Luxemburg and Belgian governments. The wrong—I speak openly—that we are committing we will endeavor to make good as soon as our military goal has been reached. Anybody who is threatened, as we are threatened and is fighting for his highest possessions, can have only one thought—how he is to hack his way through."

The plan of campaign which the German military staff—as busy almost in time of peace as in time of war—had prepared contemplated the invasion of France from three points by three armies:

The Army of the Meuse, with its base at Aix-la-Chapelle was to enter Belgium, reduce the forts at Liége and march on Paris by a westerly route, taking in passing the forts at Namur and at Lille.

The Army of the Moselle already concentrated in Luxemburg was to enter France at Longwy and proceed to Paris, subduing by the way the

Belgian field pieces masked by being placed amongst bushes and partly screened by straw

No army of all history ever took the field so splendidly equipped with new and terrible engines of war

fortresses at Verdun and Rheims.

The Army of the Rhine, the only one not making neutral territory a part of its pathway, was to have its base at Strassburg and cross the French frontier near Nancy. By this last route the Prussians thrice before had reached the French capital.

The Army of the Meuse was made up of the very flower of the German army, for to it was assigned the task which was expected to be the most glorious and the most spectacular, and, proving to be both of those, was the most arduous as well. Upon it the eyes of the civilized world were riveted for weeks. Against it fought Belgians, British, and French from the very outset of its operations, and before it merged its identity in the general German line it had withstood the assaults of infantry, cavalry, and artillery —and all with hardly a stop for food or sleep; it had met and fought Turcos from French Africa, and Sikhs and Hindoos from British East India. Commanded by General von Emmerich, it numbered at its entrance upon Belgian soil about 200,000 men, which number, oft depleted by heavy fighting, was continually reënforced until it approached the impressive total of a half million armed men.

as the armies of Germany, and particularly the Army of the Meuse in this campaign. Aeroplanes and dirigibles spied out the way, reported the positions of the enemy, and indicated to the artillery the range. Motor cars carried soldiers swiftly from point to point and hurried light guns into action; heavily armored, they had their place on the line of battle, and marked with the Red Cross they carried the wounded to places of safety. Rapid-fire guns poured out streams of bullets like water from a hose, and were so compactly built that one could be packed on a horse, or carried on two motor cycles. Siege guns with a range of ten miles, of a calibre and weight never before thought capable of passage along country roads, were dragged by traction engines or by their own motors at a rate of eight miles an hour—guns that twenty years ago would have been useless in any field because of their immobility. By the use of flat platforms on the circumference of their wheels—"caterpillar wheels" they called them—these cannon could be dragged by motors even over plowed fields. They throw an armor-piercing shot weighing 800 pounds, and at seven miles will demolish a target of a few feet square. It was their deadly accuracy that beat down Belgian resistance at Liége and Namur.

Early in the afternoon of Tuesday, August 4, 1914, the first gun of the war of the nations was fired, when the outposts of General von Emmerich's army exchanged shots with the Belgian outposts at Liége. The moment will always be historic. Not only did it mark the beginning of the greatest war that has ever devastated Europe, but it was forty-four years to the day, and almost to the hour, since the forerunners of these invaders had crossed the French frontier at the beginning of the Franco-Prussian War.

At the time the whole world attached too great importance to the character of the early battles of Belgium. But too much importance could not be attached to their significance for the delay caused by the heroic resistance of the little Belgian army at the outset unquestionably saved Paris by enabling the French to shift their dispositions of troops to meet an attack from an unexpected quarter, and in thus saving Paris and France probably determined the ultimate outcome of the war.

Over the action of the Belgians directed by their heroic king, Albert, in thus sacrificing themselves and exposing their country to the most cruel and indefensible ravages recorded since the Dark Ages, there has raged some conflict of opinion.

The Germans and their sympathizers throughout the war bitterly denounced King Albert for his course, which they declared to be dictated partly by sentimental reasons, and partly through personal arrogance. They pointed out that the Duchy of Luxemburg,

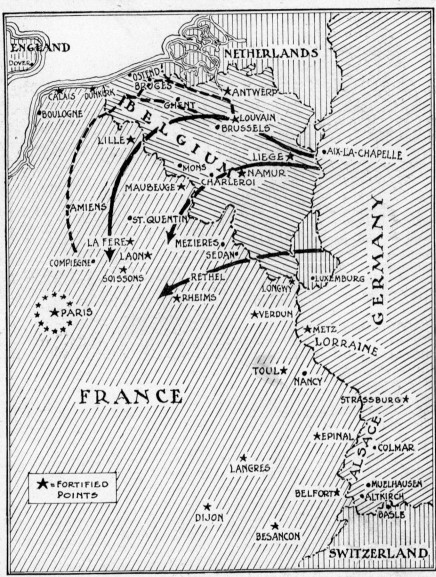

The map shows approximately the extent of the German advance to September 6, 1914. The heavy lines with arrow-tips show in a general way the main German advance; the heavy dotted lines, routes of parallel, but lesser columns. All the territory between the line touching Antwerp, Ghent, Bruges, and Amiens and the main line was filled with German troops. Raiding parties also reached Ostend and Boulogne

having accepted the inevitable and allowed its territory to be used at once as a place of concentration and a highway for German troops preparing for the invasion of France, had suffered no spoliation nor destruction of property and had been reimbursed for whatever damage the passing troops inflicted upon the property of its inhabitants. They declared that had Belgium been equally acquiescent in the German plan of campaign, the troops marching through would have been instructed to respect property, whatever incidental damage had been done would have been paid for, and the word of the German government would have been pledged to maintain thereafter the complete independence and the

House in Antwerp smashed by a German shell

neutrality of Belgium.

The answer, of course, was complete. The word of Prussia was already pledged to respect and to protect the neutrality of Belgium. If that pledge was violated at a time when Germany really needed Belgian assistance against a hostile Europe, what chance was there that it would be respected by the triumphant government of the Kaiser after the rest of Europe had been brought to his feet? Hopeless as resistance appeared, the Bel-

The vanguard of the Russian army marching upon Austria-Hungary

gians felt assured that if they were to save their integrity as a nation they must fight, and trust to the Allies to win for them that independence which they could not secure by their own independent effort and for the protection of which they could not trust to German assurances.

As a result their country suffered as no nation has in modern times. Their people, such as survived the immediate shock of combat, were reduced to the point of starvation and for years lived only through the

Bridge over which thousands escaped. This picture of the bank of the Scheldt shows the slender pontoon bridge across which the army and many refugees escaped from Antwerp

charity of the other nations of the world. Their beautiful and historic towns were reduced to ruins, their commerce laid prostrate, their industry destroyed except as it was operated by their people working as slaves under the eyes of German officers for the advantage of the German cause.

No other such record of national self-sacrifice is recorded in history.

But great as was the significance of the Belgian resistance there has been a tendency to exaggerate the

French infantry in action bore frequent testimony to the spirited personal initiative of the soldiers

Czar Nicholas tasting a sample of the soup that was served to the Russian army

character of the battles fought there in the first ten days of the war of the nations. What really happened was that with the very first action the German artillery proved so vastly superior to the Belgian forts, and the German cohorts so enormously outnumbered the Belgian defenders that there could not for a moment be any question as to the issue.

Liége, the point of first attack, had been

Belgian troops manned these forts, or defended the gaps between them. Two hundred thousand Germans demanded that the way be opened. Worse than all, the equipment of the forts had not been kept up to date and their armament was entirely inadequate for their defence. In fact, the first and largest fort, Fleron, was practically silenced by the field guns of the Germans, who had not yet had time to bring up their heavy siege

Refugees from the outlying villages fleeing to Brussels for protection against the advancing German army

looked upon as a fortified point of prodigious strength. Its fortresses were of the type which military science up to that time had fixed upon as approaching the impregnable. They were wrought steel turrets, curved so as to offer the poorest possible target for shells, looking like great black mushrooms, squatting close to the ground with a ditch surrounding each and a broad cleared space on every side. Underground passages connected the nine turrets, and there was the usual provision of mines, ditches, electrified barbed-wire entanglements, and other devices for defence. But only twenty thousand

guns, which afterward proved the sensation of the first weeks of the war. The fall of this, the most powerful of the Belgian works, opened a gap in the defences of Liége, which was held with unprecedented gallantry for forty-eight hours by a comparatively few men, the greater part of whom were little better than civilians in training. During this period the Germans brought up their big howitzers, smashed two supporting fortresses, and opened the way to the city to the German advance.

Ignoring for the time the other works still held by the Belgians, the Germans entered Liége, made it a base of supplies, and pressed

German volunteers

on to the interior of Belgium. While their armies were thus advancing, the other forts were reduced by a savage artillery fire. General Leman, the Belgian commander in the city, established himself in the fort of Loncin, which was to the west of Liége and intended to defend that city, not to sustain an attack from it. The German possession of Liége enabled them to attack the fort from its so-called blind side. Almost wholly unable to return the fire, the gallant defenders held their ground until after a resistance of days the fort was literally battered to pieces, its garrison all killed or wounded and the General himself found by the attacking force apparently dead in the ruins.

Liége furnished the first proof of the utter worthlessness in the face of modern artillery of the type of fort which the nations of Europe up to that time had been relying upon. Thereafter the few forts that were able to resist artillery were simply left for the time, while the invading army swept by into the desired territory, leaving a comparatively small detachment to prevent any

offensive operation on the part of the garrison. This was done at Lille, Namur, and Maubeuge. Namur, which all France thought would hold back the German tide for a month at least, detained them but a day. As the war progressed and new solutions were found for the problems it offered, the trench and the barbed-wire entanglement, hastily thrown up by the troops in the very moment of action and readily replaced by other like works when abandonment became necessary, took the place of the huge fortresses. Even Verdun, whose resistance for months, indeed, for more than two years, to the persistent attacks of the Germans under the Crown Prince was saved not by its own guns, but by the network of trenches and concealed field artillery by which it was surrounded on every side.

The very first test of the great German and Austrian siege cannon forced the abandonment as worthless of that long line of ponderous fortresses that France had built along the German frontier and upon which the Republic had spent more than $1,500,000,000, or more than the whole South African War cost Great Britain or the Manchurian War had cost Russia.

It was on Saturday, the 15th of August, the two chief German armies began their

All that was left from the disaster. This dog cart and its contents were all that a once prosperous family saved from ruin

advance along the Belgian railways which have their point of concentration in Liége across the Belgian plain. The delay which had occurred on the frontier had enabled the French to hurry back part of their forces from Alsace-Lorraine which they had invaded immediately upon the declaration of war. In passing it may be noted that at first the French forces in these former provinces of the Republic had carried all before them, the main attention of the German military command being directed toward the Belgian frontier. But the French advance there was speedily checked and the necessity for calling back a large portion of the troops to meet the German advance through Belgium destroyed the importance of the Alsace-Lorraine campaign during the first half of the war.

An Impromptu Registration. Refugees from Antwerp writing their names and addresses on a fence to let their friends know their whereabouts

To meet the greater German menace the French troops were hurried into a position near Namur, where in coöperation with the British expeditionary force they formed a line crossing the River Sambre at Charleroi and forming a sharp angle behind the River Meuse. Along this line were arrayed about 250,000 men of whom the British numbered about 100,000. Pressing down upon them in parallel lines through Belgium were not less than 500,000 Germans, delayed somewhat but not long restrained by the gallant resistance of the Belgians.

The advance was one continuous fight, not as in the Franco-Prussian War, or the American Civil War, a succession of pitched battles with days, even weeks, between for recuperation. So steady and determined was the fighting that even the customary armistices for the burial of the dead after sanguinary combats were refused by one or the other combatant, and the gruesome practice became customary of piling the bodies in huge pyramids with combustibles and thereto applying the torch. Visé, Montaud, Mons, Haelen, Tirlemont were clashes which in any other war would have been reported as pitched battles. The official reports of this gigantic struggle dismiss them with the curt statement, "Our forces were in contact with the enemy at Haelen," or a reference to the "affair of outposts at Visé." But they were very real, very savage, and each contributed its

The English recruit's introduction to army life. Volunteers arriving at Aldershot training camp are first taught to form in line and are given instructions in marching in step

kingdom in the neighborhood of Ostend, where the fragment of the Belgian army which had been beaten indeed, but not annihilated, maintained itself gallantly.

It was holding this corner of the kingdom of Belgium free from German occupation at the end of the war's second year.

The action of the authorities of Brussels in offering no resistance to the incoming Germans was dictated by consideration of the methods of revenge and terrorism adopted by the Germans in their march through Belgium. War has never been more remorseless. In every town and village prominent men were seized as hostages and were relentlessly put to death if any citizen, maddened by the destruction of his property or insults offered to his womenkind, dared to attack the aggressors. The story of German atrocities in Belgium is not to be told here. It formed the subject of heated diplomatic discussion

Boot inspection at Aldershot. Owing to a short supply new shoes cannot be issued to all volunteers at once, and so the most needy are supplied first

quota to the tens of thousands of lives offered up on the altar of imperial ambition and national vainglory.

In the course of this advance the Belgian capital, Brussels, was entered without fighting. The burgomaster of the city, wisely advised by the United States Minister, Brand Whitlock, met the approaching invaders with the assurance that there would be no resistance offered and that every effort would be made to prevent unauthorized attacks on the German troops. The city was thereupon made the headquarters of the Army of the Meuse, and by imperial proclamation the Kaiser declared Belgium to be part of the German Empire. King Albert and the remnant of the Belgian government retired to Antwerp, and when that city subsequently fell into the German hands they retired further to the extreme southwestern corner of the

Doing signal corps work. Some of the more intelligent recruits are detailed for signal corps duties and are given a rigorous training. The primary lesson is in "wig-wagging" with flags

A RUINED LIÉGE FORT
A steel turret overthrown and masonry demolished by German siege guns

Germans find work for their prisoners of war. This photograph shows British soldiers captured by the Germans engaged in building fences near Berlin

in all the countries involved. It was investigated by a distinguished commission, headed by Viscount James Bryce, whose name alone carries conviction of intellectual honesty to all informed readers. In every war men lose in some degree the semblance of humanity and cast off the veneer of civilization. It is impossible, however, to read both sides of the discussion of German methods during the first weeks of the invasion of Belgium without being convinced that the extreme severity, approaching barbarism, was both definitely ordered and systematically encouraged by the German commanders in pursuance of the "policy of frightfulness," and with the purpose of over-

The effect of one shell. Hole torn in the pavement by a shell in Antwerp

awing at the very outset a population which they knew they would hold in military subjection during the period of the war, and hoped to retain as vassals thereafter. It is significant that as the conquest of Belgium became more complete the savagery of the invaders was mitigated.

Most shocking to the sentiment of the world was the almost complete destruction of the quaintest and most picturesque part of Louvain, a Belgian town richly stored with treasures of Gothic art and architecture dating from the period of the Middle Ages. This town was destroyed by the Germans systematically, with military precision, by soldiers who went from street to street filling the first stories of the buildings with combustibles and then applying the torch. The excuse given by General von Lutwitz, in command, was that a shot fired by the burgomaster's son killed a high German officer and seemed to serve as a signal for snipers in the windows and on roofs. He asserted that investigation showed that the inhabitants were plotting a general attack upon the troops. All these charges were earnestly denied by the authorities and citizens of Louvain. Both parties to the controversy sent commissions to the United States to lay before the President the facts in the case.

Nothing in the course of the war indicated more strikingly the changing tenor of military sentiment than the earnestness with which all parties to this great conflict besought the good opinion of the United States. All war is cruel, bloodthirsty, barbaric, but every charge that either belligerent had exceeded the necessary ruthlessness of battle was at once indignantly repudiated and every effort made to marshal facts in its disproof. Charges of the sort there were in plenty and the destruction of Louvain, coming in the very first week of the war, was fought over as bitterly in the organs of public opinion as it had been in the streets of the town. Whatever the excuse—and, concerning that, doubt will never be settled—the destruction was complete. A most graphic description of it was written by Richard Harding Davis, the well-known American author, who was held prisoner in a railroad car in Louvain by German soldiers while the town was burning:

"When by troop train we reached Louvain, the entire heart of the city was destroyed and fire had reached the Boulevard Tirlemont, which faces the railroad station. The night was windless and the sparks rose in steady, leisurely pillars, falling back into the furnace from which they sprang.

"In their work of destruction the soldiers were moving from the heart of the city to its outskirts, street by street, from house to house.

How the surrender of Rheims was demanded. When the fall of Rheims was imminent the Germans demanded the surrender of the city and sent two officers to parley with the French. These men were admitted to the city blindfolded

"In each building, so German soldiers told me, they began at the first floor, and when that was burning steadily passed to the one next. There were no exceptions—whether it was a store, chapel, or private residence, it was destroyed. The occupants had been warned to go, and in each deserted shop or house the furniture was piled, the torch was stuck under it, and into the air went the savings of years, souvenirs of children, of parents, heirlooms that had passed from generation to generation.

"The people had time only to fill a pillowcase and fly. Some were not so fortunate, and by thousands, like flocks of sheep, they were rounded up and marched through the night to concentration camps. We were not allowed to speak to any citizen of Louvain, but the Germans crowded the windows, boastful, gloating, eager to interpret.

"On the high ground rose the broken spires of the Church of St. Pierre and the Hôtel de Ville, and descending like steps were row beneath row of houses, roofless, with windows like blind eyes. The fire had reached the last row of houses, those on the Boulevard de Jodigne. Some of these were already cold, but others sent up steady, straight columns of flame. In others at the third and fourth stories the window curtains still hung, flowers still filled the window boxes, while on the first floor the torch had just passed and the flames were leaping. Fire had destroyed the electric plant, but at times the flames made the station so light that you could see the second hand of your watch, and again all was darkness, lit only by candles.

"You could tell when an officer passed by the electric torch he carried strapped to his chest. In the darkness the gray uniforms filled the station with an army of ghosts. You distinguished men only when pipes hanging from their teeth glowed red or their bayonets flashed.

"Outside the station in the public square the people of Louvain passed in an unending procession, women bareheaded, weeping, men carrying the children asleep on their shoulders, all hemmed in by the shadowy army of gray wolves. Once they were halted, and among them were marched a line of men. They well knew their fellow-townsmen. These were on the way to be shot. And better to point the moral an officer halted both processions and, climbing to a cart, explained why the men were to die. He warned others not to bring down upon themselves a like vengeance.

"As those being led to spend the night in the fields looked across to those marked for death they saw old friends, neighbors of long standing, men of their own household. The officer bellowing at them from the cart was illuminated by the headlights of an automobile. He looked like an actor held in a spotlight on a darkened stage.

"It was all like a scene upon the stage, so unreal, so inhuman, you felt it could not be true; that the curtain of fire, purring and crackling and sending up sparks to meet the kind, calm stars, was only a painted backdrop; that the reports of rifles from the dark rooms came from blank cartridges; and that these trembling shopkeepers and peasants ringed in bayonets would not in a few minutes really die, but that they themselves and their homes would be restored to their wives and children."

Thursday, August 10th, the German forces proceeding through Belgium had massed in heavy numbers before Namur, where as we have seen the Anglo-French forces awaited their attack. Namur lies at the junction of the Sambre and Meuse rivers. Its forts, which up to that time had been supposed to be impregnable, formed the whole support of the French right against the unexpectedly overpowering force of the Germans. With those forts destroyed there was no possible chance for the French to block in the open field the progress southward into their country of the German invaders. But to the amazement and the consternation of the Anglo-French forces Namur fell almost with the first shock of the attack. The Germans entered the city the very day they arrived before it. Two or three of the forts held out for a time but soon succumbed, the attack of the Germans upon the French line proceeding while these forts were still unsubdued.

The forces opposed to the German invasion, enumerated from the left of the line, or its western end which rested at Mons, were as follows: The British contingent, numbering at the outset barely 70,000 men under the command of Sir John French, extended to Charleroi, where it came into contact

A Krupp aeroplane gun. The two small tubes at the top are filled with glycerine to take up the recoil

with the fifth French army of three corps amounting to perhaps 120,000 men, under General Joffre. This French line extended as far as the angle of the rivers at Namur, then bent sharply in an angle to the south where along the Meuse lay three more army corps amounting to another 120,000 men. In all at this moment there were about 400,000 men in this allied army.

Unsuspecting the marvelous efficiency of the German transportation neither of the allies imagined that they would be attacked by more than 500,000 men at the utmost. While this was conceding a heavy superiority to the enemy, yet with the advantage of the Namur forts, the weakness of which none suspected, and with the protection of the two rivers the case did not seem hopeless. At the very worst the allied commanders looked forward only to a slow retirement to permit the further reënforcements, which were coming from England and from other sections of France, a chance to reach the firing line.

What happened was that the Namur forts gave way before the enemy's fire like so many paper boxes, and the German force, which had not been expected to reach four hundred thousand, was in fact seven hundred thousand. They had brought through Belgium five army corps, each with a separate division, under the command of General von Kluck, which confronted the two British corps under French. Four more, under Von Buelow, including the Emperor's own imperial guard, extended from Von Kluck's right to Namur, where the line was taken up by the third army under the Duke of Wurtemburg numbering five corps. The latter had reached the field of action by pressing through the difficult territory of the Forest of Ardennes through which the French authorities had no belief an army could move with anything like the celerity it attained. The effect of this

overwhelming force was that not only were the British and French brigades confronted by superior forces in their immediate front, but the right of Von Kluck's army extended far beyond the left flank of Sir John French, while the left of the Duke of Wurtemburg's army likewise extended beyond the right flank of the fourth French army. Thus the force striving to hold the invaders back from French soil was in imminent danger of being flanked at either end, surrounded, and annihilated. Had that happened nothing could have saved France. Cities, even capitals, may be lost by a nation without the loss of the war if its armies are still left in the field to continue the struggle. But with the army destroyed the nation itself falls. So we shall see later that at the moment when Paris itself seemed most in danger, the French government, notwithstanding the sentimental affection which would seem to dictate the defense of its capital to the bitter end, nevertheless prepared for its abandonment and the concentration of every effort upon saving the army. At Namur both allied armies were in the gravest peril from which they extricated themselves slowly and only by a retreat almost to the gates of Paris conducted with the most admirable skill by General French and General Joffre, and maintained with heroic endurance and daring by both British and French soldiers. The unmilitary reader is apt to think of a retreat as only an ignominious incident of war. So it is, if it is allowed to degenerate into a panic, but although the circumstances dependent upon the beginning of this retirement gave every excuse for rout, the generals and soldiers kept their heads and out of the discouragement of retreat plucked the laurels of victory on the banks of the

One of the huge German siege guns with the so-called caterpillar wheels as a precaution against soft roads

Marne almost two weeks later.

What happened at Namur was that on Saturday, the 21st of August, the Germans delivered so fierce an assault on the fourth and fifth armies that both fell back toward Mauberge. Through some error never explained, and about which the British have ever since complained bitterly, news of this retirement was not sent to Sir John French until nearly twenty-four hours later. His troops were in fierce battle with those of Von Kluck and at the moment did not understand the overpowering dimensions of the force by which they were attacked. In the midst of this action word came to French that his allies were in full retreat, and that a gap was open between the end of his line and theirs into which the German army might well have poured, cut the continuity of the allied lines, and destroyed their armies. Out of this situation, more menacing to his force than to the French because his troops were vastly more outnumbered and were enveloped on either flank, Sir John French plucked ultimate victory. Nothing is more difficult than to lead an outnumbered army to safety in a retreat extending over a number of days. You cannot merely turn your back upon the enemy and walk away, for while you are so doing his troops will be pounding away at your rear, his artillery would be in constant pursuit, unlimbering long enough to fire a few score shot into the retreating columns, then limbering up again and dashing forward to a point of closer contact. The only way an orderly retreat can be conducted is by setting aside one detachment after another to hold the pursuing enemy in check while the main body of the retreating army presses on to safety. This means, of course, heavy sacrifice of men and guns, but safeguards the integrity of the whole army. This sort of fighting was maintained by both British and French from the 22d of August until about the 2d of September, at which time the Germans had reached the neighborhood of Senlis, their nearest approach to Paris.

One Sunday, August 23d, the British were holding their enemy in check outside the French frontier at Mons in Bel-

On the road to safety. The dog is much used as a draught animal in Belgium, and many refugees were fortunate enough to get dog carts in which to escape

Every part of the German battle lines, an aggregate of almost 600 miles, has been visited by the Crown Prince

War's real victims. Hungry women and children waiting in the "bread line" at Malines, the day before the bombardment of Antwerp began. Malines was included in the storm of shell, and the building in the background was set on fire the night after this picture was taken

gium. A week later they were at La Fere, only eighty-five miles from Paris. At Rheims, whose famous Gothic cathedral became for weeks the favorite target for German guns, the French lost the town, 410 guns, and 12,000 men, and all Germany went wild because that same city had fallen on precisely the same date forty-four years earlier. Later the French retook it. While the Army of the Meuse was thus pushing back both the British and the French, the Army of the Moselle, under Prince Rupprecht, broke through a French line of from five to eight army corps between Nancy and the Vosges, defeating them decisively. The Army of the Crown Prince, advancing through Luxemburg, menaced Paris from that direction. Nothing seemed likely to intervene for the salvation of the French capital, from which the government had fled to Bordeaux while the city itself was daily menaced by the flight over it of German aeroplanes.

All Germany was

British troops passing through London streets on their way to the front

wild with joy. Her troops had reduced fortresses that had been expected to hold out for weeks, and had done nothing but pursue flying force of French and British which offered only the brief resistance of rearguard battles. "Sedan Day" approached—that glorious September 1st on which, in 1870, Napoleon Third and the last great French army were trapped by Von Moltke on the battleground at Sedan, cut to pieces, and forced to surrender. Up and down the streets of Berlin now marched cheering mobs, crying for some great new triumph on this historic anniversary, while German officers, and it is said even the Emperor himself, gayly made appointments to celebrate it in Paris at the Café de la Paix. In part the enthusiasm of Berlin was justified, for on that day came news of the overwhelming victory of Von Hindenberg over the Russians at Tannenberg in East Prussia—a victory which for more than a year held that section of Germany free from invasion.

But in France

Photograph taken amid bursting shells. This picture was taken under fire. The soldiers in the trenches were Belgians

Sedan Day marked the beginning of the end of German triumph. It was almost the critical moment which determined the result of the war. For on that day the German advance was halted so near to Paris that the city's church bells could be heard during the lulls in the clatter of musketry along the opposing lines.

The German halt was so sudden as to amaze all the world, and even Paris was dazed by the abruptness of its respite. For five weeks the enemy's advance had been practically without interruption. There had, it is true, been no great battles, as battles have come to be estimated in this colossal war. The flood of Teutons clad in gray-green had overflowed first Belgium then northern France, yielding to no obstacle whatsoever, pushing back from before them the French and English alike, until at

the beginning of the fifth week of the invasion it seemed certain that the boasts of the early days of the war, that Paris would be taken in six weeks as had been the case in 1871, seemed certain of fulfillment.

But the German generals knew better than

English convalescents amuse themselves

Making English recruits physically fit

either their soldiers or the mass of the people could know, that every day of the advance toward Paris made their problem harder. To begin with the force opposed to them was being ceaselessly reënforced. Guarded by the great gray battleships of the British navy, the transports of the British army were slipping back and forth across the Channel bringing troops by the tens of thousands to the reënforcement of Sir John French. At Namur the British line had been estimated at about seventy thousand. When the Germans were halted near Senlis it numbered not less than 150,000. At Namur, again, the French forces were estimated at about 240,000 men. When the check was imposed on Von Kluck and Von Buelow they had increased to the neighborhood of a million men. Moreover, the French brought into action at this point an entirely fresh army of nearly 500,000 men, which had been gathering under the eye of General Gallieni, commandant of Paris, for the express defence of the capital. While it is reasonable to believe that Von Kluck was aware of the existence of this army, he himself has recorded

A land of universal mourning. Women in France wearing mourning for lost relatives

English "Rookies" getting first instruction in rifle sighting

Africa, Apaches from the heights of Montmartre and Orientals from the picturesque countries of the East. Thrust entirely fresh into the conflict against the fatigued German troops, this army produced an immediate and decisive result.

Not only were the Allies stronger at the close of their retreat, but the Germans were weaker. Always during the pursuit the Germans

that he greatly underestimated its numbers. It was a picturesque and emphatically a fighting force. In it were the famous Foreign Legion, immortalized by Ouida in her novel, "Under Two Flags." Not a few adventurous spirits from the United States served in its ranks. There, too, were Turkos from northern had outnumbered their adversaries; now had come the time when they were to be outnumbered. The hostile territory of Belgium had to be garrisoned with troops withdrawn from the German fighting force. Probably more than 100,000 were thus taken from Von Kluck's army. More serious than this, how-

British Marines disembarking at Ostend and receiving a rousing welcome from the Belgians

ver, had been the necessity for sending back to the east heavy detachments to meet the unexpectedly prompt and vigorous attack of the Russians in Galicia and East Prussia. Not less than five army corps were thus disposed of.

And so it came about that when almost in sight of the coveted French capital on Sep-

end of this line on which the heaviest fighting had thus far been done. Next to him came General von Buelow, whose left flank in turn rested on the army of the Prince of Wurtemburg. Last of all, to the east, was the Army of the Crown Prince, starting at the German frontier, and enveloping Verdun, the

Uhlan patrol surprised by Belgian armored car

tember 1st, Von Kluck was forced to aban-don the method of strategy that had so far been wholly successful. He no longer had enough men to reach around the left flank of the allied army. Instead he was obliged to withdraw his own right flank, swing it to the eastward, and halt his advance.

When this check was sustained the Ger-mans held a line over one hundred miles long, reaching from Amiens in the west through Senlis, Meaux, and so eastward to Verdun and Toul. Von Kluck held the western

long struggle for the reduction of which had just begun.

Opposed to Von Kluck was the Army of Paris, fresh troops in the main. The English who had so long and stubbornly contested the German advance had now been shifted from the extreme right of the German line, many of their troops passing through Paris to their new position. Beyond this command of Sir John French extended the main line of the French army—Generals Pau, Desperey, de Langle, Foch, and Sarrail, all under the

English recruits on skirmish work

supreme command of General Joffre. More than two million men, armed to the teeth, drilled to the highest point of efficiency, equipped with every imaginable device for the prosecution of bloody and successful war, and animated on either side by motives of the highest patriotism, believing themselves fighting for their homes, their countries, and the very continuance of civilization, confronted each other along this far-flung battleline.

The country in which these colossal armies were thus aligned included some of the fairest spots in France. The harvest still stood in the fields, for the peasants were all in the army and none save women were left for the harvesting. The villages, trim and neat as are all the little hamlets of France, were swept of all men, and the women and children left behind looked wide-eyed out upon the scene of sudden martial invasion, and were soon swallowed up in the red torrent of war.

When Von

Examining the recruits' equipment

Kluck finally determined that there was no likelihood of his taking Paris in a rush —and there are picturesque stories of the unwelcome knowledge being forced upon him just as he was celebrating his "victory" in champagne—he at once recognized the need of a change in tactics. Instead of besieging the capital he determined to pierce the French army, separating its left wing, including the British, from the right, which was based on the forts at Verdun and Toul.

To this end all parts of the German line were stripped and forces concentrated at a point between Sezanne and Vitry where the great drive was to be made. Upon the army corps commanded by General von Buelow fell the burden of making the main assault. But to reënforce that command Von Kluck withdrew portions of his forces from the line confronting the French at Paris. They, quick to discover the fact advanced by their left flank reaching beyond the German right and threatening to get into their enemies' rear. This advance menaced the whole German army, and as day by day the French kept pushing forward by the left, Von Kluck withdrew his right until the whole position of his army was changed. After four days of this strategy the German general found his right wing enclosed in a sort of a monster V, with the angle to the west made up of the garrison of Paris, and that to the east, of the combined French and British armies. If the

von Kluck took a chance on the Crown Prince's being able to keep the French busy on their centre, and fairly invited a flank attack. General Joffre took a chance on the allied armies being able to resist the Crown Prince at the centre, and delivered the flank attack. Joffre more wisely estimated the chances of war and won.

The country about the Marne in which for a week or more 2,000,000 men swayed back and forth, charging madly and repelling charges with steel, ravaging the woods and

Thousands of Belgian refugees reaching Holland

two arms of this monstrous nut-cracker should close together, Von Kluck would be caught between and ground to powder. On September 7th they did in fact attack at the same moment, and for a time it appeared that the fate of Von Kluck's force was sealed. Only by savage fighting did he win clear.

Had the Army of the Crown Prince on the German left been successful, or had its savage effort to pierce the French centre been sufficiently menacing to distract altogether the attention of General Joffre from the weakened condition of the German right, with its exposed flank, the German grand strategy might have won out. But there the fortune of war was against the Germans. General

villages with a storm of shells and shrapnel, was one of the fairest parts of France. Its fertile fields now trampled into crimson mire were dotted by scores of trim little villages that now exist only as clusters of ruined homes with their tenants driven none knows where.

The forces engaged during the seven days' struggle exceeded 2,000,000, the Allies being credited with 1,500,000 men, the Germans with 900,000, though the superior ability of the latter to concentrate their forces at the point of attack nullified to some extent this discrepancy. More than in any prior struggle between the warring armies this battle was decided by superior strategy rather than by force of numbers, or more desperate fighting on the one side or the other. In his official report General French made it clear that for three days the apparent retirement upon Paris of the allied force had been in fact a ruse, designed by him, in conference with General Joffre, to draw the Germans into a more untenable position. In fact, Von Kluck detected the stratagem before his enemies were quite ready for the joint attack with which they intended to open a decisive battle, and his columns were in full retreat on the 6th before the French attack was delivered. By the 9th the Germans were forced back across the Marne. From the moment that the Army of Paris began to swing to the north and west enveloping Von Kluck's right and menacing his communications there was left for him but one hope —that the Crown Prince could pierce the French centre near Sezanne. But the French saw this as a menace as clearly as the Germans saw it as a hope, and their centre stood like a Holland dyke against the onrush of the German tide. Soon, instead of the French centre it was the German centre that was imperilled, for the retirement of Von Kluck left its right flank exposed. By the 10th of September the whole German army was in retreat from the ground it had won with such dash and daring, and the form of its retreat on the extreme right where Von Kluck commanded was very like a rout, with cannon and munitions of war abandoned, and whole regiments cut off and captured. Four days of hard fighting that followed turned the fortunes of war against the Germans, who had already exulted in the prospect of feasting on the fleshpots of Paris.

In ultimate history it is not improbable that the fame of Von Kluck will rest quite as

Explaining the rifle to English recruits

securely on his successful retreat from the Marne as upon his almost unopposed march upon Paris. The former was by far the more difficult test of his generalship. Caught between the hammer and anvil, outnumbered, with the morale of his army sorely suffering by the sudden transition from enthusiastic advance to precipitate retreat, he yet saved his army from the destruction which for a time seemed imminent. It was demonstrated in this retreat that the German soldier is not at his best in rearguard fighting. Advancing he comes on in dense columns, heedless of the execution done by artillery to which so solid a formation affords the best possible target, singing his war songs, and pressing on irresistibly. But in retreat he is more inclined to straggle, and the forlorn fighting of the rearguard, falling back as it fires with no hope of glory, but only the forlorn hope of escape, seems not to accord with the Teutonic temperament. Airmen flying high over the route of Von Kluck's retreat described the scene as one of the greatest confusion. The retreat was by no means confined to the highways. Men alone and in groups could be seen running across the fields, jumping fences, or worming their way through hedges, without order or discipline. The fields were covered with abandoned arms and accoutrements, the roads blocked with wagons and disabled artillery.

But the panic was only on the fringe of the army. In the main the movement was an orderly retreat, conducted with truly Teutonic precision to a new position prepared in advance by the prescience of the German General Staff.

For amidst all the shouting and the triumph of the march upon Paris tha'

Belgian refugees resting on their way out of Antwerp.   Knitting helps to quiet the nerves

prudent and omniscient board of strategists had foreseen that something might happen to force their armies away from Paris again at the very point of victory. This possibility was never admitted to the soldiers in the ranks, or to the people of Berlin. The latter were stirred by constant reports of victories, roused to riotous enthusiasm by parades of captured French cannon drawn down Unter den Linden, and reassured when Sedan Day passed without the news of the capture of Paris, by the assurance that for strategic reasons General von Kluck was seeking a new line. But all the while along the Hills of Champagne and the Hills of the Ile-de-France men with picks and shovels—captured Belgians many of them—were working industriously under the eye of German engineer officers, digging trenches, throwing up redoubts, laying concrete emplacements for cannon, and making all arrangements for a line of defence at which the retreating Germans could make a stand against their now triumphant enemy.

This line, indeed, was one originally designed by the French for their second line of defence against an invad-

Belgian girls in holiday costume

ing foe. From La Fere to Rheims stretched a line of French fortresses which, when the hour of trial arrived, proved of no avail, the Germans cutting in between the most westerly and the Channel, thus turning the allied flank and forcing the abandonment of the forts without defence. At Laon and La Fere the German artillery now held the very ground once occupied by the French forts, now dismantled. At Rheims the invaders were driven from and through the town back to the heights beyond, whence their heavy artillery, brought to France for the reduction of Paris, poured upon the cathedral city, and upon the cathedral itself, that deluge of shot and shell which brought ruin upon one of the noblest monuments of Gothic art in Europe, and roused the art-loving world to an agony of fruitless protest.

The new line thus formed was at an average distance from Paris of about eighty miles. When the German fighting men, scarred and exhausted after the retreat of five days, threw themselves into the trenches and faced again the foe that only a few days earlier they had thought to be beaten, they looked back over a territory

Refugees in a Church in France

the fighting was fiercest about Vitry, and there it seemed that the Crown Prince's Army was to be beaten back and the German centre pierced. Had this advantage been gained by the French, nothing could have saved the wing commanded by Von Kluck. The Crown Prince, however, held his ground stubbornly. On that part of the line the most notable change in the German position was that the forces which had enveloped the historic fortress of Verdun, so that news of its capture had been daily expected —was indeed falsely reported more than once—were forced back to the north. Toul, too, was wrested from German occupation, and Nancy was swept clear of the Kaiser's troops which, however, fortified themselves strongly just north of the town. At only one point along the French eastern frontier was there a break in the line of defence; that was at St. Mihiel, and from that point too, the Germans were destined to be driven.

of sixty miles, extending from near the Channel almost to the eastern boundary of France, which they had won in a rush, but from which they had been fairly driven. They had lost heavily in men and guns. Driving rains and swampy country along the right of the German line took toll of the heavy artillery which the invaders had been rushing on to Paris, and which they could not withdraw with sufficient speed in the face of the advancing French. Amiens, Nancy, Luneville, all considerable towns, they had had to abandon after a brief occupation.

While the right wing of the German army was thus forced far back to its new line, the more eastern line maintained more nearly the advanced position it had won. For a time

In the main, however, the great and striking gains of the Allies were made in the west, where the retreat of the Germans at points extended over sixty miles. While the English and French were strongly pressing the foe in front, the sorely shattered Belgian army was harassing him on the flank and rear, reoccupying Bruges, Ghent, and Courtai and even menacing Brussels. When Von Kluck's and Von Bue-low's armies finally dropped, torn and exhausted, into the trenches prepared for them on the heights beyond Rheims, and on the hill crests along the Aisne, they found a shelter sorely needed, for disaster was very close upon them. Nor were they given time to recuperate, for almost without appreciable interval the Battle of the Marne was succeeded by the even longer and fiercer Battle of the Aisne.

An English correspondent, George Renwick, following the army in the rear—the ig-

Desperate stand of British artillery against odds. During the Battle of Mons a German battery of ten guns surprised Battery L, Royal Horse Artillery, and killed most of its horses and men before it could get into action

noble position to which in this war all war correspondents were relegated—gathered from wounded soldiers left behind some narratives illustrative of the fighting which they had seen. It must be remembered, however, that the individual soldier's knowledge of a general battle ranging along a front of one hundred miles or more is but fragmentary. Mr. Renwick's narrative, in part, follows:

"Let me here give a short description, provided by an officer wounded in the fighting, of the struggle which took place on the River Marne.

"'We were in our positions early on Friday, September 4th,' he said, 'but we did not take part in the fighting on that day. During the whole of Friday and Saturday we

had nothing to do but to listen to the sound of firing which was not far distant and to speculate as to the result. Late in the evening the order came instructing us to retreat, but in the course of our retirement during the night that order was countermanded, and we advanced once more, taking up a strong position on sloping ground facing the river.

"'Early on Sunday Germans approached in considerable numbers, with the apparent intention of outflanking us, for they poured in on our extreme left. "Hold the position," was the order we received, and I can tell you it was just the order we wished, for how they swarmed toward our position! Wave after wave approached, turned, slowed down, and

Ghent, Belgium. In the tower at the left is the bell which for centuries has called the Belgians to war

fell away before the hurricane of lead with which we greeted them.

"'God, but they were brave! One can't deny them that tribute. But their artillery for once did not seem to be as effective as usual, and their fire was strangely erratic.

"'German soldiers, by the way, do not aim at all at times. They came near enough to allow us to see through our glasses the curious methods of the German riflemen. They do not put their rifles to their shoulders and take aim. They put the butt of the rifles under their arms and simply fire away, trusting to the effectiveness of volleys.

"'In the evening we received reënforcements from the direction of Meaux, and as darkness fell we had pushed back for the time being the forces which had been thrown against us.'

"Another officer, who was also wounded in the fighting somewhat further from the extreme left near La Ferte-Gaucher, told me that the general engagement there was an extremely hot one. It went on with varying results during the whole of Sunday night, but the most severe fighting took place on Monday morning.

"'Then,' he said, 'the enemy's resistance collapsed in a strangely sudden manner. Just as we began to advance I was knocked down, but I am told we advanced something like

twenty miles, driving an enemy before us which did not put up even a show of fight. They seldom turned even to treat us to a volley. It looked as though they

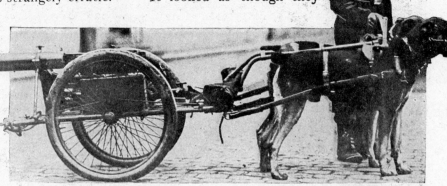

These are the real dogs of war. The Belgians use them to draw batteries of Lewis guns

had suddenly run completely out of ammunition.'

"Another soldier was able to take up the story. In the course of their hurried retreat the Germans left the ground simply littered with dead and wounded, though they could be seen carrying off many of the latter. A German detachment was cut off and the advancing forces took ten guns and several hundred prisoners. Some of the prisoners confirmed the statement that the enemy were very short of ammunition, and added that they were compelled to husband their rations.

"The German losses must everywhere have been exceedingly heavy. An infantry officer wounded near

Making friends with the Belgians

Dutch soldiers on their way to guard the frontier

A company of the Royal Engineers of the British army spent three weeks
in a sand pit

Meaux on the 8th told me two German army corps were in action during that day and on the 7th, and that in one trench alone he counted 600 dead. Even on Tuesday, it would appear, the German commander did not perceive that his southward movement was placing him in very considerable danger. On that day the battle changed with dramatic swiftness. The Allies assumed a vigorous offensive at the very point at which the German General had supposed them not to be strong enough to make his southern advance dangerous.

"Here the British were in great strength, and for the first time in the war, on anything like a large scale, they showed the Germans what a British frontal attack was like. 'They shelled us with their big guns,' said a Frenchman who took part with the French force aiding the British, 'but the fire was not very effective, and then we moved forward. It was a sight to see. There was almost too much "élan" at times in our moves forward, and some severe losses were experienced at times, I noticed, by the troops neglecting to make trenches and contenting themselves with what proved to be ineffective cover. But nothing could stay the steady advance.

"'At one little village we got right home with the bayonet, and we could see that we were driving dead-tired men in front of us. At times, however, they rallied with an effort.

"'Beyond the village they had made trenches, and it required a costly charge to clear them out. We had to advance over barbed wire, and as we did so it was terrible to see how one's comrades fell. We reached the trenches and cleared them. Then came ten minutes or so of unopposed advance, and

A Bavarian corps passing the old Hercules Fountain at Augsburg, Germany

then another fusillade, followed by a quarter of an hour of unceasing slaughter.

"'On again, but that's where I got shot in my foot. We kept straight on, I know.'"

In ultimate history it is not improbable that the fame of Von Kluck will rest quite as securely on his successful retreat from the Marne as upon his almost unopposed march upon Paris. The former was by far the more difficult test of his generalship. Caught between the hammer and anvil, outnumbered, with the morale of his army sorely suffering by the sudden transition from enthusiastic advance to precipitate retreat, he yet saved his army from the destruction which for a time seemed imminent. It was demonstrated in this retreat that the German soldier is not at his best in rear-guard fighting. Advancing he comes on in dense columns, heedless of the execution done by artillery to which so solid a formation affords the best possible target, singing his war-songs and pressing on irresistibly. But in retreat he is more inclined to straggle, and the forlorn fighting of the rear guard seems not to accord with the Teutonic temperament.

Wounded but still firing

What a Zeppelin bomb did in Antwerp

CHRONOLOGY OF EVENTS TREATED IN CHAPTER II

August 4. Germans attack Liége, and cross the French border near Mars-la-Tour.

August 7. Germans enter Liége, leaving some forts in Belgian possession.

August 8. British expeditionary force lands on Continent. French take Mulhausen, after battle at Altrich.

August 9. Germans retreat in Alsace.

August 11. German victory at Liége complete. French forced back in Alsace. Germans pushing into France between Verdun and Longwy.

August 12. Germans move on Brussels.

August 13. Battles at Diest, Haelen, and Egheeze in Belgium. Stories of German atrocities in Belgium first become current.

August 15. Armies of Germany and Allies face each other on 248 mile battlefront.

August 16. Battle at Dinant. French take the offensive at Luneville.

August 17. Belgian government moves to Antwerp.

August 20. Germans enter Brussels.

August 21. Germans capture Ghent and begin assault on Namur.

August 22. Battle along twenty-mile front near Charleroi begun. English and Germans fight on historic field of Waterloo.

August 23. Beginning of battle of Mons.

August 24. British retreat from Mons beginning Sir John French's prolonged and skillful retreat upon Paris.

August 25. Germans capture five Namur forts and pursue French to the southward.

August 27. Germans push Allies back, take Malines, an Paris prepares for a siege.

August 28. Germans sack and burn Louvain.

August 29. German force withdrawn from Belgium to mee Russians. Germans march on La Fère.

August 30. German advance upon Paris uninterrupted.

September 2. French move their capital to Bordeaux.

September 3. Germans take La Fère and Amiens and move t attack Laon and Rheims. Invaders now twenty-five mil from Paris.

September 4. Germans suddenly abandon Paris drive an move eastward. Right wing under Von Kluck driven bac by French under General Gallieni, commandant of Par and British under Sir John French.

September 5. Germans take Rheims and three forts at Ma beuge. Belgians flood country around Malines and tra Germans.

September 7. Allies drive Germans back in 160 mile batt from Nanteuil to Verdun. Paris saved.

September 8. British and French win great battle on t Marne and the Ourcq.

September 9. British cross the Marne, Germans steadil retreating.

September 10. British and French pursuing Germans. Ge eral von Stein admits defeat. Belgians renew activitie retaking Termonde, Aerschot, and Diest.

September 14. Amiens and Rheims reoccupied by t French. Germans after seven days' steady retreat establis themselves on heights along the Aisne and await battle.

GERMANS, WEARING GAS MASKS, STORMING A BRITISH TRENCH NEAR YPRES

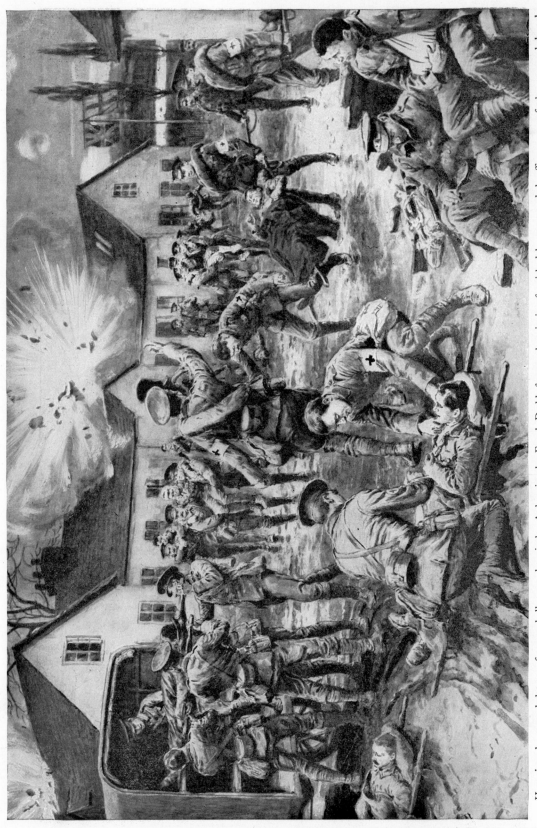

Hurrying the wounded away from a shell-swept hospital. A drawing by Frank Dadd, from a description furnished by a wounded officer, one of those saved by the hospital corps. A dressing station had been established in a village behind the British lines in France and when it was filled with wounded, German batteries began to rain shells on it. The wounded were hastily moved farther to the rear, but a number were killed, as were several Red Cross men. The battles around Ypres, where the Germans made a powerful attack on the Allied lines, cost the British dearly

CHAPTER III

WHAT is called the Battle of the Aisne is described as lasting twenty-two days, or from the 12th of September to October 4, 1914. But the name of the battle and its duration are alike fixed arbitrarily. It was quite as much the Battle of the Somme or the Oise, for it raged along the banks of both of these rivers as well as in territory far removed from all three.

its plan may be roughly determined by a study of the map on page 70. This shows the line of the two belligerents confronting each other and extending across France to the southeast with Rheims at the centre. The Germans once across the Aisne and on the heights back of Rheims had speedily dug themselves in and made their position what may properly be called impregnable, as despite continuous fighting they still maintained themselves in that position as late as August, 1916. All along this line the fighting was constant. The Franco-British attack took the form of the extension of their lines to the northwest as shown by the arrowhead at the end of the allied line on the map. At this time the Allies outnumbered the Germans heavily. When General French found on September 12th that he was no longer pursuing a retreating army, but face to face with the Germans, halted and awaiting attack

A Belgian sentry

As for duration it might most be said to have continued for eighteen months or more for it merged insensibly into the fighting in Flanders, and the names of the principal towns and cities which occur in the story of the Battle of the Aisne were still in the day's news that told of the allied drive in midsummer of 1916.

As a detached battle, therefore, the Battle of the Aisne was practically inconclusive. In a way

Belgian recruits parade London streets

Searching for wounded by night. The Red Cross Corps sees almost as much fighting as the combatants, since its members go on the firing line to assist the wounded

regiment for having crossed the river "in single file under considerable shell fire by means of a broken girder of a bridge which was not entirely submerged." When beyond the river the allied forces found themselves on a level plain rising gently as it receded from the river to a line of hills, the crests of which were crowned by German artillery or prepared emplacements, while on the rising slopes were lines of German rifle pits. Nor were the assailants permitted to prepare in security for their attack on this strong position. Twice the Germans poured out of their trenches and in solid columns late at night rushed on the French and English in vain efforts to dislodge them from the foothold they had won. There was fighting for weeks back and forth over the Plateau of Craonne. Now the charging line sung

behind heavy intrenchments, he recognized the necessity for a change in tactics from any further direct frontal attack. His first task was to get his troops across the Aisne. This was done by both British and French on pontoon bridges, constructed under heavy fire, and in his report General French compliments one

the "Marseillaise," or "Tipperary," and then the German cries for Deutschland rung out over the same blood-stained plain. There were villages occupied twice in a week by each of the warring hosts, villages in which the fighting was hand to hand in the streets, and on which, though within easy range, neither side ared to turn its rtillery for fear f killing its own men. Rheims was eld in turn by oth enemies and inally bom- arded by the Germans with re- ults that shocked he art-loving orld—but of hat more here- fter. A condi- ion of war which fterward became ommonplace nough, but vhich at the time eemed to all the vorld unprece- ented for its old-blooded bru- ality, shocked he American ournalist, Irvin S. Cobb, into writ- ng this ghastly lescription:

"As I recall ow we had come hrough the gate f the school- ouse to where he automobiles tood when a puff f wind, blowing o us from the eft, which meant rom across the attlefront, rought to our oses a certain mell which we all knew full well.

"'You get it, I see,' said the Ger- man officer who stood alongside me. 'It comes from three miles off, but you can get it five miles distant when the wind is strong. That'—and he waved his left arm toward it as though the stench had been a visible thing—'that explains why tobacco is so scarce with us among the staff back yon- der in Laon. All the tobacco which can be

Belgians in their rifle pits. Note the complete cover secured by bridging the openings made for the guns

spared is sent to the men in the front trenches. As long as they smoke and keep on smoking they can stand—that!

"'You see,' he went on painstakingly, 'the situation out there at Cerny is like this: The French and English, but mainly the English, held the ground first. We drove

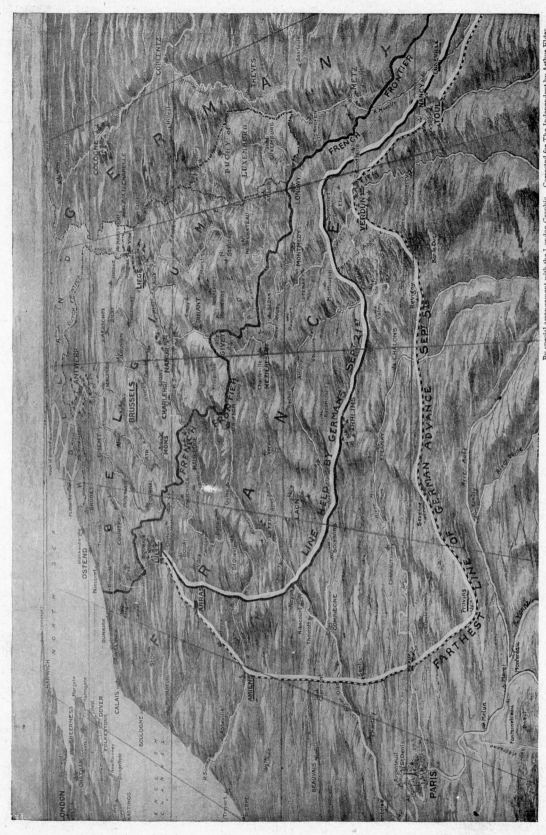

The receding line of the German invaders showing the nearest approach to Paris.

By special arrangement with the London Graphic.   Corrected for The Independent by Arthur Elder.   The intersecting lines form squares of fifty miles to a side

English sportsmen's battalion on the march.   Great Britain has a unique regiment in her new army, made up exclusively sportsmen, including polo players, huntsmen, football stars, amateur boxers, big game hunters, and devotees of all sorts of letic recreations

m back and they lost very heavily. places their trenches were actually full dead and dying n when we took se trenches.

"'You could have ried them merely filling up the nches with earth. d that old beetgar factory which u saw this noon en we were at neral von Zwehl's adquarters—it was wded with badly unded Englishmen. "'At once they ralld and forced us ck, and now it was r turn to lose avily. That was arly three weeks o, and since then e ground over which fought has been batable ground, lyg between our lines d the enemy's lines

General Sir Horace Smith-Dorrien, credited with having saved the British left wing

—a stretch four miles long and half a mile wide that is literally carpeted with bodies of dead men. They weren't all dead at first. For two days and nights our men in the earthworks heard the cries of those who still lived, and the sound of them almost drove them mad. There was no reaching the wounded, though, either from our lines or from the Allies' lines. Those who tried to reach them were themselves killed. Now there are only dead out there—thousands of dead, I think. And they have been there twenty days. Once in a while a shell strikes that old sugar mill or falls into one of those trenches. Then—

enders of Antwerp harassing the Germans.   Belgian infantry firing from hastily constructed trenches, during the investment
of Antwerp

ll, then, it is worse
those who serve in
front lines.'
"But in the name
God, man,' I said,
hy don't they call a
ce—both sides—
d put that horror
derground?'
'He shrugged his
ulders.
"War is different
w,' he said. 'Truces
not the fashion.'"
Despairing of fur-
r progress in the
e of the sturdy re-
tance of the Ger-
ns, Sir John French
the fighting at that
int to the French,

Hospital wrecked by the German invaders.   Patients fled to the open fields

French artillery in action, the gunners trying to protect their ear-drums from the shock.   During Von Kluck's great driv[e] Paris, the French artillery did wonderful service in holding their ground to the last possible moment then retreating and tak[ing] up another defensive position

and began reaching around the German right flank with the purpose of cutting Von Kluck's communications. Had the effort succeeded there would have been a fair chance of destroying at least Von Kluck's army, but the Germans met the menace in two ways. As fast as General French advanced Von Kluck extended his right swinging it back and northward un[til] it formed almost a right angle with the m[ain] line of the German armies.   But this strate[gy] itself endangered the German line.   If G[er-] man troops were continually rushed to t[he] right their line would have been weakened [at] the centre, and might have been pierced b[y a] determined attack by the French.   Acco[rd-]ingly the Germans attacked fi[rst] trying to drive the French out [of] Rheims, and also to pierce the all[ied] lines near the Argonne Forest. H[ad] this been effected Verdun wo[uld] have fallen, and the quickest pa[th]way from Germany into Fra[nce] which that fortress barred for t[he] early years of the war would ha[ve] been opened.   The long, circuito[us] route through Belgium which [re-]quired more than 150,000 men [to] guard could then be abandon[ed.] But although the Crown Prince a[nd] General von Heeringen united i[n a] drive against the French lines th[ey] were beaten back.   Virtually

French infantry awaiting the order to advance

Siege guns in action under cover of a forest. This picture shows two heavy German mortars firing on the French. The guns are elevated at a high angle so that the heavy projectiles fall almost vertically on the enemy's forts

the operations conducted by either side which we sum up under the name of the Battle of the Aisne resulted in failure, and the end of the grand strategy was but a drawn battle. For months the long curved line across France remained so little changed that it is almost impossible to depict the different positions on a map, while a gain of a few hundred metres by either side was triumphantly announced as a victorious advance.

Only to the westward, where Sir John French was trying to outflank von Kluck, did the line change. There, as each belligerent continually extended his lines toward the northwest, new territory was continually occupied until the serried rows of trenches, bomb proofs, and wire entanglements reached all the way to the sea.

In the course of the fighting on the centre of the line there was inflicted on the Cathedral at Rheims that irreparable damage which awakened at once deep regret and bitter resentment throughout the civilized world. The Germans claimed for a time that the de-

struction wrought upon this historic and beautiful piece of Gothic architecture, long held to be the most perfect in Europe, was due to accident. But when several official commissions demonstrated the fact that this was impossible, that the Cathedral rising in its colossal bulk in the midst of the two and three story houses of Rheims was so prominent an object that it could not have been struck save by design, German officials at

French prisoners with their morning soup

Stone bridge destroyed at Liége; new pontoon bridge in distance

Berlin said that it was the fault of the French who made Rheims a fortress. Later they claimed that the French had mounted guns on the tower of the Cathedral thereby making it properly the subject of artillery attack.

Mr. E. Ashmead Bartlett, who visited the Cathedral shortly after the bombardment, gathered from eye-witnesses the material for a picturesque account of the disaster which he published in *Collier's Weekly*. After commenting upon the fact that the Cathedral had survived the supposedly barbarous wars of the Middle Ages only to be irreparably wrecked by exponents of twentieth century culture, he goes on to say:

"Our knock wa

Namur, looking down upon the town from the fortifications

Bridge at Termonde, blown up to check the German advance

answered by a priest, who, on seeing that we were English, at once allowed us to enter. The sacred father then told us in language that was not altogether priestly, when speaking of the soldiers whose guns were still thundering outside, of how the Germans had bombarded the Cathedral for two hours that morning, landing over fifty shells in its immediate neighborhood, but, luckily, the distance being very great, over eight kilometres, the solid stonework of the building had resisted the successive shocks of these six-inch howitzers, and how it was with that ancient and priceless glass which had suffered the most.

"'Monsieur, they respect nothing. We placed scores of them inside and hoisted the Red Cross on the spire in order to protect the Cathedral,

A bridge at Amiens, repaired by the Germans

Rheims Cathedral before it was shattered by German shell fire

Ruined Rheims as seen from one of the Cathedral towers

and yet they fire at it just the same and have killed their own soldiers. Pray Monsieur make these facts known all over Europe and America.'

"A great wave of sunshine lit up a sombre picture of carnage and suffering at the western end, near the main entrance. Here, on piles of straw, lay the wounded Germans in all stages of suffering. Their round, shaven heads, thin cheeks, and bluish-gray uniforms contrasted strangely with the sombre black of the silent priests attending them, while in the background the red trousers of the French soldiers were just visible on the steps outside. Most of the wounded had dragged their straw behind the great Gothic pillars, as if seeking shelter from their own shells. The priest conducted us to one of the aisles beneath the window where the shell had entered that morning. A great pool of blood lay there, staining the column just as the blood of Thomas à Becket must have stained the altar of Canterbury seven centuries before.

"'That, Monsieur, is the blood of the French

Food for the seventy-fives.   Shells for the famous French field-gun

gendarme who was killed at eleven th[e] morning. But he did not go alone.' Th[e] priest pointed to two more recumbent figure[s] clad in the bluish gray of the Kaiser's legion[s] There they lay stiff and cold as the effigi[es] around them. All three had perished by th[e] same shell. Civilian doctors of Rhein[s] moved among the wounded, who for th[e] most part maintained an attitude of stoic indifference to everything around then[.] Food is scarce in the town, and meat almo[st] unobtainable, but in the centre of the Cath[e]dral transept lay the raw quarter of a slaug[h]tered ox, a horrid touch of materialism amid[st] a scene otherwise lacking a[ll] sense of reality. We move[d] around collecting fragments [of] the precious glass which th[e] Kaiser had so unexpectedl[y] thrown within our reach. W[e] were brought back to realities b[y] hearing the unmistakable whist[le] of an approaching shell, followe[d] by a deafening explosion, an[d] more fragments of glass cam[e] tumbling from aloft. The wear[y] war-worn Teutons instinctivel[y] huddled closer to the Goth[ic] arches.'"

It will be remembered that [in] the fierce eagerness of the Ge[r]mans to reach France they swep[t] by Antwerp without stopping [to] take it. Now, balked of the[ir] prize, Paris, and driven bac[k] their attention was turned aga[in]

A military bluff. With a wine barrel and an old cart the Germans constructed what, at a distance, looked like a mortar

oward this considerable / seaport,
he strategic position of which is such
hat Napoleon once said of it, "Ant-

Antwerp was surrounded by a ring of forts
at a distance of about twelve miles from the
city. They were of the sort deemed impregnable before this war, but withstood
the fire of the great German guns
called "Busy Berthas," after the
daughter of Herr Krupp, only three
days. It would have been wise had
the authorities of Antwerp, when the
first fort fell, imitated the prudent
course of the burgomaster of Brussels
and made prompt surrender to the
German invaders. For there was no
adequate force present to defend the
city. The Belgian army had already
been so badly cut to pieces that a
scant twenty thousand garrisoned the
town and its defences. A foolish relief
expedition of about 8,000 British
marines and blue jackets was sent to
the city, but about 2,000 were disabled by
the enemy's fire and as many forced over the
line into Holland, where in accordance with
international law they were disarmed and
interned for the period of the war. Indeed
their mission proved more harmful than
helpful, for they enraged the Germans and

Teaching "Tommy Atkins" to use the
bayonet

erp is a pistol aimed at England's heart."
Now the extension of the German line to
eet Sir John French's flanking movement
npelled Von Kluck to undertake the capture
f the city. It was a constant
enace in Belgian hands to his
ank and rear. As a fortress it was
cond only to Paris. Its harbor,
ne River Scheldt, opened
the sea. Holland con-
olled the river's mouth so
at only respect for the
eutrality of that nation—
which the Germans could
ardly appeal after their
eatment of Belgium—
ood in the way of Ant-
erp's being continually
pplied with fresh troops
nd munitions of war by
e British. Moreover, it
quired 150,000 troops to
vest it, and these men Von
luck needed sorely on his
ttleline. They could only
relieved by making Ant-
erp a German possession,
d accordingly on the 29th of Sep-
mber, while the Battle of the
isne was being fought bitterly all
e way from Verdun to Arras,
e attack was made.

Boys play only one game in England now

General Pau, the one-armed veteran of the French army

fying. That flight of a whole people wa
strikingly described by E. Alexander Powe
a British correspondent in *Scribner's Maga
zine*, from which the following account
taken:

"No one who witnessed the flight fron
Antwerp will ever be able to erase it fron
his memory. No words can describe it
pathos, its miseries, and its horrors. I
was not a flight; it was a stampede. Th
sober, slow-thinking, slow-moving Flemis
townspeople were suddenly transforme
into a herd of terror-stricken cattle. S
complete was the German envelopin
movement that only three avenues of e
cape remained open: westward, by th
St. Nicholas-Lokeren Road, to Ghent an
Bruges; northeastward into Holland, an
down the Scheldt toward Flushing. C
the four hundred thousand fugitives—for th
exodus was not confined to the people of An
werp, but included the entire population c
the countryside for thirty miles around—
probably a quarter of a million escaped b
river. Everything that could float wa

caused a bombardment of the city for which,
but for their presence, there would have
been no excuse. The bombardment, however, was conducted more as an object
lesson than with intent to destroy. The
artillerists avoided hitting historical edifices
or great public buildings with such complete
success as to entirely discredit the plea that
in the case of the Cathedral at Rheims the
destruction had been due to accident. While
the bombardment lasted about thirty-six
hours it resulted only in the destruction of
certain limited quarters in the town, and the
loss of life was not serious. The panic,
however, caused by it and by the rapid and
successful capture or passage of the forts
by the German storming parties was terri-

Sir Douglas Haig—successor to Sir John French—wi
King George

pressed into service: merchant steamers, dredgers, ferry-boats, barges, canal-boats, tugs, fishing-smacks, yachts, scows, rowboats, launches, even extemporized rafts. There was no attempt at maintaining discipline or order. The fear-frantic people piled aboard until there was not even standing-room upon the vessels' decks. They were as packed with humanity as are the New York subway trains on a Saturday noon. Of all the thousands who fled by river but an insignificant proportion were supplied with food, or with warm clothing, or had space in which to lie down. Yet through two nights and two days they huddled together on the open decks, while the great guns tore to pieces the city they had left behind them. As my launch threaded its way up the crowded river after the first night's bombardment, we seemed to pass through a wave of sound—a great moan of mingled anguish and misery and fatigue and hunger from the homeless thousands adrift upon the waters.

"The scenes along the highways leading

Field Marshal of the British Army, Kitchener of Khartoum

Enlisted to fight England; now fighting for her. Ulster volunteers being inspected by Sir Edward Carson

toward Ghent and to the Dutch frontier were even more appalling, for here the soldiers of the retreating field army and the fugitive civilians were mixed in inextricable confusion. By mid-afternoon on Wednesday the main highway from Antwerp to Ghent was jammed from ditch to ditch with a solid stream of hastening humanity, and the same was true of every road, every lane, every foot-path leading away from the advancing Germans.

"I doubt if the world has ever seen so pathetic, so heart-breaking, so terrible a procession. It seemed as though no wheeled vehicle had been left in Antwerp. There were people in motor cars, with others standing on the running-boards and clinging to the hoods and mud-guards; there were people in

Obsolete gunboats harass the Flanders coast. Great Britain has resurrected some queer old craft from the naval junk yards to assist in bombarding the German positions along the coast of Flanders

carriages, in delivery wagons, in moving-vans, in farm-carts, in omnibuses, in carts drawn by dogs, on bicycles, on horseback, and thousands upon tens of thousands in the frantic throng afoot. I saw men pushing their wives and children in wheelbarrows piled high with bedding. I saw sturdy young peasants carrying their aged parents in their arms. I saw monks in woollen robes and sandals bearing wounded men on stretchers. I saw white-faced nuns urging forward groups of war-orphaned children who had been confided to their care. I saw mothers, so weak and ill that they could scarcely totter forward, with week-old babies in their arms. I saw priests assisting the feeble and the wounded. I saw women of fashion, in fur coats and high-heeled shoes, staggering under the weight of the belongings they were carrying in sheet-wrapped bundles upon their backs. I saw white-haired men and women grasping the harness of the gun-teams or the stirrup-leathers of the troopers who, themselves exhausted from days of fighting, slept in their saddles as they rode. I saw springless farm-wagons filled with wounded soldiers, with bandaged heads and arms, and

Keeping watch in Flanders. German scouts trying to locate the enemy from a tree

with piteous white faces, and through the straw beneath them the blood dripped . . . dripped . . . dripped, leaving a crimson trail along the road.

"The confusion was beyond all imagination, the clamor deafening: the rattle and clank of batteries, the trample of hoofs, the cracking of whips, the throb of motor cars, the curses of the drivers, the moans of the wounded, the cries of women, the whimpering of frightened children, threats, pleadings, oaths, screams, imprecations—and the shuffle, shuffle of countless feet. And the fields and ditches between which these processions of disaster passed were strewn with the prostrate forms of those who, from sheer exhaustion, could go no farther. Within a few hours after the exodus began, the countryside for miles around was as bare of food as the Sahara is of grass. By this I do not mean that there was a scarcity of food; I mean that there was literally nothing to eat. Near Capellen a well-to-do resident of Antwerp eagerly exchanged his $5,000 motor car for food for his starving family. Time after time I saw the famished fugitives pause at farmhouses and offer all of their pitifully few possessions for a loaf of bread, and the country people, with tears streaming down their cheeks, could only shake their heads. I saw prosperous looking men and smartly gowned women, and wounded soldiers, pull up turnips from the fields, and devour them raw—for there was nothing else. It will probably never be known how many people perished during that awful flight from hunger, exposure, and exhaustion; many more, certainly, than lost their lives during the bombardment. Near one small town on the Dutch frontier twenty children were born during the night, in the open fields, the mothers being without beds, without shelter, and without medical attention."

Just at the end the Belgian troops which for hours had conducted their retreat through the city in good order were thrown into panic.

By some blunder the pontoon bridge, the sole means of crossing the Scheldt, was blown up. Thirty thousand soldiers were still in and about Antwerp and when these reached across to safety. Others fled across the country to be captured by the enemy or driven across the line into Holland, there to be interned until the end of the war. The road to Ghent, the chief way of escape, was so packed with soldiers and civilians that a correspondent said that to proceed against that panic-stricken mob would have been as impossible as to paddle a canoe up the rapids at Niagara. The river was as crowded with vessels, their decks packed with refugees, as Fifth Avenue is with vehicles on a pleasant afternoon in winter. In all 250,000 of the 400,-000 inhabitants of Antwerp fled. The rest were hiding in cellars or in the backs of their houses when the triumphant Germans marched along the empty streets to the strains of their military bands or the more exultant notes of their own songs.

It was a marvelous army that marched through the old Belgian town. It was little scarred by conflict, for the prize had been taken at but slender cost. Battery after battery of field artillery rumbled along the streets, and eye-witnesses report that although these guns had been in action for thirty-six hours the horses were groomed as for a parade and the harness polished till it shone again. Every regiment had its band. The cavalry was preceded by rumbling kettle drums and blaring trumpets, behind which followed the Uhlans with their forest of lances and fluttering flags, the cuirassiers in helmets and breast plates of burnished

An aërial duel within sight of Ypres. A German aeroplane, flying high over Ypres, was attacked by four British biplanes, and in spite of the heavy shrapnel fire from German guns the British machines closed around their quarry and forced it to the ground

the river front and found their escape cut off they lost all semblance of discipline or order. Some commandeered the few vessels remaining in the river, and made their way

steel, bluejackets from the ships which had not yet dared to take the sea, Bavarians in dark blue, Saxons in pale blue, and Austrians in uniforms of silver gray made up the triumphal procession which poured through absolutely deserted streets. But leaving behind this spectacular army the main body of the German troops pressed straight through Antwerp in pursuit of the thoroughly discouraged Belgian army. Of King Albert's troops there were hardly more than 50,000 left. They had every reason to be discouraged, disorganized, and demoralized. Brussels, their capital, had fallen, their king and government had fled first to Antwerp, and were now fugitives along the road to Ostend. They had seen the speedy fall of their greatest fortresses, Liége and Namur. They knew of the obliteration of such beautiful and picturesque unfortified towns as Louvain, Termond, and Malines. They had been left to bear the burden of conflict practically alone, for the little aid rendered by the handful of British sent to their assistance had been more of an irritation to their enemies than a help in time of need.

Yet this disheartened army pulled itself together and on the banks of the sluggish Yser and amidst the network of canals in Flanders fought desperately and successfully for the retention of the last bit of their native soil left to them.

While their main army pursued the retreating Belgians the German staff, with the

admirable system which characterizes their nation, set to work to restore Antwerp to its normal condition. The waterworks cut by shells were repaired. Scientific sanitation

Warneford destroys a Zeppelin. Few men have won greater fame in this war than Flight Sub-Lieutenant R. A. J. Warneford, R. N., who was given the Victoria Cross for destroying a Zeppelin near Ghent by dropping a bomb on it from his aeroplane. Warneford was killed a few days later

checked at its very start an epidemic that was threatening the city. The odor of disinfectants supplanted that of powder smoke. The electric lights, long extinguished for fear

Watching for Germans

Bruges. Neither of these ever proved serviceable for naval operations, being too shallow.

The fleeing Belgian army, now in the very southwestern corner of Belgium, had come into touch with the left wing of the allied armies which we have seen menacing Von Kluck's communications by extending northward. When this junction was affected the allied line extended unbroken from Nieuport, on the English Channel, through France to the meeting-place of that country with Germany and Switzerland, a distance of about 260 miles. While there was fighting all along this line, it became apparent early in October that the ambition of the Germans for the capture of Calais would cause the main struggle to

of German Zeppelins, blazed forth once more, for Antwerp was now a German city. The reopened post office sold German stamps, and those bearing the head of King Albert disappeared. Surest sign of all the German word "Verboten" stared at the passerby almost as frequently as in Germany itself. Proclamations posted in every public square called upon the citizens to refrain from any hostile act which "might lead to the demolition of your beautiful city."

Meanwhile the main German army swept on to the westward, partly in pursuit of the fleeing Belgians, partly in order to secure seaports on the North Sea and English Channel. The entrance to Antwerp was blocked by the control of the Scheldt's mouth by neutral Holland. Kiel and Cuxhaven were too far from the English coast to serve as effective bases for German naval demonstrations. Calais was the port for which the Germans really yearned. But for the moment they were compelled to be content with Ostend and Zeebrugge, the port of

This fieldpiece was hit squarely on the muzzle by a shell. The rifling inside the barrel can be plainly seen

be in that section of France and Belgium known as Flanders. So great was the struggle which raged there for months that it seems extraordinary to know that the territory affected was less in area than the District of Columbia, hardly greater indeed than that included within the city limits of New York or Chicago. Yet in that tiny corner of the world, not a mere battle, but practically a war was fought.

A French outpost, in advance of the first line trenches

It was a difficult country for the operations of armies. Sand dunes bordering the cold gray waters of the North Sea; sluggish tidal rivers making their way inland and connected for plodding barges by canals locked against the rise and fall of the tides; the country everywhere water-logged and at points as much as nine feet below the level of the sea, protected by dykes which the troops used first for breastworks, and afterward as a refuge from the angry waters when the Belgians flooded their fields rather than surrender this last bit of their native land—such was the topography of the country in which the hostile armies grappled early in October after the fall of Antwerp, and in which they were still battling when the midnight chimes ushered in the Happy New Year of 1915. The reflections of the soldiers in the flooded, frozen trenches must have been rather cynical at that midnight hour.

No equal period of time in the world's history, no such limited space in the globe's geography ever witnessed so much of the horrors of war as Flanders during that struggle in dreariest winter. Not the soldiers alone, but hapless civilians felt war's scourge in its utmost savagery. The district was densely populated by a people mainly agricultural, but engaged in some degree in small home manufacturing in·

How a road was blocked. Belgian trenches near Ghent

dustries. Little towns like Ypres, Ramscappelle, Furnes, Nieuport, and Dixmude, for centuries the homes of happy and thrifty people, possessing the quaintness and charm that attaches to the Flemish cities in which ancient architecture has withstood the test of time, lay in the tract of war and were ruthlessly blotted out.

It became clear early in October that the German strategy contemplated a drive down

How a modern battle looks. This is a picture of the battle as viewed from a housetop in Soissons

the coast of the Channel to Calais. About 250,000 men, Belgian, French, and British, opposed the Germans on this part of the line. The Belgians, about 50,000 strong being on the extreme left, bore the shock of the conflict. The fighting raged for weeks without material advantage to either side. Indeed after two years of the war the opposing lines through Flanders were practically identical with those taken when the German advance first reached Ostend. But nowhere and at no time in the history of the war has there been more savage fighting, nor have ever troops dared more or suffered more than those in the water-logged fields of Flanders.

Dunkirk was the first objective of the Germans. After it Calais. The activities of the British monitors, in the Channel, which could readily have been reënforced by numbers of light-draught vessels, made the advance along the coast hazardous. Accordingly at Westende the invading columns turned inland. But at once they encountered the River Yser, with canals extending in all directions from it. Behind these natural defences the Belgians, perhaps 50,000 of them, and the French had established themselves in force. Later a British corps, including several regiments of East Indians from Lahore, came to the aid of these forces. It had become apparent to General Joffre and Sir John French that in this water-logged corner of Europe the Germans intended to strike at their enemies with all the power of their marvelous morale, superb equipment, and overwhelming numbers.

Five months of fighting without cessation followed. A bleak, chill October passed into the bitterness of winter. The men who had long fought knee-deep in water now stood with freezing feet upon sheets of ice. Day by day news went out to the world of trivial successes or reverses. An advance of ninety yards was worth chronicling in the official reports. Villages were taken and retaken. In the same day's news the same town would be noted as occupied by both armies, which, paradoxical as it might seem, was true as neither occupied more than a small part of it, though destruction and death possessed it all. Not for years will the losses sustained by the armies struggling for the Yser be known —accurately they will never be known. For the first thirty days of fighting, however, the total losses of the Germans were estimated at 120,000 by one of their high officials. The French estimates were higher, while they put the losses of the Allies in the neighborhood of 75,000.

The German troops engaged during October and early November numbered about 00,000 men, according to French authorities. They were commanded at different points in the line by the Crown Prince of Bavaria, General von Fabeck, General von Demling, and the Duke of Wurtemberg. Animated by high ambition they were still further stimulated to daring by proclamations declaring it the will of the Kaiser that all Belgian resistance be stamped out before November 1st, in order that on the birthday of the Kaiser the announcement might be made to the world of the annexation of Belgium to the German Empire, the first spoil of war.

At the outset this seemed an ambition easy of attainment. The Belgian army fleeing from Antwerp was utterly demoralized. The English army moving northward from the Aisne was delayed for lack of transportation. On the coast and in Flanders the chief French force was made up of cavalry, territorials and drafted men from the navy—all under General Foch, and not strong enough to interpose a sufficient defence to the German assault. To the right of Foch, around Lille, was General Maudkin, and beyond his division was that of General de Castelnau near Arras.

As rapidly as possible the French concentrated in the neighborhood of Dixmude, holding the railroad line, and protected by the river and canals in their front. Behind them the Belgians were rapidly reorganizing. The Germans, avoiding for the time a frontal attack, sought to get around the left flank of the Allies, menacing Dunkirk and Calais and cutting the British off from their base on the Channel. In this endeavor the antagonists fought in a flooded country, where trenches became ditches, and deep canals cut through the flooded fields lured on unsuspecting troops to watery graves. The savagery of the fighting exceeded anything known in war. At one

point a ferryman's stone house, an object of attack alternately by both armies, was taken and retaken, until the fields awash around it were filled with floating bodies. Along the Yser, at Ypres and Ramscappelle, the armies were in such close contact that the fighting was much of the time hand-to-hand, and in the end neither force had gained any material advantage.

All authorities agreed that the losses of the

Training English schoolboys for future officers

Germans in this fighting far exceeded those of the Allies because of their stubborn adherence to the attack en masse. They charged in dense columns, eight abreast, offering a target no artillerist could possibly miss. "In certain trenches 120 metres long," says a French official report, "there have been found more than 2,000 corpses. This in spite of the fact that we know the Germans, whenever it is possible for them to do so, remove their dead from the field of battle."

As a result of three weeks' hard fighting along the Yser and about Ypres, the Belgian army was buttressed in its final hold upon its own land, and the desire of the Kaiser to an-

An Egyptian camel corps on review

nex Belgium was, for the moment at least, thwarted. Dunkirk, Calais, and Boulogne were saved for the Allies. The spirit of the Belgian troops was renewed, and that of the French and British greatly stimulated by the decided check to the German onrush. The Germans were not driven back, however. They dug themselves in, in Flanders, as they had done all across France, and the year closed without any indication of the ability of the Allies to drive them out. Nevertheless the check was essentially an allied victory.

The territory over which the hostile armies were fighting so tenaciously and savagely was devastated as no land since we began to talk of "civilized warfare" has ever been. Dixmude, Ypres, Ramscappelle—all beautiful towns—were reduced to ruins. The destruction seems almost to have been wanton, the artillerists hurling their shells upon historic edifices apparently for the mere pleasure of

seeing them crumble. Of the 18,000 inhabitants of Ypres, virtually all were driven out—only the dead remained. The houses that were not destroyed by shell-fire were pillaged and burned by the German invaders. A correspondent visiting the city after the bombardment had continued a month describes its appearance thus:

"For a distance of three hundred yards German shells had ploughed their way through parallel streets, forming a new ruthless avenue through the town of Ypres.

"The most terrible sight of all lay farther on. The Cathedral of Saint Martin, a magnificent edifice of the Fifteenth Century, containing the tomb of Jansenius, is nothing but a mass of ruins. It was dusk when we reached it.

"Climbing a heap of stone débris, discolored by the fumes released from shells, I saw in the gloom of the ruined aisle a red glow which for a moment I took to be that of an altar light. Clambering farther into the ruins of the church I found this to be nothing but the still-smouldering embers of the cathedral.

"For while we were still there the Germans, heaven knows for what reason, were busily engaged in pouring incendiary bombs upon the already ruined city. Next door to the cathedral stood the magnificent Market Hall of Ypres. It is now literally a heap of ruins. I would wish the people of half a dozen cities in

The barber in the French trenches

Some American members of the French Foreign Legion

the textile district could imagine they possessed markets of the artistic beauty of Westminster Abbey, together with their own thriving trade, and imagine the scene of utter desolation and ruin which I have endeavored to describe there at Ypres.

"The town has not only been bombarded systematically with a view to destruction rather than military advantage, but it has also been sacked with all the thoroughness of the German system. It was not only a shell; it is a burst shell. Its very streets have been destroyed. In the main road from Ypres one of those 'Jack Johnson's,' which the French troops, with the same light-heartedness which characterizes our own have given the name of marmites, or soup kettles, has made a hole big enough to contain a London motorbus. These huge pits yawn in every road along the front.''

A British official report, setting aside for the moment cold officialism, described strikingly the conditions of life in the trenches along the Yser:

"The condition of the trenches became wretched beyond description. From having to sit or stand in a mixture of straw and liquid mud, the men had to contend with half-frozen slush. 'It is an ill wind, however,' and one good point about the wet weather is that it made the ground so soft that the enemy's howitzer shells sink some depth

before they detonate, and expend a great part of their energy in an upward direction, throwing the mud about.

"Nevertheless the wet and cold have added greatly to the hardships of the troops in the trenches, and the problem how to enable them to keep their feet reasonably dry and warm now is engaging serious attention.

"At one place, owing to the kindness of the proprietor, certain works recently were placed at our disposal as a wholesale bathhouse, lavatory, and repair shop. In the works are a number of vats large enough to contain several men at one time. They serve most excellently for the provision of hot baths for the men on relief from the trenches.

"While the men are enjoying their bath, their clothes are taken away, their underclothing washed or burned, and replaced by a new set. At the same time their uniforms are fumigated, cleaned and repaired and buttons sewed on. The repairs are done by a band of women who are employed for the pur-

Sodding a dugout. These underground habitations are covered with sod to keep enemy airmen from locating them

pose. By this installation some 1,500 men are catered to in every way."

Digging in, shivering day and night in the trenches, killing now and then with a rifle shot some other poor fellow quite as weary of the war as his killer, dodging bombs or throwing them, starving, hopelessly and endlessly pursuing vermin, going unwashed and often unfed—so both Allies and Germans spent the winter months with practically no advantage

through the mountains that the Germans had taken early in the war were slowly regained. Instead of the German capture of Verdun, which had so long been expected, the news came daily of French successes near St. Mihiel and St. Die. The former of these positions, marking the extreme German advance into France along that line, was the scene of constant fighting. Could the French but break through at that point, they would

Three blind soldiers at St. Dunctan's Villa, a magnificent London property given by Otto Kahn, an American banker, for a home for blinded soldiers and sailors

won or lost. December passed; 1914 gave way to 1915; and still the Germans clung to the soil they had won, still the French and English barred their way to any further conquest. But the Allies were steadily growing stronger while the needs of Von Hindenberg in the west, where the fighting was again savage, compelled the sending thither of heavy reënforcements from France and Belgium.

As a result of this the French pushed their way ahead in Alsace, and on the right of their line became the aggressors. The roads

cut the German communications with Metz, and put the entire Army of the Crown Prince in jeopardy. But week after week the pounding went on without serious result. The line of the Meuse still held practically as the limit of the Germans' advance though at one to two points they had indeed crossed the river.

Verdun alone among the fortresses of France gave that example of stubborn defiance and protracted resistance which had been expected of the forts at Lille and Namur. And it indeed was protected rather than a protector, for, seeing the impotence of their

Louvain, city of learning, the Oxford of Belgium, wrecked by war

Louvain laid waste. Curiously enough, statues in the streets were seldom injured

forts before the heavy new German artillery, the French determined to defend Verdun from without rather than within, and threw forward their trenches with infantry defenders to such a point that the Germans were never near enough to the fortress to bring their heaviest artillery to bear. The lines of hostile trenches approached each other so closely that the soldiers shouted messages across the field, and patching up temporary truces went amicably together down to the

the towns within twenty miles of the frontier, setting up their own governments and courts. They say that when the first crier opened the court "in the name of the French people," old men who had been annexed with the country by Germany in 1871 burst into tears and the young people ran about the streets waving the tricolor.

By the end of the year the French had possession of the whole Vosges region, the valley of the Thur, and many strategic

Indian soldiers on their way to France

neighboring stream to bathe—putting off, it would appear, their enmities with the uniforms that symbolized them.

While holding the invaders back from their territory the French were making inroads—small, indeed, but to the French mind immensely gratifying—upon German lands. For Alsace, which had been lost in 1871, into which at the opening of this war the soldiers of the Republic had exultantly streamed only to be driven out again, was now coming once more into their possession. From Belfort, the most southeasterly of the French fortresses, they poured into Alsace, occupying

mountain passes. Their material gains were little. Mühlhausen and Altkirch were still holding out against them. But their positions were such as to promise an active advance in the spring when the heavy snows that blocked the mountain roads should have melted away. Yet their successes in that region were no offset to the tremendous advantage held by the forces of the Kaiser in the west.

For, checked in his advance, forced to a standstill as he was, the Kaiser still held at the end of 1914 the position in the west practically of a conqueror. All Belgium,

Her husband slain, her home destroyed

Homeless in the path of the invaders

The ruined church of St. Pierre, Louvain, from the rear

So thoroughly were his troops entrenched in France and Belgium, it seemed nothing could drive them out. "The march upon Berlin," said a German general in answer to a French boast, "would take years and cost 5,000 men a day." Probably this was no over-statement. The German positions in Belgium, at least, seemed almost impregnable, while the past had been for the German Emperor one

save perhaps 35 square miles in its extreme corner, was his. Belgian cities like Brussels, Antwerp, and Ghent were ruled by his officers, and paid tribute to his treasury. His armies held about 8,000 square miles of French territory, inhabited by 2,500,000 Frenchmen. Save for a little corner of East Prussia, all the fighting was on the soil of his enemies; his own land knew little of the horrors of war.

General Joffre, directing the French force

long record of victory.

Yet the victories were of a sort that, as the event shows did not hasten the end of the war but rather prolonged it. The callous and cynical indifference to neutral rights manifested in the invasion of Belgium not only brought England into the field as a foe to Germany but more than a year later was a powerful argument for the entrance of Italy upon the struggle as one of the Allies.

The work of a shell in the Malines Cathedral

General von Buelow of the German army

The atrocities perpetrated in Belgium were awakening an ever louder chorus of indignation from neutral nations. The presence of a foe on their soil aroused the French to such prodigies of valor and sacrifice as awakened the admiration of the world. In the end it seems likely that 1914 will be looked upon as the time when the glory of the Kaiser reached its culmination, for thereafter the tide of success no longer carried him smoothly to victory.

Strassburg, next to Metz the most important city in Alsace-Lorraine, toward which the French forces first marched

CHRONOLOGY OF PERIOD TREATED IN CHAPTER III

September 15.   Beginning the Battle of the Aisne, extending from Noyon to Verdun.

September 17.   French advancing in Woevre.

September 18.   Allies, left and right wings advance.   Heavy fighting at Rheims.   Beginning of the German bombard ment of Cathedral of Notre Dame in that city.

September 20.   Heavy fighting at Rheims and Soissons.

September 21.   Allies gain between Rheims and the Argonne.

September 23.   Germans bombard Verdun. (The German attack upon this famous fortress will be treated in a chapter by itself.   Verdun was first bombarded September 4, 1914. On August 1, 1916, it still defied its assailants, although for six months prior to that date the most strenuous efforts of the German army, led by the Crown Prince, had been put forth for its subjection.)

September 26.   Germans take Fort des Romaines and cross the Meuse.

September 29.   Germans take Malines and shell the outer forts of Antwerp.   The fighting on the Aisne still continues.

October 1.   Belgians repulse German attacks on Antwerp forts.

October 2.   Allies' northern advance in the west checked at Arras.

October 4.   Germans capture three forts defending Antwerp. Allied relief expedition reaches Antwerp,

October 6.   Heavy fighting along the Oise, Soissons, Lille, and Ypres.

October 8.   Bombardment of Antwerp.

October 10.   Antwerp surrenders.   Belgian army escapes.

October 11.   British and Belgian forces from Antwerp make a stand at Ostend.

October 12.   Belgians occupy Ghent and press on toward Ostend and Bruges.   Lille taken by Germans.

October 14.   Belgians abandon Ostend and join Allies in the field.   Allies reoccupy Ypres.

October 16.   Germans occupy Ostend.   Their battleline reaching the sea for the first time.   Their attempt to take Dunkirk checked.

October 18.   Fighting along Ypres canal and River Yser. The beginning of a deadlock lasting fully eighteen months in the water-logged section of northwestern France and southwestern Belgium.

AUSTRIAN TROOPS FORDING A RIVER AS THE RUSSIANS WITHDRAW

Russian regiment storming the stronghold of Josepovo. The attackers encountered great barricades of logs and rocks so placed that they could be cut loose to slide down the embankment like avalanches. Hundreds of men were crushed, but the regiment swept on to the top and captured the fort

CHAPTER IV

THE WAR IN THE EAST—SWIFT INVASION OF EAST PRUSSIA BY RUSSIANS—THEIR
DEFEAT AT TANNENBERG—RUSSIANS ADVANCE INTO GALICIA—CHARACTER OF
AUSTRIAN ARMIES—THEIR FAILURE BEFORE RUSSIAN ATTACK—GERMANS COME
TO THE RESCUE—TIDE OF BATTLE BEFORE CRACOW—WARSAW AND PRZEMYSL

S O ALL-COMPELL-ING and spectacular was the march of the German hosts through Belgium and France to the very gates of Paris that during the first six weeks of the war attention was little directed to its progress in eastern Europe—on the borders of Austria and Servia where the conflagration started, and on the Russo-German frontier where lay from the very first Germany's point of greatest weakness. The world knew, of course, that beyond the little-known banks of the Vistula, the Dneister, and the San the great Russian monster was slowly rolling together its masses of armed men ready to overwhelm Germany and Austria by sheer weight of numbers. But the world knew not the new Russia. It considered the boundless steppes, the widely separated villages, the single-track railroads, the highways which a rain turns into a bottomless bog, and it dismissed the thought of Russia becoming a factor in the war for at least two months after its declaration. This was obviously the anticipation of Emperor William, and was the second of the two illusions which led him to embark upon the struggle with a supreme confidence which the event ill-justified—the first being his misconception of the isolated position of Germany among the nations of Europe.

Among military experts generally August 26th was fixed as about the earliest date upon which the Russians could complete mobilization and take the offensive. But fully two weeks earlier the Czar's legions were in motion. The swiftness of the Russian advance found Germany most inadequately prepared. Only three army corps, less than 150,000 men in all, were available for defence in East Prussia when the Russians first struck at Gumbinnen on August 20, 1914. So thoroughly had the Kaiser stripped his eastern frontier of troops in order the more certainly to overwhelm Belgium and France that the Russians, with more than 750,000 men, at first seemed able to sweep all before them. In a week the greater part of East Prussia was in their possession and Königsberg, a fortified town of 250,000 inhabitants on the Baltic, and the fortresses of Thorn and Gradenz, were besieged. The country is a difficult one for military operations, being marshy and plentifully interspersed with small lakes. The progress of the Russian armies, too, was checked at the frontier by a change in the gauge of the railroads, Russia using a wider gauge.

Examination of the map will show the nature of the strategic problem with which the Russians had to grapple. That part of the Czar's domain known as Russian Poland projects to the westward between East Prussia and Austria-Hungary until it reaches a point only 140 miles from Berlin as the crow flies. From the first Berlin was the Czar's objective though the topography of the country in which his armies operated made it equally easy for him until late in his campaign to strike at either Vienna or Berlin, while the magnitude of his armies made it perfectly possible for him to menace both capitals. But by agreement with the Allies he was to threaten Berlin from the very beginning of his operations in order that the Kaiser might be compelled to recall some of his troops from France to protect his own capital.

Though it would appear that the westward thrust of Russian Poland made it simple for the Russians to begin their invasion of Germany within 140 miles of Berlin, the principles of safe strategy would not permit this. The frontiers of East Prussia to the north and

forces operating before Paris, and dispatch them to the danger point in the east. That was the moment when Von Kluck halted his hitherto resistless march upon the French capital. It was the critical incident which showed that the delay in Belgium and the unexpected swiftness of Russian mobilization had defeated the Kaiser's plan of first crushing France and then turning upon the Russian Bear. The moment when the diversion of German troops from France to East Prus-

Polish women work for the relief of refugees. Poland has its relief problem no less than Belgium, and the hardships endured by the citizens of its destroyed towns are almost beyond description

Galicia to the south were lined with forts protecting hostile Germans and Austrians who would close in behind the Russian troops, should they take the most direct route to Berlin, and cut them off from their base.

Russia struck first at East Prussia, where there were only three German army corps, or about 150,000 men to meet. For the overwhelming force which the Czar put into the field this was hardly a stumbling block. Despite the gallant resistance, despite, too, the difficult nature of the campaign the invaders moved resistlessly onward until the menacing progress of their armies forced the Kaiser to recall two army corps from the

sia was compelled was as fraught with importance to the history of Europe, as was to the history of the United States the appearance of the *Monitor* in Hampton Roads on the very day when, but for it, the *Merrimac* would have completed the destruction of the Union fleet and put to sea to lay the cities of the North under tribute.

Under command of General Rennenkampf, a dashing cavalryman who brought back from the war in Manchuria the title of "the Russian Tiger," it took the Russians scarcely a week to sweep so far into German Poland that the non-military world began to think that Germany's downfall was destined to

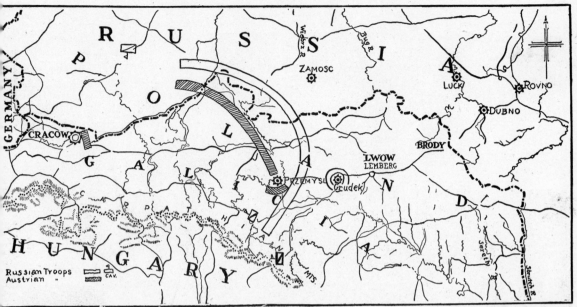

The Russians were long halted on the line shown in Galicia. Cracow and Przemysl were both relieved by the Germans on the verge of surrender

General map of the Eastern Theatre of War, the shaded portion showing extent of the Russian advance. During the period covered by Chapter IV the Russians menaced Königsberg, were beaten at Allenstein, and in Galicia progressed as far as Przemysl, while their cavalry passed beyond the Carpathians. The Germans pushed east in Poland almost to Warsaw

Cossacks raid a German motor supply train

ome from that quarter. Looking back upon that moment, so critical to Germany in every phase of her many-sided campaign, one can but admire the magnificent determination with which the Kaiser and his General Staff closed their ears to the cries for help from East Prussia and stubbornly adhered to their purpose to crush France before turning to meet the Russian peril. Königsberg, Thorn, and Grandenz, all fortresses of the first class, were invested before the German force under General Hindenburg was sufficiently reënforced to make headway against the invaders. To secure these reënforcements, Belgian towns that

Spies taken from a haystack by Cossack soldiers

had been taken at the sacrifice of thousands of German lives were stripped of their garrisons, and the line of communication of the army before Paris, with its base at Aix-la-Chapelle, was left so scantily guarded as to tempt the Belgian army to new activity.

But when the Germans did turn their attention to the Russians in eastern Prussia the work they did was sharp and effective. In all, General Hindenburg had about 50,000 troops to oppose to a vastly superior Russian force, but within a week he had pushed them back from the fortified positions they menaced, forced them to fight the pitched battle of Tannenburg, and defeated them decisively, capturing nearly 80,000 men.

A difficult and treacherous country and a German general who from youth had studied the characteristics of this country and knew instantly and precisely how best to apply them to the needs of any military situation that might confront him, were the two factors which contributed chiefly to the Russian disaster in East Prussia.

The district in which occurred the battle, which the Germans call Tannenberg and the Russians Allenstein, is sparsely inhabited with few railroads and bad highways. It is part of what is known as the Masurian Lake district, a region of sandy hillocks, scant patches of

Russian commissary officers determining the portions of food for the soldiers

forest, and innumerable bodies of water ranging from small pools to considerable lakes. Much of the land that seems to the eye solid is in fact a bog which refuses to support the weight of man. The lakes are doubly treacherous because across some extend fords of sand or gravel capable of carrying the heaviest burdens, while the bottom of a sheet of water only a few hundred yards away will be of illimitable mud. In places ridges of sand or clay extend into the lake and come to a sudden end, leaving any body of troops that think to use them as fords, entrapped in deep water or deeper mud. By ages of labor the Germans had laid out narrow turnpikes between the lakes, but these were insufficient for the passage of any large army and out of touch with each other. There was no possibility of deploying troops between the roads. If the road was so crowded that the marching men spread out into the adjacent fields they would find themselves mired. It was almost impossible to judge by the appearance of the surface whether the ground might be trusted to bear any considerable burden.

The physical menace of this treacherous territory would have been as great to either side had it not been that the Germans were commanded by a man who had foreseen years before the possibility of a great battle in this territory and prepared himself to utilize to the fullest extent all its treacherous qualities against any possible enemy. General von

Russian machine guns, captured by the Germans and exhibited in Berlin

Hindenburg was born in his section of eastern Prussia, served all his life in the army, and years before asked to be assigned to duty in this section the very nature of which might well repel any soldier. His furloughs were spent among the lakes, and he knew intimately the nature of the bottom of each, the character of its ford, and the degree of reliance that might be put upon the stability of the strips of soil separating them. "The Old Man of the Lakes" his soldiers came to call him.

What the Russians did to a bridge at Przemysl

With his knowledge of the nature of the battlefield to which he was inviting the Russian invaders, Hindenburg calmly awaited their attack. He was confident that once they were enmeshed in that water-logged region his superior knowledge of the territory would make amends for any possible shortage in his men. The first clash between the two forces had resulted in Russian victory. With two armies, numbering in the neighborhood of 200,000 men, they had advanced into East Prussia both from the east and from the south. They encountered the Germans first at Gumbinnen, defeated them there and drove them back upon Königsberg. A few days later another Russian army, again enjoying the superiority in numbers, overwhelmed a German army corps near Frankenau. By the 25th of August a vast crowd of refugees was fleeing to the westward and it seemed that nothing would block the Russian advance. But by this time Von Hindenburg had secured

The ghastly task of clearing a battlefield

what he believed to be a sufficient force and
was ready to make a stand. His troops were
drawn in part from the German line as far
away as Flanders. In all he had probably
200,000 men or nearly as many as the Russian, General Samsonoff, who opposed him.
Within forty-eight hours after the opening of
battle he had dealt the Russians such blows
that nothing was left for them but retreat.

an impassable bog in which horses, men, an
guns slowly sank from sight. They essaye
the passage of the lakes by fords which le
them as far as the middle of the waters an
then dropped them off to destruction. Ther
was no possibility of rearguard fighting tha
would cover such a retreat. There was n
chance of coöperation between the variou
bodies of the army which rapidly became de

A German masked battery

Then followed the greatest disaster of the
early days of the war to the allied forces.
For Hindenburg had so utilized his knowledge
of the Masurian Lake country that he had
penned the unfortunate Russians in that be-
wildering and fatal maze of marshes, creeks,
lakes, and quagmires. He was well provided
with field artillery, and the heavy fire of his
guns made the orderly retreat of the Russians
along the narrow road impossible. They
broke and took to the fields, only to find that
what appeared to be solid ground was in fact

moralized. Regiments and brigades were
swallowed up, and the toll of death taken by
Hindenburg's merciless artillery was moderate
in comparison to the numbers of men swallowed up in the mud and water. The accounts of eye-witnesses are ghastly in their
descriptions of the cries of whole battalions of
men rising out of the night from some dark
quicksand in which they were being slowly engulfed.

   The portion of the Russian army that was
caught in this colossal trap was fairly an-

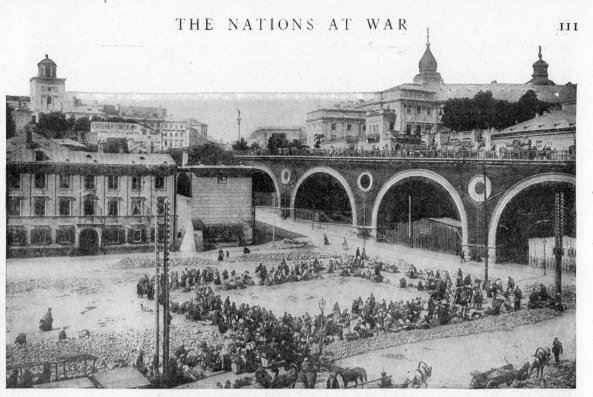

Civilians preparing to leave Warsaw as the Germans approach

German troops, attend service in the garrison church at Przemysl

Cossacks clash with Austrian cavalry

Russian infantry and civilians evacuating Przemysl

ihilated. More than 80,000 men were captured by the Germans, and it is estimated that almost as many more lost their lives. The fragments of the army recoiled upon Russia and it was long before they recuperated sufficiently to take up again the task of invading Prussia. Numbers of the prisoners and hundreds of the captured cannon were sent to Berlin where they arrived in season to be paraded in triumph before the people on the anniversary of Sedan. It was at least some compensation to the German nation for the failure of the army in the west to enter Paris on that day. Hindenburg became the idol of the German people, and though in later actions his good fortune did not adhere to him, he never lost the heroic position he attained by the battle of the Masurian Lakes.

By the 1st of October the whole of eastern Prussia had been cleared of Russians, the Germans having concentrated there their main endeavors in the east. Besides freeing their own territory of the enemy, they were trying to divert the Russians from the invasion of Galicia to the south, which by this time was shown to be the main feature of the

Russian prisoners after being bathed, shaved, and fumigated by the German sanitation corps

Russian campaign. But from this the Russians refused to be diverted. Rennenkampf, having lost the battle of Allenstein, and retreated as far as the banks of the Neiman, made a brief stand there, then attacked in his turn, driving the Germans back to their own frontier. There we may leave him for a time, and turn our attention to the main Russian campaign in Austrian Poland or Galicia.

If the reader will consult again the general map of the scene of the war in the east he will see that just south of that part of Russian Poland which juts out into German territory lies the Austrian province of Galicia. If natural boundaries formed in fact the boundaries of states in Europe, Galicia would belong to Russia, and the frontier be pushed back to the south where the line of the Carpathian Mountains rears a natural barrier between the two countries. International politics, however, made Galicia Austrian nearly forty years ago, and as nature had left it peculiarly exposed to Russian invasion, it became to the war in the east what Belgium was in the west —the great field of battle of the warring nations.

Austria was in no way fitted to cope with Russia in the field. An intensely military nation, if the tone of her society in time of peace is at all representative, she has had a more inglorious record of defeats and unsuccessful wars than any power of Europe. The nominal war strength of her armies, 1,360,000 with a maximum strength of 4,320,000, is far more impressive than their history. The last time Austria-Hungary appeared in panoply of war—except in petty

Balkan quarrels—was in 1866 when her forces were decisively beaten at Königgratz by the Prussians, their allies in the war of 1914.

After having lighted the fuse that fired the war magazine of all Europe, Austria settled

General Popoff watching the battle of Prazasnysz. During this fight a single division of the Russian army repulsed a superior force of Germans and took 10,000 prisoners. It was here that Hindenburg's "lightning drive" into Russian Poland was stopped

back to an inglorious career of futile self-defense. Her armies did indeed bombard Belgrade and begin a brief invasion of Servia, but were speedily called back to meet the Russian menace to the north. A brief rush into the territory of the Bear carried the Austrian standards as far as Lublin in Russian Poland. There they stopped. The Russian army, estimated at a million strong,

Danzig—a strong maritime fortress and seaport of Germany on the left bank of the western arm of the Vistula

The *Rathaus* in Breslau

German Taube brought to earth by Cossacks in Russian Poland

struck in its turn. Remorselessly, over-whelmingly, rolling resistlessly onward like a tidal wave, it bore back the Austrians by sheer power of weight. The Russian left rested in the passes of the Carpathians, its right reached as far into Russian Poland as Lublin. Two rivers barred the progress of this army, the Bug and the San, but despite the savage resistance of the Austrian artillery —the most efficient branch of that country's military force—both were passed. The country was a difficult one in which to operate. The rivers were either bordered by wide marshes or flowed tumultuously through

deep, rocky canyons. The roads in the main were wretched, and had the Russians or Austrians possessed the great guns which the Germans dragged so rapidly along the level highways of Belgium, they could have made no use of them.

There were, however, no such ponderous fortresses to stay the Russian progress in Galicia as confronted the Germans in Belgium. Lemberg, a place of moderate strength, was taken September 1st, the victory being accompanied by the capture of an enormous body of Austrians, estimated at the time at 80,000, and the killing or wounding of half as many more. To Russia the victory was an offset to the disaster of Tannenberg which befell the same week. Practically as many men were lost to Austria here as were lost to Russia in the battle of the Masurian Lakes.

This victory had its prompt

The horror of war—one of the Austrian dead

effect on the German lines before Paris. It was only too clear that with Lemberg fallen and the Russians outnumbering the Austrians nearly three to one, there was a new danger threatening Berlin from the south and east. At the beginning of the war Austria, thinking like her ally that Russia was too big to move swiftly, had lent two army corps to Germany. These were hastily recalled. With them came five German corps, snatched from Von Kluck and Von Buelow while the Battle of the Marne was in progress. The new-comers set themselves stubbornly across the Russian path and there fol-lowed weeks of fighting as des-perate as that in the fair fields of France and Bel-gium.

The objective points were Przemysl and Cracow, and in the struggle for these fortified positions a host of battles were fought in fields that history will scarce record, though the numbers engaged exceeded those at Waterloo or Sedan.

Despite the overpowering numbers of the Russians, however, the operations of September, 1914, showed them quite incapable of overcoming the superior discipline and strategic skill of the Germans. The Austrians, indeed, they fought to a standstill. After the victory of Lemberg the Russian advance toward Cracow was steady, opposed by the Austrian forces in battles like that at Dukla, but never long halted. Przemysl, an important stronghold with an unpronounceable name, which long troubled disputants on war strategy, was invested

Burning the bodies of the dead in Russia. Cremation is frequently resorted to as a substitute for burial when vast numbers of bodies must be disposed of in a short time. This method of disposal of the dead is most resorted to when the ground is deeply frozen, making the digging of graves a difficult and tedious task

and left for later attack as the Russian advance pressed on. The invaders were greatly helped by the fact that they were operating in a country the Polish inhabitants of which, though subjects of Austria-Hungary, were nevertheless covertly friendly to the Russians.

A portion of the town of Kalvaria, Poland after it had been shelled by the Germans

They showed their friendship by eagerly giving information as to the movements of the Austrian troops, and many curious devices were employed to convey the information. A coal fire making black smoke signified one thing; a wood fire making whitish smoke, another. In the village streets the position of the images on the Eikons, or shrines, told one story to the invading Cossacks, while a seemingly innocent display of household utensils, or linen hanging from a window, would put the

pursuing cavalry on the track of the retreating enemy.

By the end of September the Austrians had successfully withdrawn their troops which had invaded Russian Poland, and which the world had been informed, falsely, had been cut off and captured by the Russians. Forming a junction with the right wing of the Austrian army, these troops took up a line with their left resting on the Vistula River, and their right resting on Przemysl, whose ring of forty-one forts connected by railroads and garrisoned by 60,000 men long held the invaders in check. Jaroslav, another fortress of less power, also proved a serious stumbling-block in the Russians' path. Beyond it, and extending to Cracow, the force opposed to the Russians was mainly composed of Germans, and against them the forces of the Czar made but little headway. September ended with these two armies beating against each other with but little decisive result. The ceaseless attrition of the Russian hordes, however, had told heavily upon the Austrians, who are estimated to have lost during the month's campaigning 300,000 men and 1,000 guns, or nearly a third of their entire force. During this period, too, the Serbs and Montenegrins had been busy on the southern borders of Austria, compelling that nation to keep at least 500,000 men there.

Essentially the Russian army at this time might be taken as a single line of battle, numbering about 2,300,000 men, extending from the Baltic Sea to the Carpathians. In East Prussia it was confronted by a German army of 1,000,000 men. In Russian Poland the Germans had about 500,000, and, though outnumbered by the Russians, held them

Clash between advance guards. One of the hundreds of small skirmishes in which many lives are lost without any decided advantage being gained. A detachment of Germans pushing into Russian territory is met by a patrol

long in check on their own soil. In the south the Germans and Austrians together had perhaps 1,000,000 more.

At the beginning of the month of September it appeared that the Russian advance was irresistible. German troops were withdrawn from Belgium and France and rushed to the east. The advance on Paris was checked. The long struggle along the banks of the Somme and the Aisne dragged its slow length along, and the world thought that the Russian Bear had awakened in time to balk

ONE OF THE FORTS AT PRZEMYSI AF

BOMBARDMENT BY KRUPP HOWITZERS

Austrian prisoners captured in the Carpathians

Germany of her French prey and transfer the scene of the struggle to German soil. But the world was deceived. That marvelous fighting machine the Kaiser and his General Staff had so patiently builded proved equal to this new emergency, and the Russians were roughly checked before they had been able to make more than a slight inroad on the soil of the Fatherland.

and abandoned their advance to the south of the Carpathians. The world wondered at this retreat in the face of continuous victory, but it was learned in time that the Russian supplies of munitions of war had been exhausted. It was months before the armies of the Czar were suitably equipped to resume the offensive. Meantime the Germans pushed into Russian Poland and soon it was War-

Circassian troops in bivouac

Indeed the sudden check to the Russians, and the counter-attack delivered by the Germans in the first half of October were little less remarkable as military achievements than the rush of Von Kluck's army upon Paris in August. The world had settled down to see the Russian Bear stride into Germany, crushing down all opposition. Berlin itself, despite messages of encouragement and reassurance from the Kaiser, began to show signs of unrest and approaching panic. But scarcely had the real fighting force of Germany come into contact with the Russian advance when all was checked. The invaders receded from Cracow and from Przemysl,

saw, a Russian capital, instead of Cracow, the Austrian stronghold, that was endangered.

After the German successes in the Masurian Lake region Von Hindenburg began that invasion of Russian Poland which, with varying fortunes but with the general trend of success on the German side, was still in progress when the first six months of the war closed, February 1, 1915.

Warsaw was the objective, and for these six months was the point upon which converged all the German lines of attack. These lines came from the north *up* the Vistula, from the south *down* the Vistula, and directly from the west with Breslau for the German

Königsberg, an East Prussian stronghold

Russian troops in the trenches, waiting for a German attack

ase. The first army was commanded by General von Hindenburg in person, the second by General Dankl of the Austrian army, and the third by the Crown Prince of Bavaria. The concerted movement was begun October 4th, and the forces then engaged numbered on the German side about 400,000 with about 200,000 Austrians. They were heavily outnumbered by the Russians under the Grand Duke Nicholas, but nevertheless pressed to the very suburbs of Warsaw without serious check in the first week of the fighting. Here their path was blocked by not less than a million Russians, who held the trenches in the German front while their great numbers enabled them to flank the invaders with both cavalry and infantry. Before this overwhelming force the invaders retreated, and by the end of the month were virtually expelled from Russian soil.

Russian infantry advancing under fire

Photograph by James F. J. Archibald

Stragglers from the Russian line of march

Russian armies in Galicia and in East Prussia could close in behind the audacious invaders and cut them off. This was precisely what they did, and, beginning November 15th, ten days of continuous fighting ended in Russian victory. The newspaper reports from Petrograd were delirious with claims of victory, and even Berlin admitted disaster. Warsaw had been saved after the Kaiser's troops had come within sound of its bells. Von Hindenburg was reported, falsely, a prisoner. At Lodz and at Mlwa the Germans were decisively beaten. East Prussia was still occupied by the Russians in force, and in Galicia the Czar's successes were daily augmenting, and the Austrian armies were rapidly disintegrating. Though in the neighborhood of Lodz and Lowicz German successes were reported, the main story of the fighting along the eastern battleline was one of German disaster.

When December was ushered in it appeared that the Russians by mere force of numbers had checked finally the German advance upon Warsaw. Not much was heard of the earlier

But to accomplish this Russia had been compelled to recall in part her armies from Galicia and the Carpathians. The siege of Przemysl was raised, to be renewed later, the troops of the Czar were withdrawn from Jaroslav, and Hungary was freed from their presence. These sacrifices had been compelled by the menace of Von Hindenburg's westward drive. With his retreat it appeared that Russia would retake her lost ground. Again Russian troops flowed over into East Prussia and Galicia. By the middle of November Przemysl was again invested, the Cossacks were in the passes of the Carpathians, and the Czar's guns pounded at the gates of Cracow. Before November was half ended the Russians, save for their heavy and irreparable losses at Tannenberg, had regained the advantage they had lost.

But it was again only the ebb of the German tide. Once more it turned to the flood and flowed back across the territory. Ending their retreat about the middle of November, the General Staff hurriedly concentrated their eastern armies in the neighborhood of Thorn and again turned their faces toward Warsaw. Their advance menaced Russian communications and did in fact cut the railroad lines which tied the chief Russian army to Warsaw. But the movement had its perils. As the Germans had cut the Russian communications, so the

Cossacks capture German spies on the thatched roof of a Polish farmhouse

Russian infantry, in hastily constructed trench, awaiting Austrian attack

Russian promise of "Berlin in three weeks," but the decisiveness with which the German advance upon Warsaw had been stopped without compelling the Russians to withdraw from either East Prussia or Galicia was generally accepted by observers as indicative of the end.

Then in a few weeks Von Hindenburg, backed by the marvelous efficiency of the German army, turned the tables for the third time, and once again Berlin rang with the praises of her new war-lord.

All of Von Hindenburg's plans centred upon a descent upon Russian Poland from East Prussia. Much of the territory in which he planned to operate was marshy, full of small lakes, and intersected with sluggish streams.

Russian prisoners just as captured. They usually require vigorous attention from the sanitary corps

The roads were mere dirt highways difficult in wet weather for ordinary luggage vans, but utterly impassable for the heavy artillery

A view of the banks of the river San in Przemysl. This picture was made while the Russians had possession of the Galician fortress which they took after a protracted siege but were unable to hold

Cossacks entering the captured fortress of Przemysl

which Von Hindenburg intended to marshal against his foe. In December, then, the Germans began to prepare for a winter campaign and a third attack on Warsaw. The frozen roads and rivers were to be the highways; the snow should bear the German baggage trains newly mounted on runners. The familiar gray-green of the German infantry disappeared, or was covered up by heavy sheepskin coats, white and invisible against the snow. Cannon were mounted on runners. Motor sledges of new types appeared. Scouting parties on foot were equipped with skiis. Great depots of winter supplies were established at Thorn and Posen. Lodz, the chief manufacturing town of Poland, and Lowicz, an important railroad centre, were heavily fortified, the industrial edifices of the towns being torn down to supply material for the forts, and guns brought from the Krupp Works in Essen for the armament.

In the struggle for Warsaw, which became toward the end of the year the chief bone of contention in the eastern theatre of war, the price paid by each of the contestants was a heavy one. Owing to the policy of secrecy adopted by all the governments involved, the precise losses of each in any given battle,

campaign, or month of the war will not be known definitely for years, or until official historians begin to give out the authorized

Fighting with the bayonet in a Polish cemetery

accounts of the campaigns. Petrograd, however, claimed that the Germans had lost more than 200,000 men in their efforts to reach Warsaw up to January, 1915. Prisoners to the number of 135,840 were claimed by the

Russians. These figures were strenuously denied by the Germans who claimed themselves to hold 306,290 Russian prisoners, besides 3,575 officers.

On the last day of the year the Germans claimed to have taken 136,000 prisoners, 100 cannon, and 300 machine guns in the Poland campaign within two months.

Yet despite this fierce fighting, this marshaling of legions of men and multitudes of guns from prodigious distances — Von Hindenburg was said to have 30,000 auto trucks for transportation purposes—this campaign ended with the struggling forces just where they began.

But early in the spring of 1915 the Russians, being in possession of Przemysl, determined to invade Hungary by way of the Carpathian passes. For the time operations in East Prussia were confined on the part of the Russians strictly to the defensive. The Germans indeed were pressing them hard enough there to keep them busy. The advance through the Carpathian Mountains went well enough at the outset. As in the earlier attacks the Austrians proved no match for the multitudinous soldiers of the

Austrians laying a field telephone line across a stream

Great White Czar. But the Germans rushed reenforcements and leaders to the threatened point and just at the most critical moment struck the Russian line on the Dunajec River, broke it and thereby flanking the line through the Carpathians, forced the hurried retreat of the Russians. Almost simultaneously up in East Prussia the Germans started a drive with the idea of forcing the Russians back against Warsaw. North and south the Teutonic offensive was successful. The Russian line which had extended in an approximately direct line from the border of East Prussia to the Carpathians was bent into an acute angle like a pair of partly open dividers with Warsaw at the point of junction. It soon became impossible for the Russians to maintain their line of communications from Warsaw to the south, and just as the second year of the war was beginning in August, 1915 that capital was evacuated and eagerly seized by the Germans.

The fall of Warsaw was the signal for another general Russian retreat—the third apparently irretrievable reverse suffered by the armies of that country since the beginning of the war. Once again East Prussia was

Austrian portable disinfecting apparatus

swept clear of the invaders. The Carpathian passes saw their marching columns recoiling in disorder toward Russian territory. Galicia and the fortified towns taken at such

tion of Petrograd, the capital of the Czar's empire.

This high ambition, however, was not destined to be gratified. The line the Russians

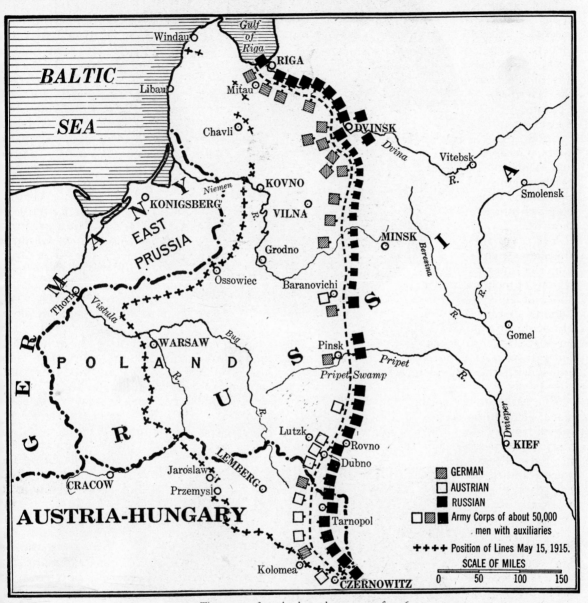

The eastern front in the early summer of 1916

heavy cost were abandoned. Worse than all, the Germans swept triumphantly through Russian Poland, not content with Warsaw alone, but seizing smaller cities and the railroads which gave them control of all that part of Russian territory. The retreat of the Russians did not end until their right flank was rested on the Gulf of Riga, and the exultation of the Germans did not hesitate at predicting their own speedy occupa-

established with their right resting on Riga stood firm. The shortage of ammunition that had cost the followers of the Czar so dear was met by rushing trains across Siberia bringing the output of Japanese factories— the chief contribution of Japan to her allies. The dogged Russian courage suffered not a bit by the army's reverses, and after brief recuperations the Russian banners swept forward again over the thrice fought fields

Homeless Poles in flight before the Germans

Making 16,000 loaves of bread for daily consumption in the German army

CHRONOLOGY OF PERIOD TREATED IN CHAPTER IV

July 28. Austria declares war on Servia. Russians mobilizing.

July 30. Kaiser demands that Russia halt mobilization within twenty-four hours.

August 1. Germany declares war on Russia.

August 2. Russians cross German frontier.

August 5. Austria declares war on Russia.

August 8. Germany invades Finland.

August 9. Russians invade Austria; are repulsed by Germans near Tilsit.

August 10. Germans concentrate on Russian frontier.

August 11. Russians press on into East Prussia.

August 14. Russians defeat Austrians on the Dniester.

August 17. Russia demands from Turkey the unrestricted use of the Dardanelles.

August 19. Russians victorious over Austrians at Padolia.

August 20. Russians occupy Gumbinnen and Lyck in East Prussia.

August 23. Continued Russian successes carry Czar's armies fifty miles into Prussia.

August 24. Austria abandons Servian campaign to meet invading Russians.

August 26. Russians sweep over Prussia menacing Königsberg and Posen.

August 27. Russians take Tilsit. Germans still steadily retreating.

August 28. Russians reach Allenstein.

August 29. Russians invest Königsberg in East Prussia and Lemberg in Galicia.

August 30. Russians advance to the Vistula and bombard Thorn and Graudenz. Battle of Tannenberg begun.

September 1. Germans inflict crushing defeat on Russians at Tannenberg.

September 2. Russians victorious around Lemberg, but retreating in East Prussia.

September 5. Russians take Lemberg and Halicz. Begin new march on Prussia.

September 7. Russians closing in on Przemysl.

September 9. Last Austrians driven from Russian Poland.

September 10. Russians invade Silesia and menace Breslau.

September 11. Serbs and Montenegrins take the offensive against Austria.

September 13. Russian victories near Lemberg. Russo-Serb army menaces Budapest.

September 17. Austrians retreat before Russians toward Cracow.

September 20. Russians attack Jaroslav and Przemysl.

September 24. Relieving force of Germans occupy Cracow.

September 26. Russians enter Przemysl.

September 28. Russians cross the Carpathians and invade Hungary.

October 3. Germans begin evacuating Russian Poland.

October 5. Russians advancing along all lines. Approach Allenstein and Cracow.

October 7. Germans bring reënforcements from Königsberg and check Russians.

October 9. Russians bombard Przemysl.

October 12. Russians abandon siege of Przemysl and retreat from Galicia. (Many weeks later it was learned that this sudden retreat of the Russians in the face of apparently uninterrupted successes was caused by a sudden failure of their supply of ammunition.)

October 13. Russians defeated before Warsaw, and fall of the city believed to be inevitable.

October 17. Heavy fighting around Warsaw and Przemysl.

October 18. Germans repulsed at passage of the Vistula with heavy losses.

October 24. Russians drive Germans back forty miles from Warsaw.

October 28. Germans admit the retreat of their army along the Vistula and in Russian Poland in the face of heavy Russian reënforcements.

November 2. Russians advance upon East Prussia. Warsaw apparently out of danger.

November 6. Steady retreat of the German and Austrian armies in Russian Poland.

November 10. Russian offensive unchecked. German army driven toward Masurian Lakes. Russian sieges of Cracow and Przemysl renewed. For the ensuing week all the advantage in the fighting is with the Russians.

November 25. Main German army seriously menaced in Russian Poland. Heavy reënforcements sent forward, but the retreat continues with no change of fortune until the end of the month.

December 1. Germans break through the Russian wing near Lodz, capturing 12,000 prisoners and twenty-five guns. Russians claim they have taken 50,600 Austrian prisoners in two weeks in Galicia.

December 3. Germans claim the capture of 100,000 prisoners in battles in Poland. Austrians report the taking of Belgrade with the bayonet.

December 6. Germans occupy Lodz.

December 9. Austrians defeated near Cracow. Russians claim that they have 750,000 Austrian and German prisoners in Russia.

December 13. Germans are defeated in the Mlawa region.

December 16. King Peter enters Belgrade at the head of an army. Servia now clear of invaders.

December 17. Germans declare Russian offensive against Silesia and Posen to be broken. Russians deny the report, claiming they are shifting their battleline.

December 20. Von Hindenburg again advancing upon Warsaw.

December 31. Germans claim to have taken 140,000 prisoners, 100 cannon, and 300 machine guns in Poland since November. Russians declare that the Germans lost 200,000 men in the battle of the Bzura.

January 9, 1915. Germans renew offensive from direction of Mlawa.

January 15. New Russian army marches north in Poland. Germans near Mlawa are in peril.

January 16. Austrians bring up heavy artillery to hold the Donajec River.

January 21. Austrians rout the Russians on the Donajec.

January 22. Budapest alarmed by approach of the Russians.

January 27. Austrians mass ten army corps in southern Hungary; many German regiments among them.

January 28. Great struggle for the Carpathians opens. Austro-German forces advance on an eighty-mile front.

February 3. Russians gain in Hungary. German position north of the Vistula menaced.

February 4. Von Hindenburg attacks Russian lines near Warsaw with 50,000 men.

February 7. Germans compelled to withdraw troops from France to defend East Prussia.

February 8. Germans begin transport by motor cars of 600,000 men from Poland to East Prussia.

February 12. Von Hindenburg wins a great battle in the Masurian Lakes, captures more than 30,000 prisoners with fifty cannon and sixty machine guns. Russian loss a proaches 50,000.

February 15. Russian retreat from East Prussia checke Russians force the fighting in Galicia and the Carpathians.

March 2. Russians win Dukla Pass.

March 5. Russians on the offensive from the Baltic Sea the Roumanian border.

March 11. Number of men engaged in battles in northe Poland estimated at one million with a battleline of eigh miles.

March 15. Russians capture the outer defences of Przemys

March 19. Von Hindenburg starts a new offensive in centr Poland.

March 20. Statistics published in Petrograd show that towns and 4,500 villages in Russian Poland have been de astated as the result of German invasion with a dama; of $500,000,000.

March 22. Przemysl falls after being besieged since Septen ber 2d.; 125,000 men, including nine Austrian Genera taken; the strategic value of the place regarded as great.

March 30. Russian advance in the Carpathians caus alarm. 160,000 German troops said to be rushing to tl rescue.

April 1. German Headquarters Staff reports that in Marc the German army in the east took 55,800 Russian prisonei nine cannon, and sixty-one machine guns.

April 11. After steady fighting, during which at times tl armies operated in seven feet of snow, the Russians occuj all the main ridges of the Carpathians; 280,000 Germans, seven army corps, are helping the Austrians in Hungary.

April 14. Petrograd estimates that 4,000,000 combatant including both sides, are engaged in the Carpathians.

April 18. Reviewing the Carpathian campaign the Russi: General Staff declares that since the beginning of Marc the Russians have carried seventy-five miles of the princip chain of the Carpathians, have taken 70,000 prisonei thirty field guns, and 200 machine guns.

May 3. Sudden Russian weakness apparent. General v Mackensen defeats the Russians in west Galicia takii 30,000 prisoners and many guns. A continued Austr German advance begins lasting with slight checks until tl last of the month. Jaroslav is retaken by the Teutons ar Przemysl menaced.

May 21. Austrians announce that since May 1st they ha taken 194,000 Russian prisoners; Germans declare th General Mackensen since May 1st has taken 104,000 pri oners, 72 cannon, and 253 machine guns; the Russian stat ment declares that the losses of the Austro-Germans are ave aging 10,000 a day and that they have used between tw and three million shells in the recent fighting.

June 3. Austro-German troops capture Przemysl which h been held by the Russians since March 22d.

June 10. Russians again take the offensive in the Balt provinces and Galicia.

June 22. Lemberg falls to the Austro-German forces, aft having been held by the Russians since September 3 Russians retreating throughout Galicia.

July 3. Berlin reports that from May 2d to June 27th, 1,6 officers and 520,000 men of the Russian army have been ca tured besides more than a thousand field and machine gun

July 15. Germans renew their drive toward Warsaw. Hi denburg advancing from the north and Mackensen from tl south.

July 22. Russians in retreat everywhere laying waste tl country as they retire, and clinging desperately to Warsa"

August 5. Warsaw taken by the Germans under Prin Leopold. Russians retire in good order, saving the entire army.

ZEPPELIN L-15 BROUGHT DOWN BY ANTI-AIRCRAFT GUNS OFF THE COAST OF KENT

The crew were rescued by English trawlers and treated as ordinary prisoners of war

German cruisers go down firing to the last. In the naval battle off Heligoland, when the British fleet sunk five German war vessels, the most wonderful courage was displayed by the Germans. Their three cruisers went down with flags flying and guns firing until swallowed up by the sea. It is said that the crew of the *Mainz* sang a patriotic song as the vessel was plunging, stern first, to the bottom

CHAPTER V

THE WORK OF THE NAVIES—DISAPPEARANCE OF GERMAN MERCHANT SHIPS—
COMMERCE DESTROYERS—GERMAN NAVAL STRATEGY—CAPTAIN WEDDIGEN'S
EXPLOIT—THREE FLEET BATTLES—NAVAL RECORD FOR TWO YEARS

AT THE beginning of the war the one thing which seemed absolutely inevitable in the conflict was that the British fleet would promptly and efficiently sweep the seas of all signs of German naval power.

It had long been the policy of Great Britain to maintain a naval force at least as great as that of any two of her possible rivals. In 1914, notwithstanding the rapid development of the German fleet under the ambitious care of the Kaiser, Great Britain maintained an even more overpowering standard of superiority. Indeed the increase of the British fleet had been spurred to almost feverish activity by the indication of a determination on the part of Germany to attempt to equal, if not to exceed it, in power. In 1900 the preamble to the German navy act frankly expressed the purpose of the German nation to build a fleet which should cope on no unequal terms with that of Great Britain. That started the race in naval construction, and in 1906-8 England was aghast at the discovery that while she had laid down eight ships of the dreadnought type, Germany had laid down nine. From this moment rivalry in ship building was unlimited. Battleships were described as old when they had been in commission but four years. Nothing smaller

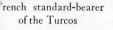

rench standard-bearer
of the Turcos

than the dreadnought with ten of the largest rifles was considered worth while, and the type soon developed into the superdreadnought class of 25,000 tons with ten 13-inch and twelve 6-inch guns with an armor belt a foot thick at its point of greatest weight. Such a ship would carry more than a thousand officers and men and cost about $10,000,000. Of vessels of this type Great Britain had eleven complete and three nearly so in 1914; Germany had none, though three were under construction. Of the next type, the dreadnought battleship, Germany and England had each thirteen.

During the course of the war the shipyards of both England and Germany had been busy day and night, but the secrecy which enveloped all governmental activities at that time preclude any statement of the war-time additions made to the belligerent fleets. At the beginning of the war the sea power of the hostile nations may be roughly estimated as follows:

Reduced to its very lowest terms of statement the British navy at the opening of the war consisted of 60 modern battleships, 9 battle cruisers, 34 armored cruisers, 17 heavy protected cruisers, 70 light cruisers, 232 destroyers then ready and 16 building, 59 torpedo boats (and 50 old ones), and 75 submarines, besides 52 sea-going auxiliaries of the fleet, such as mother ships for destroyers, mine-layers, distilling ships, oil ships, repair and hospital ships.

The French navy, though fourth in the list of naval powers, naturally follows here as England's ally. It had 18 battleships, together with eight building at the war's commencement, 19 armored cruisers, 2 protected cruisers, and 10 light cruisers. The French navy was peculiarly strong in destroyers, torpedo boats, and submarines, having 84 of the first class, 135 torpedo boats, and 78 submarines with a number on the stocks at the beginning of the war.

Russia, as a naval power, was of little importance in the conflict. Her losing war with Japan had left her with but three of her old

The Kaiser and his naval heads—Admiral von Tirpitz, in centre, and Admiral von Holtzendorf at the right

battleships, and these with three of later construction, 6 armored cruisers, 91 destroyers, and 55 submarines made up her effective fleet which at the beginning of the war was mainly in the Black Sea.

The navy of Japan, though powerful and highly efficient, may be ignored here as its service was mainly in the Pacific.

To meet this naval strength Germany offered naturally the most powerful fleet, which at the outbreak of war was tied with that of the United States in the struggle for second place. On her ships' roster at the declaration of war were 36 battleships, 5 battle cruisers, 9 armored cruisers, and 43 cruisers as the seagoing fleet. She had also 130 destroyers and 27 submarines. The first loss to the navy was that of a submarine, sunk by a British cruiser. For some reason Germany was weak in torpedo boats.

Austria-Hungary entered the struggle with 9 battleships, 10 light cruisers, 18 destroyers, 63 torpedo boats, and 6 submarines.

It has already been pointed out that the obvious design of the Germans to challenge British supremacy on the ocean had much to do with the entrance of Great Britain upon the war. It was international gossip that the German officers were eager for the test, and stories were common of a toast of singular brevity and cryptic meaning that was drunk at the German naval dinner boards when no foreign guests were present: "Der Tag"—"The Day"—always brought the officers to their feet with brimming glasses, for it hailed in anticipation the day when they should do battle of Great Britain on the seas she had so long professed to rule.

That day, however, did not come soon, nor did it bring glory. Almost instantly upon the declaration of war the German flag disappeared from the high seas. Merchantmen

swiftly noti-
fied by wire-
less sought
the shelter of
neutral ports
—more than
$100,000,000
worth of Ger-
man liners be-
ing tied up in
the port of
New York
alone. The
British navy
swiftly de-
scended upon
Germany's
colonies
throughout
the world and
took posses-
sion of them.
A few German
commerce de-
stroyers re-
mained at sea
and preyed
upon the mer-
chant ship-
ping of the

Copyright by Underwood & Underwood

One of the most remarkable of photographs, taken from the bridge of a Zeppelin
during a battle in the skies in a German air raid on England

Allies until
run down by
the British
navy and de-
stroyed. But
the great
fighting fleet
of Germany
took refuge in
the harbors of
Kiel and Cux-
haven and
waited long
there before
offering even
partial battle
to the British
fleet. This
was wise
strategy but
hardly glori-
ous. The Brit-
ish sneered
at the re-
fusal of the
Germans to
fight against
overwhelming
odds, and
Winston

German battleship squadron with its guardian Zeppelin

Photo by Paul Thompson

Churchill, first Lord of the Admiralty, foolishly assured Parliament that "the rats would soon be dug out of their hole."

It was a braggart metaphor and a foolish one. The rats came out of the hole when they had a chance of inflicting serious damage upon the waiting British. The latter for their part never in the first two years of the war sought to follow the Germans into their retreat. The British strategy of this period offered no parallel to that of Farragut in our Civil War who damned the torpedoes and went ahead at Mobile and New Orleans, or Dewey when

It became an outpost far at sea from which submarines could continually menace the British fleet and guard against the nearer approach of enemy vessels to the German naval bases, Cuxhaven, Bremerhaven, and Kiel. At Kiel is the canal connecting the North Sea with the Baltic, which in effect multiplies the German North Sea fleet by two. If menaced by the British fleet in the North Sea the German ships of war could retire through this canal to the Baltic. Should the British attempt to pursue through the difficult, tortuous, and well-mined channels of the Skagerak and Cattegat north of Denmark, the German fleet could slip out into the North Sea and ravage the British coasts before their

The deadly British destroyers.   A 1,000-ton destroyer in a heavy sea

he pushed at night into the harbor of Manila, careless alike of the strength of the forts or the presence of the mines that guarded its entrance. The Admiralty ordered Sir John Jellicoe, commander in-chief of the home fleet, the day war was declared to "find the enemy, capture or destroy him." The Admiral had no trouble in finding the enemy, but at the end of two years he had neither captured nor destroyed him.

The island of Heligoland, which stands thirty-two miles from the German coast, was sold to Germany in 1890 by Lord Salisbury and was immediately made by its new possessors a fortress as impregnable as Gibraltar.

defenders could return. This situation enabled the Germans to play fast and loose with the British and avoid any serious conflict in the North Sea until the latter part of January, 1915.

Prior to that date there were occasional losses inflicted upon the British navy by floating mines or by submarines. Most of these may be ignored in this rapid narrative as none of them seriously affected the strength of the British navy as a whole. At the battle off Heligoland a British squadron of battle cruisers and destroyers under command of Rear-Admiral Sir David Beatty fell upon four German cruisers and a number of de-

British destroyers sinking a German submarine

action said, "There really was nothing for us to do except shoot the enemy as Pa shoots pheasants." None the less London went wild over the news of this first victory, much as in 1898 all American journalism rushed out extras to tell of the triumph of Admiral Sampson when he captured a Spanish steamer, the captain of which, not knowing that war had been declared, took pains to bring his ship close to the American fleet, in order, as he said, that he "might salute all those beautiful warships."

The Germans, however, quickly had their revenge. On the morning of September 22d three British cruisers, the *Aboukir*, *Cressy*, and *Hogue* were patrolling the North Sea not far from the Hook of Holland. They were all three cruisers of the same class; 12,000 tons each, with a 6-inch armor belt amidships, with a main battery of two 9.2 inch guns and twelve 6-inch, and a complement of 755 men each. Well within the range of action of the German submarine and torpedo boats, their officers may well be supposed to have been all vigilance. At such a time a warship is all eyes.

Nevertheless, from none of these ships was a warning cry raised until a German submarine had slipped up to within a mile, fired her torpedo, and sent the *Aboukir* to her destruction. Gallantly, but as the event showed, rashly, her sister cruisers rushed to the aid of the stricken ship, but were themselves torpedoed by the same unseen enemy and sent to the bottom. Its deadly work completed, itself too small to be of aid in rescuing any of the survivors, the German submarine *U-9*, Captain Otto Weddigen, with 26 men aboard, slipped away as secretly as it had stolen up and reached its base at Wilhelmshaven in safety.

At the moment this was the most notable achievement in the history of submarine warfare. Only the vaguest details of the exploit were permitted to leak out, the German War Office not being anxious for any intelligence to be made public that might interfere with the success of subsequent raids of the same

Zeppelin over London spotted by a searchlight

sort, while the British Admiralty was not desirous of giving any additional publicity to so disquieting an illustration of the helplessness of even armored ships before the sinister submarine. An American newspaper, the New York *World*, secured and published the following description of the exploit from Captain Weddigen himself. After telling of his voyage, the duration of which he conceals, he says that when eighteen miles northwest of the Hook of Holland he sighted through his periscope three British cruisers.

"I submerged completely and laid my course so as to bring up in the centre of the trio, which held a sort of triangular formation. I could see their gray-black sides riding high over the water.

"When I first sighted them they were near enough for torpedo work, but I wanted to make my aim sure, so I went down and in on them. I had taken the position of the three ships before submerging and I succeeded in getting another flash through my periscope before I began action. I soon reached what I regarded as a good shooting point.

"Then I loosed one of my torpedoes at the middle ship. I was then about twelve feet under water and got the shot off in good shape, my men handling the boat as if she had been a skiff. I climbed to the surface to get a sight through my tube of the effect, and discovered that the shot had gone straight and

The French adaptation of the war Zeppelin

true, striking the ship, which I learned later was the *Aboukir*, under one of her magazines, which in exploding helped the torpedo's work of destruction.

"There was a fountain of water, a burst of smoke, a flash of fire, and part of the cruiser rose in the air. Then I heard a roar and felt reverberations sent through the water by the detonation. She had been broken apart and sank in a few minutes. The *Aboukir* had been stricken in a vital spot by an unseen force that made the blow all the greater.

"Her crew were brave, and even with death staring them in the face kept to their posts, ready to handle their useless guns, for I submerged at once. But I stayed on top long enough to see the other cruisers, which I learned were the *Cressy* and *Hogue*, turn and steam full speed to their dying sister, whose plight they could not understand, unless it had been due to an accident.

"The ships came on a mission of inquiry and rescue, for many of the *Aboukir's* crew were now in the water, the order having been given, 'Each man for himself.'

"But soon the other two English cruisers learned what had brought about the destruction so suddenly.

"As I reached my torpedo

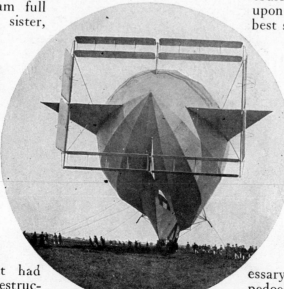

Stern view of a war Zeppelin

depth I sent a second charge at the nearer of the oncoming vessels, which was the *Hogue*. The English were playing my game, for I had scarcely to move out of my position, which was a great aid, since it helped to keep me from detection.

"On board my little boat the spirit of the German navy was to be seen in its best form. With enthusiasm every man held himself in check and gave attention to the work in hand.

"The attack on the *Hogue* went true. But this time I did not have the advantageous aid of having the torpedo detonate under the magazine, so for twenty minutes the *Hogue* lay wounded and helpless on the surface before she heaved, half turned over, and sank.

"By this time, the third cruiser knew, of course, that the enemy was upon her and she sought as best she could to defend herself. She loosed her torpedo defence batteries on both starboard and port, and stood her ground as if more anxious to help the many sailors who were in the water than to save herself. In common with the method of defending herself against a submarine attack, she steamed in a zigzag course, and this made it necessary for me to hold my torpedoes until I could lay a true course for them, which also made it necessary for me to

H. M. S. *Lion* racing into action

get nearer to the *Cressy*. I had come to the surface for a view and saw how wildly the fire was being sent from the ship. Small wonder that was when they did not know where to shoot, although one shot went unpleasantly near us.

"When I got within suitable range I sent away my third attack. This time I sent a second torpedo after the first to make the strike doubly certain. My crew were aiming like sharpshooters and both torpedoes went to their bull'seye. My luck was with me again, for the enemy was made useless and at once began sinking by her head. Then she careened far over, but all the while her men stayed at the guns looking for their invisible foe. They were brave and true to their country's sea traditions. Then she eventually suffered a boiler explosion and completely turned turtle. With her keel uppermost she floated until the air got out from under her and then she sank with a loud sound, as if from a creature in pain.

"The whole affair had taken less than one hour from the time of shooting off the first torpedo until the *Cressy* went to the bottom. Not one of the three had been able to use any of its big guns. I knew the wireless of the three cruisers had been calling for aid. I was still quite able to defend myself, but I knew that news of the disaster would call many English submarines and torpedo-boat destroyers, so having done my appointed work I set my course for home."

More than 1,200 men went down with the three cruisers—done to their death by a handful of but 26. Thirty-six thousand tons of modern

Sir John Jellicoe's flagship the *Iron Duke*

steel warships, packed with heavy guns and equipped with all the latest devices for maritime warfare, were destroyed in an hour by a pigmy craft of 450 tons. What wonder that men the world over began to predict the abandonment even of the dreadnoughts, for all their weight of armor on their sides will avail them not a whit against attack from below. As the iron-clad sides of the *Merrimac*, and the revolving turret of the little *Monitor* relegated to the scrapheap the

that were either actively at war or allied with some of the belligerents, were absolutely closed to them. In neutral ports they could stay but one day and could take on supplies of coal and provisions only sufficient to take them to the nearest German port. At one time British, French, Japanese, and Russian warships were hunting these cruisers which somehow managed to keep the ocean, renew their stocks of coal, and sink or burn British ships in every one of the seven seas. By

The French battleship *Justice* leading the French fleet

"wooden walls of England," so the submarine, and its scarcely less sinister coadjutor, the airship, may put an end to the $12,000,000 floating forts of steel which the Powers have been building.

Except for submarine activities, the German navy was heard from chiefly in the earlier months of the war by the work of its commerce destroyers. Of these four were at sea when war was declared: the *Emden*, *Karlsruhe*, *Prinz Eitel*, and *Kronprinz Friedrich*. Of these the first two alone were man-of-war built, the others were converted merchantmen. The expedients by which the Germans kept these ships at sea for months after the declaration of war showed extraordinary cunning and executive genius. Most of the ports of the world, being in countries

British admission the *Emden* had sunk twenty British merchantmen and the *Karlsruhe* thirteen by the 15th of October. The *Emden* had been particularly adventurous. Late in October she astonished the world by rigging up a fourth smokestack to disguise her identity, and slipping into the harbor of Penang under a Japanese flag. The sentinels on the parapet were completely deceived and all the shipping in the harbor was amazed when the strange ship without anchoring let slip a torpedo which sunk a French destroyer, turned her guns upon the Russian cruiser to her complete destruction, and turning about, steamed safely out of the harbor.

But the seas are too populous for the career of a raider to be a long one. The inevitable end came to the *Emden* November 10th, when she was overhauled by the Australian cruiser, *Sidney*, nearly double her size and carrying eight 6-inch guns to the *Emden's* ten 4-inch guns. The battle was but short, a running one so far as the German ship was concerned. After two of her smokestacks had been shot away and the flames were sweeping her fore and aft she was driven ashore on Cocos Island and burned. During her entire career she had captured and destroyed 31

the war than did Germany, but as the German fleet remained in hiding behind the battlements of Heligoland and Kiel, submarines could not reach them. The British fleet in the open North Sea, and the thousands of British merchantmen going back and forth on all the lanes of ocean travel afforded ample opportunity for the activities of the undersea terrors of the German navy. A frightful feature of submarine warfare is the enormous

Destruction of the cruiser *Mainz*. This photograph was taken by a sailor on one of the British ships engaged in the fight off Heligoland. At the moment the picture was taken the two funnels of the *Mainz* had been shot away and flames were bursting through her deck. A few minutes later the doomed vessel sank, still defiantly firing to the last

vessels, sending several others home as transports for prisoners taken.

The other German commerce destroyers met similar fates, with the exception of one, the *Prinz Eitel*, which amazed the nautical world by eluding all pursuers and slipping into Hampton Roads, where she was interned until the end of the war.

The story of the submarines is one almost for a volume in itself. The fruit of their activities was mainly gathered by the Germans. This was chiefly due to the fact that the British shipping, both naval and merchant, being at sea afforded the greater number of targets. Both Great Britain and France had more submarines at the opening of

proportion of the death list to the total numbers on the attacked record. The submarine can save no one. The torpedoed vessel goes down in but a few minutes. As a result practically all its crew are carried down to death. We have seen that more than 1,200 men went down with the three cruisers that Weddigen sunk. Later 475 out of 544 men on the British cruiser *Hawk* were sacrificed to submarine attack. The British cruiser *Pallada* carried down practically her entire crew of 558 men. The *Formidable* was sent down with 600 men. In the first ten weeks of the war submarines destroyed seven British cruisers with a tonnage of 48,370 and crews numbering 3,397, of whom 2,298 were lost—a frightful percentage illustrating the deadliness of submarine attack.

Nor did the German submarines limit their activities to attacks upon vessels of war. Early in the war the British declared a blockade of the entire German coast, including the Baltic ports. The form of this blockade was new to international law. A lawful blockade has hitherto been held to require the actual blocking of entrance to the enemy's ports by many. This raised one of the new questions of international law of which this war has been prolific and which are yet to be determined. The Germans met this policy by decreeing the blockade of the British coasts, although they had no way of enforcing it, since their fleet could not venture forth in the presence of the enormously superior British force. They could only partially enforce it by the use of submarines, and with these vessels in the

The wreck of the famous cruiser *Emden* which, before her destruction off Cocos Island by the Australian Cruiser *Sydney*, had destroyed 2 warships and 25 merchant ships

warships stationed outside them. A blockade of this sort we maintained during the Civil War with the utmost rigor, and it contributed largely to the downfall of the Confederacy. Such a blockade, however, can never again be maintained owing to the perfection of the submarine. A fleet, stationed off the mouth of a harbor, like that at New York, or at Charleston, would be subject at all times to the attacks of submarines which would be held safely inside the harbor until the propitious moment for delivering their assaults. Accordingly the British undertook to blockade Germany by stationing their ships hundreds of miles from the ports, but in the regular lanes of commerce and seizing any ships which they might detect bound for Germany crowded waters immediately surrounding the British Isles they inflicted enormous damage upon British shipping. Neutral ships suffered as well, and from this sprung an issue between Germany and the United States which narrowly escaped leading to war and which did result in materially curbing the German submarine activities.

It has long been the recognized law of nations that a peaceful merchantman, suspected of violating a blockade, must be boarded by an officer from the warship which has halted her and if her character as a blockade runner is proved she must either be taken with all her passengers and crew into a home port of her captor or the human beings aboard must be taken off and provided

The German cruiser *Blücher* being torpedoed by the *Meteor* during the battle in the North Sea on January 24, 1915

with a safe means of escape before the vessel is sunk.

The Germans insisted that observation of this rule would put their submarines in danger. They are fragile vessels, carrying no heavy guns, readily destroyed by either ramming or a single shot from a gun of 4-inch calibre, such as many of the British merchantmen were armed with. Accordingly under the orders of Admiral Von Tirpitz, chief of the

matic controversy between the United States and Germany. It was dragged out for a year, greatly to the impatience of a large section of the American people who demanded swift and punitive action. In the end, however, Germany promised that in future no unarmed passenger vessels would be torpedoed at all, and that other vessels would only be destroyed after due warning and the removal of passengers and crew. During the progress of

Great Britain arrays her war strength. The naval review at Spithead, just before the outbreak of the War, was probably the greatest display of armed sea power ever made

German navy, the German torpedo boats began sinking merchantmen either without warning or with at most a very brief warning, and the allowance of perhaps ten minutes for the captain of the doomed vessel to remove his people in his own boats. The submarine, of course, can take no prisoners aboard. Repeated instances of the heavy and wanton sacrifice of the lives of peaceful, and often neutral, citizens caused bitter protest on the part of neutral nations. The controversy reached a climax by the torpedoing, May 7, 1915, without warning, of the great British passenger liner, *Lusitania*, by which 1,392 men and women, many of them of national eminence, lost their lives.

Out of this incident grew a prolonged diplo-

the diplomatic discussion several submarine attacks occurred by which American lives were lost, and the irritation of the American people reached the point that almost forced an unwilling administration into war.

As the efficiency of the submarine became more apparent German shipyards were rushed with construction. The size of the boats increased. Their cruising area was so extended that before the second year of the war submarines voyaged as far as the entrance to the Mediterranean and even circumnavigated the British Isles. There was no part of British waters closed to them, and the Admiralty was aghast when the 23,000-ton battleship *Audacious* was sunk in the Irish Sea by one of these invisible foes. The

The *Lusitania* sailing on her fatal voyage

British were no laggards. In 1915 one of their submarines sailed from England, made its way through the Mediterranean and the Dardanelles, dived under five rows of mines, and sunk the Turkish battleship *Mersudieh*. So greatly was the field of action of the submarines extended that in July, 1916, one of them, the *Deutschland*, built expressly for carrying cargo, steamed all the way across the Atlantic and safely entered Chesapeake Bay despite the vigilance of British and French ships that had been warned of her coming. The vessel carried 1,500 tons of cargo, and

from buoys, which were so equipped with signals that the thrust of the nose of an unseen submarine would be shown along the whole line of the net. Once entangled the submarine's case was hopeless. Thereupon destroyers and small cruisers would gather at the spot, and after waiting a day or two for the ghastly purpose of allowing the crew of the strangled vessel to be smothered so that no resistance or explosion could be caused, would raise the submerged vessel and tow it to a British dock yard to be refitted for further use under a new flag.

South African field artillery embarking on the auxiliary cruiser *Armadale Castle*

enough fuel oil for a voyage of twice the distance.

For the purpose of meeting the menace of the submarines, the British employed all the known weapons at their command such as destroyers and mines, and enforced vigilance on the part of trawlers in the North Sea. New expedients were adopted. Scouting aeroplanes, hanging over the surface of the water, could readily detect the presence of a submarine within fifty feet of the surface and by signalling to watching destroyers and torpedo boats often secure its destruction. The most deadly defence against the submarines, however, were the great steel nets hung by the British at various points in the English Channel and North Sea. These nets hung

Among the first of the true naval battles, involving more than single ships, was one fought on November 1st, far from the main scene of hostilities. When war broke out Germany had a considerable naval force in the Pacific which it was the immediate purpose of the British and Japanese navies to destroy. Early in the war the German and Japanese squadrons had fought an inconclusive battle in the Bay of Tsing-Tau, and later the Japanese had sunk the German cruiser *Æolus* off Honolulu. But the main German naval force in Pacific waters was a scattered squadron, including the *Scharnhorst*, *Nurnberg*, *Gneisenau*, and *Dresden*, so widely dispersed that probably no two of the fleet were within 2,000 miles' steaming distance of

Sinking of the *Falaba*. The South African liner, *Falaba*, was torpedoed without warning and sank so rapidly that many passengers had no time to take to the boats

each other. The way in which these ships were concentrated, though the Pacific navies of Japan and Great Britain were scouring the sea in pursuit of them, showed remarkable seamanship and an extraordinary efficiency on the part of the German bureau by which these vessels were guided safely through seas swarming with hostile craft. The concentration was successfully effected, and when the pursuing British squadron, under Rear-Admiral Sir Christopher Craddock, met Vice-Admiral Graf von Spee's fleet off Coronel on the coast of Chili, it was a sorry meeting for the British. The German squadron was superior in weight of metal and in speed. In respect to their heavy batteries only they compared thus:

GERMAN		BRITISH	
Scharnhorst	Eight 8.2-inch;	Monmouth .	Fourteen 6-inch guns
Gneisenau	six 6-inch guns		
Leipzig	Ten 4-inch guns	Good Hope .	Two 9.2-inch; sixteen 6-inch guns
Nurnberg			
		Glasgow . .	Two 6-inch; ten 4-inch guns
Dresden . .	Twelve 4-inch guns	Otranto . .	Merely an armed transport

The battle was fought in the evening between six and seven o'clock in rough weather with a driving rain. The result was wholly disastrous to the British; the *Monmouth* was sunk, the *Good Hope* destroyed by an explosion and fire, and the other ships, sorely crip-

Admiral Sir David Beatty, who commanded the British battle cruiser squadron at the battle of Jutland

Picture taken from the British ship *Arethusa*.   Smoke to the right shows where the last torpedo struck.   The *Blücher* is afi

"BLÜCHER"

sinking with about 800 men clustered on her sides and bottom.   She floated about ten minutes after this photograph was taken

pled, limped away to the nearest ports of refuge. The German ships were practically unhurt and escaped without loss of life, six men on the *Gneisenau* being wounded.

Twenty British ships had now been brought down by the German policy of attrition, and without commensurate losses by the enemy.

who had the battleship *Canopus* and the two battle cruisers *Invincible* and *Inflexible*, besides five cruisers in squadron. Without the two battle cruisers, however, the British were not markedly superior to the Germans, and as these were at first concealed, the Germans went gallantly into action believing that they

Saloniki's harbor thronged with boats of many nations. The port of Saloniki is one of the busiest in the world, but all its activities are those of war. Ships of all the allied nations come and go, and the surface of the bay is literally covered with small boats of every conceivable form

For the moment the boasted superiority of the British navy seemed a myth.

But the world did not have long to wait for news that the British had taken full revenge upon the triumphant Admiral von Spee. On December 8th, off the Falkland Islands, an English fleet under Vice-Admiral Sir Frederick Sturdee overtook the victorious Germans and utterly destroyed them, sinking the *Scharnhorst*, *Gneisenau*, *Leipzig*, and *Nurnberg*.

This time the weight of metal and superiority of speed were on the side of the British

had at least a fighting chance. But the British had not less than twenty 12-inch guns for which the Germans had no match whatsoever besides four of 7½-inch and thirty-eight of 6-inch. The Germans were not only hopelessly outclassed in weight of metal, but they were quite as far behind in the vital matter of speed. With their longer range, the British could batter their foes to pieces without exposing themselves, and did so. The Germans fought gamely and grimly, and save for the *Dresden*, which escaped, went down with colors flying.

The first period of the war ended January 24, 1915, with a disaster to the German navy in the North Sea. On that day a German squadron of four battle cruisers, the *Blücher*, *Moltke*, *Seydlitz*, and *Derflinger*, under command of Admiral Hibben, was steaming west, not far from the coast of England. Why the ships had left the snug refuge of Heligoland to brave the British guard is not explained. Probably it was hoped that they might elude British vigilance, round the northern end of Scotland, and get out into the open sea there to prey on the shipping of the Allies as had the *Emden* and the *Karlsruhe*. If this had been the plan, the German authorities bungled it badly by attaching to the three fast ships of the squadron, which were capable of a speed of 26 to 28 knots, the *Blücher* which was barely able to turn off 24 knots.

Whatever the purpose of this expedition may have been, it was clearly not to fight, for, encountering a British squadron of five battle cruisers near the English coast the Germans instantly turned to flee.

In Admiral Beatty's squadron were the *Lion*, *Tiger*, *Princess Royal*, *New Zealand*, and *Indomitable*. The *Lion* had 13.5-inch guns; the main battery of the others was of 12-inch guns. In the German fleet only the *Derflinger* mounted guns of 12-inch calibre. According to statistics the gunfire of the British was to that of the

Diagram showing fleet formation in Battle off Jutland

German squadron as 23 to 13—a heavy disparity which justified Admiral Hibben in taking to flight. Unfortunately for him the disparity in speed was quite as much in favor of the British; and this fact, added to the longer range of their guns, put the whole German fleet at the pursuer's mercy, should the chase last long enough. When the battle opened the Germans were about 100 miles from Heligoland, with the leading British ship, the *Lion*, about 9.6 miles astern of her principal target the *Blücher*.

At a distance of nine and a half miles the British gunners, themselves on a ship tossing on the turbulent waters of the North Sea, were aiming their shots at a mark not more than 90 feet wide, barely discernible on the horizon and rushing through the water at the rate of more than 25 knots an hour. It seems incredible that under such conditions great damage could be done, but the accounts of survivors tell how deadly was the marksmanship. One German bluejacket, saved from the waves after his ship had gone down, told to his captors this story of the fight as seen from the *Blücher*:

"We saw the big English ships steadily overhauling us. We knew that as we had more than a hundred miles to sail we would never get away. The first British ship opened fire at something like ten miles' range, and the carnage on the *Blücher* began.

English dirigible balloon at manœuvres

"We were under fire first in the action and last. Practically every English ship poured projectile shell upon us. It was awful. I have never seen such gunnery and hope that as long as I live I never shall again. We could not fight such guns as the English ships had, and soon we had no guns with which to fight anything. Our decks were swept by shot, guns were smashed and lying in all directions, their crews wiped out.

"One terrible shell from a big gun—I cannot forget it—burst right in the heart of the ship and killed scores of men. It fell where many men had collected, killing practically every man.

"We all had our floating equipment. We soon needed it. One shell killed five men quite close to me, and it was only a matter of time when nothing living would have been left upon the ship.

"When we knew we were beaten and that our flag was not to come down many of us were praying that the ship would go down, in order that no more men might be killed.

"We would rather trust to the English picking us up after our ship had sunk than to missing us with those terrible guns.

"I do not know what it was that finished the *Blücher*. She was battered to pieces above decks and had many holes. I heard she was struck by a torpedo and went down after that. If that is true, we have to thank the ship that torpedoed us for saving hundreds of lives.

"When the ship was going down, I jumped clear and tried to swim off. When she turned over some caught hold of some part of her but she sank from under us. It was terribly cold in the water. There were wounded men and dead men. Terribly shattered swimmers shouting for help were all around me.

"My mind is confused after that. I was picked up by a small English warship, as I hoped. The men were very kind. We were warmed, fed and clothed."

The final stroke to the *Blücher* was delivered by a torpedo, though she had been put out of action before that *coup de grâce*. Of her crew of 835, more than 700 were lost, and it is a striking evidence of the inadequacy of the German gunfire that the loss on the *Lion* which led the British pursuers was only eleven wounded. None were killed in the British fleet. In this disparity of losses the action

Armored car of a dirigible balloon. Showing the relative size of the car, which will accommodate more than a dozen men. It is armed with machine guns and bomb-dropping devices

A French triplane

was somewhat reminiscent of the battle of Santiago in the Spanish - American War. But any comparison of the two battles rebounds very greatly to the superior credit of the American navy. For at Santiago the pursuit was not checked nor the fires slackened until the last Spanish ship lay helpless, smoking wreck on the coast of Cuba. But in this North Sea battle three of the German ships escaped, despite the superior strength and speed of their British pursuers.

It was eighteen months before the two great rival fleets met again in combat. Meanwhile the naval activities of the Allies were confined mainly to some single ship actions in the Mediterranean and Adriatic, and to the determined but abortive effort of the British fleet to pass the Dardanelles. The former were of no material bearing on the progress of the war, and of the latter an account will be published in another chapter.

Copyright by Underwood & Underwood

The latest product of the Krupp works is a specially designed gun for defense against the enemy of the clouds

May 31, 1916, the advance ship of a British fleet, cruising off Jutland, came into contact with a German fleet and there followed a fierce battle lasting all day and part of the night, the outcome of which was very nearly a draw. The Germans at first claimed complete victory, and for that matter, still do. The British at the outset were inclined to admit, if not defeat, at least such heavy losses as to indicate the equality of the German sea fighters with what had been supposed to be the irresistible British navy. Later, however, knowledge of the extent of the German losses led the British to claim that the victory rested with them.

The day was hazy, the surface of the sea calm, affording every opportunity for skilful marksmanship. The British fleet, extending over an area of nearly 300 square miles, was sweeping across the North Sea toward the Skagerack in pursuance of the policy of patroling those waters periodically. In advance was the light squadron of battle cruisers and light cruisers under Admiral Sir David Beatty. In advance of the cruisers, in accordance with British naval tactics, was a line of steam trawlers and destroyers. At about 3:45 P. M. a cloud of smoke in the distance told of the coming of a fleet which could be only the Germans. It was, in fact, the full German High Seas Fleet under command of Admiral Scheer. These vessels were cruising in the hope of encountering some detached British force which they might attack and cut off before the full fleet of Admiral Jellicoe could come up. The situation seemed to afford them this opportunity, for that branch of the fleet under Admiral

Beatty was distinctly inferior to the German force, while Admiral Jellicoe was far in the rear with the dreadnoughts. Whatever the odds might be, on either side the men were eager for the fray. Beatty with his swift battle cruisers gave no heed to the slowness of the battleships behind him, but plunged into the attack which the Ger-

the battle cruisers, with their lighter armament and with their weight of armor sacrificed to speed, were in this case opposed to battleships. The result proved the contention of naval experts the world over that the battleship is absolutely essential to the strength of the navy. Even while the battle was in progress a debate was going on in the Ameri

London watching for aërial foes by night

mans for their part invited and cheerfully sustained. Such was the mist that the hostile lines were not visible at a distance of more than six miles. This was at the outset greatly in favor of the Germans, who had their heavier vessels, with their bigger guns, in action at the very first. As a result of this, although possibly in the case of the *Invincible*, because of a mine, three of Beatty's ships, the *Indefatigable*, the *Invincible*, and the *Queen Mary*, were sunk within twenty minutes of the beginning of the action. An additional handicap to the British was that while their foes were enveloped in mist, they themselves were outside of the bank of fog and clearly outlined against a yellowish sky. Moreover,

can Congress over the question whether if our future navy battleships should not be wholly replaced by battle cruisers. The news from the North Sea caused an abrupt abandonment of this theory.

While the main execution done among the principal ships on either side in this battle appears to have been due to the fire of great guns, the destroyers and torpedo boats were busy from the start. The duty of these little craft was twofold: namely, to attack the enemies' capital ships and to protect their own from like attack. It would appear however, that the value of the torpedo in a pitched battle between fleets has been largely overestimated. This war has demonstrated sufficiently its deadliness when launched from an unseen submarine, or, for that matter, from any unexpected quarter. But in a general action the capital ships already engaged, warned of the presence of torpedoes and protected in part by their watchful destroyers, do not appear to be gravely menaced by torpedo attacks. Only one of the British dreadnoughts, the *Marlborough*, appears to have been torpedoed, and she survived the shock. The British claim that two of the German ships were sunk by torpedoes, but this claim the Germans contradict.

When the battle had been in progress for almost two hours, with the odds strongly in favor of the Germans, the British Grand Fleet came into action and the tide of battle turned.

Count Zeppelin, at the left, with Colonel Schmiedcke and Professor Heigesell

An account of this battle, the greatest in history, evidently written in collaboration by several British naval officers who were present during the action, summarizes very clearly the strategy employed and is made the more understandable by the diagrams on page 159, which were prepared by the naval expert of the *Scientific American:*

"FIRST PHASE, 3:45 P. M., May 31.— Beatty's battle cruisers, consisting of the *Lion, Princess Royal, Queen Mary, Tiger, Inflexible, Indomitable, Invincible, Indefatigable,* and *New Zealand*, were on a southeasterly course, followed at about two miles, distance by the four *Queen Elizabeths.*

"Enemy light cruisers were sighted and shortly afterward the head of the German battle cruiser squadron, consisting of the new cruiser *Hindenburg*, the *Seydlitz, Derflinger, Lutzow, Moltke,* and possibly the *Salamis.*

"Beatty at once began firing at a range of about 20,000 yards (12 miles), which shortened to 16,000 yards (9 miles) as the fleets closed. The Germans could see the British distinctly outlined against the light-yellow sky. The Germans, covered by a haze, could be very indistinctly made out by our gunners.

"The *Queen Elizabeths* opened fire one after another, as they came within range. The German battle cruisers turned to port and drew away to about 20,000 yards.

"SECOND PHASE, 4:40 P. M.—A destroyer screen then appeared beyond the German battle cruisers. The whole German High Seas Fleet could be seen approaching on the northeastern horizon in three divisions, coming to the support of their battle cruisers.

"The German battle cruisers now turned right round 16 points and took station in front of the battleships of the High Fleet.

"Beatty with his battle cruisers and supporting battleships, therefore, had before him the whole of the German battle fleet, and Jellicoe was still some distance away.

"The opposing fleets were now moving parallel to one another in opposite directions, and but for a master maneuver on the part of Beatty the British advance ships would

ble also were lost at the turning point, where, of course, the High Seas Fleet concentrated their fire.

"A little earlier, as the German battle cruisers were turning, the *Queen Elizabeths* had in similar manner concentrated their fire on the turning point and destroyed a new

British sailors, their cruiser sunk, are picked up by one of their own submarines

have been cut off from Jellicoe's grand fleet. In order to avoid this and at the same time prepare the way so that Jellicoe might envelop his adversary, Beatty immediately also turned right round 16 points so as to bring his ships parallel to the German battle cruisers and facing in the same direction.

"As soon as he was round he increased to full speed to get ahead of the Germans and take up a tactical position in advance of their line. He was able to do this, owing to the superior speed of our battle cruisers.

"Just before the turning point was reached, the *Indefatigable* sank, probably from striking a mine, and the *Queen Mary* and the *Invinci-*

German battle cruiser, believed to be the *Hindenburg*.

"Beatty had now got round and headed away with the loss of three ships, racing parallel to the German battle cruisers. The *Queen Elizabeths* followed behind, engaging the main High Seas Fleet.

SIX SHIPS ATTACKED THE WARSPITE

"THIRD PHASE, 5 P. M.—The *Queen Elizabeths* now turned short to port 16 points in order to follow Beatty. The *Warspite* jammed her steering gear, failed to get around, and drew the fire of six of the enemy, who closed in upon her.

England's strong man. Earl Kitchener, Secretary of State for War in the British cabinet, was drowned off the Orkney Islands at 2 A. M. on June 6th when the cruiser *Hampshire* foundered after being torpedoed or through striking a mine

"I am not surprised that the Germans claim her as a loss, since on paper she ought to have been lost, but as a matter of fact, though repeatedly straddled by shellfire with the water boiling up all around her, she was not seriously hit and was able to sink one of her opponents. Her captain recovered

were suffered. They had the speed over their opponents by fully four knots, and were able to draw away from part of the long line of German battleships, which almost filled up the horizon.

"At this time the *Queen Elizabeths* were steadily firing at the flashes of German guns

Crater of a Zeppelin bomb in Paris

control of the vessel, brought her around, and followed her consorts.

"In the meantime the *Barham Valiant* and *Malaya* turned short so as to avoid the danger spot where the *Queen Mary* and the *Invincible* had been lost, and for an hour, until Jellicoe arrived, fought a delaying action against the High Seas Fleet.

"The *Warspite* joined them at about 5:15 o'clock, and all four ships were so successfully maneuvered in order to upset the spotting corrections of their opponents that no hits of a seriously disabling character

at a range which varied between 12,000 and 15,000 yards, especially against those ships which were nearest them. The Germans were enveloped in a mist and only smoke and flashes were visible.

"By 5:45 half of the High Seas Fleet had been left out of range, and the *Queen Elizabeths* were steaming fast to join hands with Jellicoe.

"I must now return to Beatty's battle cruisers. They had succeeded in outflanking the German battle cruisers, which were, therefore, obliged to turn a full right angle to starboard to avoid being headed.

"Heavy fighting was renewed between the opposing battle cruiser squadrons, during which the *Derflinger* was sunk; but toward 6 o'clock the German fire slackened very considerably, showing that Beatty's battle cruisers and the *Queen Elizabeths* had inflicted serious damage on their immediate opponents.

JELLICOE'S FLEET ARRIVED

"FOURTH PHASE, 6 P. M.—The Grand Fleet was now in sight and coming up fast in three directions (divisions?). The *Queen Elizabeths* altered their course four points to the starboard and drew in toward the enemy to allow Jellicoe room to deploy into line.

"The Grand Fleet was perfectly maneuvered and the very difficult operation of deploying between the battle cruisers and the *Queen Elizabeths* was perfectly timed.

"Jellicoe came up, fell in behind Beatty's

King and Queen pay last tribute to Kitchener

cruisers, and, followed by the damaged but still serviceable *Queen Elizabeths*, steamed right across the head of the German fleet.

"The first of the ships to come into action were the *Revenue* and the *Royal Oak* with their 15-inch guns, and the *Agincourt*, which fired from her seven turrets with the speed almost of a Maxim gun.

"The whole British fleet had now become concentrated. They had been perfectly maneuvered, so as to 'cross the T' of the High Seas Fleet and, indeed, only decent light was necessary to complete their work of destroying the Germans in detail. The light did improve for a few minutes and the conditions were favorable to the British fleet, which was now in line approximately north and south across the head of the Germans.

"During the few minutes of good light Jellicoe smashed up the first three German ships, but the mist came down, visibility suddenly failed, and the defeated High Seas Fleet was able to draw off in ragged divisions.

"FIFTH PHASE, NIGHT.—The Germans were followed by the British, who still had them enveloped between Jellicoe on the west, Beatty on the north, and Evan Thomas with his three *Queen Elizabeths* on the south. The *Warspite* had been sent back to her base.

"During the night our torpedo-boat destroyers heavily attacked the German ships, and, although they lost seriously themselves, succeeded in sinking two of the enemy.

"Coördination of the units of the fleet was practically impossible to keep up, and the Germans discovered by the rays of their searchlights the three *Queen Elizabeths* not more than 4,000 yards away. Unfortunately they were then able to escape between these battleships and Jellicoe, since we were not able to fire, as our own destroyers were in the way.

"So ended the Jutland Battle, which was fought as had been planned and was very nearly a great success. It was spoiled by the unfavorable weather conditions, especially at

Fortune (destroyer)	950	100
Nomad (destroyer)	*950	100
Nestor (destroyer)	*950	100

*Not listed in last British register

TOTALS

Battle cruisers	63,000	2,550
Armored cruisers	41,700	2,163
Destroyers	9,400	900
Fourteen ships	114,100	5,613

The German Fleet whose officers have often toasted "The Day." Meaning the day when it should dispute with Great Britain for the overlordship of the seas

the critical moment, when the whole British fleet was concentrated and engaged in crushing the head of the German line.

"It was an action on our part of big guns, except, of course, for the destroyer work, since at a very early stage our big ships ceased to feel any anxiety from the German destroyers. The German small craft were rounded up by their British opponents and soon ceased to count as an organized body."

LOSSES IN NORTH SEA BATTLE OFF JUTLAND

BRITISH

NAME	TONNAGE	PERSONNEL
		[Few Survivors]
Queen Mary (battle cruiser)	27,000	1,000
Indefatigable (battle cruiser)	18,750	800
Invincible (battle cruiser)	17,250	750
Defense (armored cruiser)	14,600	755
Warrior (armored cruiser)	13,550	704
Black Prince (armored cruiser)	13,550	704
Tipperary (destroyer)	1,850	150
Turbulent (destroyer)	1,850	150
Shark (destroyer)	950	100
Sparrowhawk (destroyer)	950	100
Ardent (destroyer)	950	100

GERMAN

NAME	TONNAGE	PERSONNEL
		[Of whom many were saved]
Pommern (battleship)	13,200	729
Wiesbaden (cruiser)	5,600 (estimated)	450
Frauenlob (cruiser)	2,715	264
Elbing (cruiser)	5,000 (estimated)	450
Six destroyers (reported)	6,000 (estimated)	600

[REPORTED BY BRITISH, BUT NOT ADMITTED BY GERMANS]

Westfalen (dreadnought)	18,900	963
Derflinger (battle cruiser)	26,600 (estimated)	1,200
One submarine	1,000 (estimated)	40

TOTALS

(ADMITTED)

Battleship	13,200	729
Cruisers	13,315	1,164
Destroyers	6,000	600
Ten ships	32,515	2,493

[INCLUDING GERMAN LOSSES REPORTED BY THE BRITISH]

Two battleships	32,100	1,692
Four cruisers	39,915	2,364
Six destroyers	6,000	600
One submarine	1,000	40
Thirteen ships	79,015	4,696

The heavy loss of life in this battle is a matter that deserves attention. In the subjoined table it will be noticed that practically the entire personnel of many British ships is reported as lost, while on the German ships many were saved. This is partly due to the fact that the British ships went down during action, whereas many of the German ships, tween decks there are pneumatic rafts, but there is scant time to put on a belt or launch a raft when the steel vessel loaded with guns and armor begins to go down. Practically every man goes down with the ship, and this fact was demonstrated at the Battle of Jutland.

Both the British and the Germans con-

The British Home Fleet steaming through the Solent. From left to right, the *King George*, *Thunderer*, *Monarch* and *Conqueror*

hen crippled, were able to pull out of the one of fire and save many of their people. ome were even in friendly home waters before actually going down. In modern naval arfare the loss on a sunken vessel is apt to be omplete. One reason for this is that a ship eldom pulls out of action until she is actually inking. Their structure is so complicated hat her commander may not know that she is bout to sink until she is just on the verge of aking the plunge. As long as she is afloat at ll she is a factor in the battle. A single appily placed shot from a sinking ship might e the blow to turn the tide of battle and to ettle the destinies of the nations at war. As ong as a ship floats it fights, its men remain in he turrets, the fire rooms, and at the guns— ll hard places to get out of when the vessel egins to career. She can carry no boats or afts on her deck for the blast of the guns ould blow them to flinders. The men in ction are provided with life belts, and be-

cealed for some time the extent of their losses. Admiral Jellicoe's formal report, dated July 6th, expressly declares it inexpedient to make the loss of the personnel and the extent of the damage inflicted public. The following table, however, agrees with the official statement of losses, except the loss of life, which is estimated. The German losses claimed by the British, but denied by the Germans, are included in a separate table.

Both sides earnestly claimed the victory. The Germans insisted that the weight of British vessels sunk and the toll of death paid in Jellicoe's fleet far exceeded th elosses of their own; the British denied heavier losses and pointed out that their enemies were forced to seek the shelter of their naval bases while Jellicoe's ships continued their ceaseless patrol of the North Sea. There was justification for both claims. But the real, vital, essential point is that after the engagement the British naval power was still overwhelming, its control of the seas still unshattered, and its blockade of German ports so unrelenting as to arouse bitter complaints from the blockaded nation which denounced the British for trying to starve the women and children of an entire nation.

The interior of a submarine, showing the pilot's wheel

fering and privation to non combatants. In no war has the blockade been so mercilessly applied as in our own Civil War, when the South was literally starved into subjection. The appeals made by the Germans for milk for their babies in this war were paralleled then by the cry of the fever-ridden

There was of course no justification for this complaint. The blockade is a legitimate weapon of war, despite the fact that it necessarily causes suffering South for quinine. But special vigilance was exerted to prevent that medicine from being shipped over the border.

German merchant submarine *Deutschland* lying in Chesapeake Bay before returning across the Atlantic. In spite of the vigilance of English patrols the *Deutschland* has made two trips to the United States, landing once at Baltimore and once at New London

Copyright by Underwood & Underwood

I. M. S. *Queen Elizabeth*, perhaps the most famous warship in the world, bombarding Cape Helles (Gallipoli) to cover the landing of the Allied forces.   She was the first battleship to carry fifteen-inch guns

CHRONOLOGY OF NAVAL EVENTS TO AUGUST 1, 1916

Naval occurrences connected with the British expedition to the Dardanelles will be found enumerated in the chronology attached to Chapter V.)

August 6.   British cruiser *Amphion* sunk by a mine.   First loss of the war to the British navy.

August 9.   German ships *Breslau* and *Goeben* enter the Dardanelles.

August 17.   French sink German cruiser in Adriatic.

August 21.   French and British ships bombard Cattaro.

August 24.   Japanese bombard Tsing-Tau.

August 27.   British ship *Highflyer* sinks *Kaiser Wilhelm der Grosse.*

August 28.   Battle off Heligoland.

September 22.   *Cressy*, *Aboukir*, and *Hogue* sunk by German submarine.

October 16.   British cruiser *Hawke* sunk by German submarine *U-9.*

October 17.   British squadron, led by the *Undaunted*, sinks four German destroyers off the Dutch coast.   British fleet bombards German forces at Nieuport.

October 19.   British and Japanese vessels begin attack on German colony at Tsing-Tau.   Bombardment of Cattaro begun by French navy.

October 25.   Japanese sink the German cruiser *Aeolus* off Honolulu.

October 29.   German raider *Emden* enters Penang harbor and sinks Russian cruiser *Jempchug.*

October 30.   Russian and Turkish fleets in battle in the Black Sea.   British cruiser *Hermes* sunk off Dover.

November 1.   German squadron under Admiral von Spee defeats British squadron under Rear-Admiral Cradock off Coronel, Chili.

November 3.   British cruiser *Minerva* bombards Akabah, Arabia, and sailors occupy the town.

November 10.   Australian cruiser *Sydney* sinks the *Emden*, which had destroyed more than $5,000,000 worth of British ships.

November 14.   First news of disabling of the British super-dreadnaught *Audacious* on October 27th off the Irish Coast. Vessel subsequently restored to service.

November 17.   Russian Black Sea fleet attacks Trebizond. German squadron bombards Libau.

November 26.   British battleship *Bulwark* blown up in the Thames.   Explosion probably accidental.

December 8.   British squadron under Vice-Admiral Sturdee defeats German squadron under Admiral von Spee off the Falkland Islands.

December 10.   German submarine raid on Dover repulsed by the forts.

December 14. British submarine *B*-11 diving under five rows of mines sinks Turkish battleship *Messudieh* in the Dardanelles.

December 16. German warship shells the British coast towns of Scarborough, Hartlepool, and Whitby; about 120 persons killed and 550 wounded.

December 22. Allied fleets shell German positions along the Belgian coasts.

December 26. British make naval and air attack on German fleet without important results.

January 1. British battleship *Formidable* torpedoed and sunk in English Channel; six hundred men lost.

January 24. British squadron under Vice-Admiral Beatty defeats German squadron in North Sea. German battle cruiser *Blücher* sunk, two other German battle cruisers damaged. British battle cruisers *Lion* and *Tiger* damaged.

February 8. Russian destroyers sink more than fifty enemy sailing vessels in the Black Sea.

February 18. German proclamation declaring the waters around Great Britain and Ireland a war zone which neutral ships may enter at their own risk takes effect. United States protests against the decree; 205 merchant craft and six neutral were sunk under the decree before August 1st, with a loss of 63 lives including two Americans.

February 19. Tension between the United States and Great Britain because of use of American flag on *Lusitania* and other ships becomes acute.

April 6. German submarine caught in a steel net off Dover. First recorded success of this method of meeting submarine peril.

April 7. German converted cruiser *Prinz Eitel Friederich* enters Hampton Roads and is interned until the end of the war.

April 15. Table published in London claims that the Allies have sunk, captured, or detained 543 ships belonging to Germany and her Allies, while 265 ships belonging to the Allies have been taken or destroyed by the Teutons.

April 26. French cruiser *Leon Gambetta* torpedoed in the Strait of Otranto, 552 men lost.

May 1. Cunarder *Lusitania* sails from New York. German Embassy at Washington publishes an advertisement stating that "travelers sailing in the war zone on ships of Great Britain or her Allies do so at their own great risk."

May 7. *Lusitania* is sunk ten miles off the Old Head of Kinsale, Ireland, by torpedoes from a German submarine. 1,154, including many women and children, are drowned or killed by the explosion.

May 17. The British admiralty announces that 460,628 tons of British shipping, other than warships, have been sunk or captured by the German navy since the beginning of the war, with 1,556 persons killed; that the German tonnage sunk or captured is 314,465 with no lives lost.

June 15. An official announcement states the total loss in the British navy up to May 31st was 13,547 officers and men.

Up to August 1, 1915, according to Senate Document 3 of the Sixty-fourth Congress, the allied navies had lost a total of 71 warships, with a tonnage of 326,855. Of these Great Britain had lost 42 ships of 254,494 tons—8 battleships, 3 armored cruisers, 4 protected cruisers, 4 light cruisers, and 24 smaller craft; France, 12 ships of 28,027 tons; Russia, 6 ships of 21,775 tons; Japan, 7 ships of 4,801 tons; and Italy, 4 ships of 17,758 tons. Germany, Austria, and Turkey had lost 89 ships, with a tonnage of 262,791. Of these Germany had lost 69 ships of 283,904 tons—1 battle cruiser, 5 armored cruisers, 10 protected cruisers, 3 light cruisers, and 50 smaller and auxiliary craft; Austria, 7 ships of 7,397 tons, and Turkey 13 ships of 16,490 tons.

Up to the same date German submarines sank 205 merchant craft belonging to the Allies, and 59 neutrals with a total sacrifice of 1,641 non-combatant lives.

In the second year of the war official records in regard to the losses of submarines and auxiliary cruisers are incomplete, and transports are not scheduled as warships. In this year

the Allies lost 41 ships with a tonnage of 202,600, and th Central Empires 33 ships, with a tonnage of 125,120. Grea Britain's loss was 34 ships—2 battleships, 3 battle cruisers 3 armored cruisers, 7 protected cruisers, 2 light cruisers, an 17 smaller and auxiliary craft, with a total of 195,900 tons Germany's loss was 26 ships—4 battleships, 1 battle cruiser 6 protected cruisers, and 15 smaller craft and auxiliaries, with total of 114,620 tons.

August 8. German squadron repulsed while attempting t menace Riga. Petrograd reports that nine battleships an twelve cruisers were driven off.

November 17. Twenty-five British submarines pass Nort Sea into the Baltic.

December 30. Austrian squadrons defeated with the loss o two destroyers by Italian ships off Durazzo, Albania.

January 9. Loss of British battleship *King Edward VII* b contact with mine is announced.

February 1. German prize crew bring in British steame *Appam* to Hampton Roads, with passengers and crews o six other British merchantmen captured by the auxiliar cruiser *Möwe* or *Roon*, ship declared British prize by Unite States Court in July, 1916.

February 13. French Government admits the loss of th cruiser *Admiral Charner* by submarine off the Syrian coast

February 27. French transport *Provence* sunk by submarin in Mediterranean with a loss of 3,100 marines and troops

February 27. British steamer *Maloja*, en route for Indi strikes mine near Dover and loses more than 150 lives i passengers and crew.

March 5. German Admiralty announces the safe arrival a Wilhelmshaven of auxiliary cruiser *Möwe* after having de stroyed or captured fifteen merchant craft of the Allies.

March 24. British Channel steamer *Sussex* torpedoed b German submarine with the death of more than fifty pas sengers.

April 25. German battle cruiser squadron with submarine and Zeppelins attack Lowestoft and Yarmouth, northeast o London. This is supposed to be in conjunction with th Sinn-Fein revolt in Dublin and the landing of Sir Roge Casement on the Irish coast.

April 27. British battleship *Russell* sunk by mine in th Mediterranean.

May 31. British and German naval engagement off the coas of Denmark, North Sea. British admit the loss of six larg cruisers and eight destroyers, the Germans a battleship a battle cruiser, four light cruisers, and five destroyers 9,500 lives are lost.

June 5. British cruiser *Hampshire* sunk by a mine off th Orkney Islands on her way to Russia. Lord Kitchene Secretary for War, and his staff are lost, together with a except twelve of the crew.

June 9. Italian Admiralty announces that the transpor *Principe Umberto* has been sunk with large loss of life b submarine in the Adriatic.

July 6. Turkish *Midullu*, formerly German cruiser *Bresla* sinks Russian transport by use of Russian flag.

July 9. German merchant submarine *Deutschland* arrives a Baltimore after unique transatlantic voyage.

July 10. Turkish *Midullu* and *Sultan Selim*, the latter form erly German cruiser *Goeben*, sink four Russian transport and bombard Caucasus coast.

July 12. German submarine shells Seaham Harbor, on Eng lish east coast.

July 15. Italian destroyer *Impetuoso* sunk by Austrian sub marine in the Adriatic.

July 22. German flotilla of torpedo-boat destroyers escap after running fight with British patrols off Holland an attempt to raid the Thames mouth. Both sides claim hit

During the second year of the war German and Austria submarines sunk 518 merchant craft of which 72 were neutra The lives of 983 non-combatants were sacrificed.

SCENE OF THE BRITISH SUCCESS AT NEUVE CHAPELLE

London prays for victory.   Special service of intercession at St. Paul's Cathedral

CHAPTER VI

DEADLOCK IN FRANCE AND BELGIUM—THE HARDSHIPS OF THE TRENCHES
—A CHRISTMAS TRUCE—BATTLE OF NEUVE CHAPELLE—THE LABYRINTH—
ASPHYXIATING GAS AND LIQUID FIRE—YPRES AND THE RIVER YSER

A Japanese cruiser

PROBABLY never in the history of mankind has more of human agony, human sacrifice, cold brutality, and warm sympathy been compressed into so small a space of time and place as in the year 1915 and in that part of France and Belgium in which the warring armies strove for the mastery. It was a year of constant battling with utterly inconclusive results. Men fell by the tens of thousands to gain a score of yards in the enemy's lines. The capture of a trench was proclaimed as a magnificent victory, though the defenders had but retreated to another work twenty-five yards in its rear. Now one belligerent and then the other assumed the offensive, but all that was sought was merely to pierce the lines of the foe. The Germans had about abandoned their hope of reaching Paris, and the French cry, "On to Berlin," was stilled. The world as a whole was beginning to speak of the great war as a draw.

Throughout the bitter months of the winter of 1915 the lines of the belligerents extended for five hundred miles from the British Channel to the Vosges Mountains, seldom more than two hundred yards apart, often hardly half that. By the map it was 200 miles, but the actual extent of the trenches was many times as much. At one point which came to be known as the Labyrinth, and at which later in the year a bloody battle was fought, there were more than 200 miles of trenches between two points separated only by twelve miles in a direct line. Of this entire 500 miles of battle front fifty were held by the Belgians and the British, the remainder by the French. But the section held by the two former nations was that in which was the most savage fighting during the opening months of 1915 and in which natural conditions made the daily life of the soldiers most difficult to bear. Sir John French in his official report said of the sufferings of the men in Flanders, "The men have been called upon to stand for many hours together almost up to their waists in bitterly cold water only separated by one or two hundred yards from a most vigilant enemy." But that is the passionless and restrained description of trench life by a great commander. This extract from the description given in a letter from one of the soldiers who had suffered months of that existence gives a more graphic picture of what it really meant:

"Take a cold, damp cellar and flood it with some three to six inches of almost ice-cold mud; at a height of five feet from the floor stretch a tangle of wires; turn an electric current into the wires and let the voltage be so heavy that every wire will be as deadly as a third rail.

"Now blow out the light, crawl to the middle of the floor in the darkness, and stand erect, trusting to blind luck that your head won't touch the wire. These charged wires, in the darkness, represent the invisible deadly trails of the bullets that fly over your head in the trenches.

"Of course, if you want to be safe in the cellar you can keep your head down, but if you did that in the trenches you would be neglecting your duty. It is your duty, for instance, to fire eight bullets an hour if on guard. Watchful eyes of officers will discover whether you are shooting into the air or whether you

Behind the French lines in the Vosges. The French "poilu" is a genius at making himself comfortable in the open air. This photograph shows the camp on wash day

sunshine of the bright Christmas morning fell on it as brightly as if it were a lover's lane or the aisle in some grand cathedral.

"I don't know how the truce began in other trenches, but in our hole Nadeem began it—Nadeem, a Turk, who believes that Mohammed and not Christ was the Prophet of God. The sunshine of the morning seemed to get into Nadeem's blood. He was only an enthusiastic boy, always childishly happy, and when we noticed, at the regular morning shooting hour, that the German trenches were silent Nadeem began to make a joke of it. He drew a target on a board,

are firing with your aim fixed on the enemy's trenches, and a good sentinel is supposed to raise his head above the trench every ten minutes to see what is going on outside."

This writer, Phil Rader by name, a young San Franciscan who had enlisted in the French Foreign Legion, was prolific of graphic sketches of life in the trenches. His description of a Christmas truce and its abrupt end throws a bright light on the psychology of war:

"For twenty days we had faced that strip of land, forty-five feet wide, between our trench and that of the Germans, that terrible No Man's Land, dotted with dead bodies, crisscrossed by tangled masses of barbed wire. That little strip of land was as wide and as deep and as full of death as the Atlantic Ocean; as uncrossable as the spaces between stars; as terrible as human hate. And the

fastened it on a pole, and stuck it above the trench, shouting to the Germans:

"'See how well you can shoot.'

"Within a minute the target had been bulls'-eyed. Nadeem pulled it down, pasted little bits of white paper where shots had struck, and held it up again so that the Germans could see their score. In doing so, Nadeem's head appeared above the trench,

Borrowed from the Dark Ages. An adaptation of the old cross-bow. It will hurl a few pounds of sudden death 30 or 40 yards

and we heard him talking across the No Man's Land. Thoughtlessly I raised my head, too. Other men did the same. We saw hundreds of German heads appearing. Shouts filled the air. What miracle had happened? Men laughed and cheered. There was Christmas light in our eyes and I know there were Christmas tears in mine.

"There were smiles, smiles, smiles, where in days before there had been only rifle-barrels. The terror of No Man's Land fell away. The sounds of happy voices filled the air. We were all unhumanly happy for that one glorious instant—English, Portuguese, Americans, and even Nadeem, the Turk—and savages as we had been, cavemen as we were, the awfulness of war had not filled the corners of our hearts where love and Christmas live. I think Nadeem was first to sense what had happened. He suddenly jumped out of the trench and began waving his hands and cheering. The hatred of war had been suddenly withdrawn and it left a vacuum in which we human beings

Clothes must be clean when going into battle. The last thing the Foreign Legion did before taking its post was to put on clean underclothes and shirts. Every soldier has a horror of tetanus

rushed into contact with each other. You felt their handshakes—double handshakes, with both hands—in your heart.

"Nadeem couldn't measure human nature unerringly. He had been the first to feel the holiday spirit of Christmas Day, but, on this day after Christmas, he failed to sense the grimness of war that had fallen over the trenches during the night. Early in the morning he jumped out of the trench and began waving his hands again. John Street, an American, who had been an evangelist in St. Louis, jumped out with him, and began to shout a morning greeting to a German he had made friends with the day before.

"There was a sudden rattle of rifle-fire and Street fell dead, with a bullet through his head. The sun was shining down again on a world gone mad."

Though the French had lost heavily in the fighting of the fall months, they had so far

Shooting death from a gas pipe. Where the hostile trenches are only a few yards apart, grenades are thrown back and forth by hand

recuperated by January as to begin efforts all along their lines to accomplish what was destined to be their one compelling purpose for the next eighteen months, namely, to break the German line and force the invaders out of France. Their first serious attack was made in the neighborhood of Soissons. There the elements combined for their undoing. At the very crucial moment heavy

the line which extended between Rheims and the Argonne. Both the French and the Germans made efforts to break their enemy's front at various points in Champagne. The Germans were trying to force the Allies to weaken their line in Flanders in order that by a sudden thrust the soldiers of the Kaiser might get around French's left flank and cut him off from the sea. In this they failed

Their light has gone out forever.   Blinded French soldiers escorted by a nurse

utterly, General Joffre proving quite capable of taking care of his centre without depleting the left flank. But Joffre in his turn attacked savagely in the neighborhood of Arras, at Lens, and about La Bassee. The purposes of the French attack here were twofold. Success would have given them control of important railroad communications held by the Germans and would furthermore have driven the enemy from the highly important mining district surrounding Lens from which they were drawing huge supplies of coal. The fighting in this neighborhood lasted more than a month, and in it not less than 500,000 men were involved. But it was at best indecisive. Beginning the last of January, March found the lines of the enemies occupying practically the same relative positions. But during this period not merely were hundreds of thousands of men put out of action, but the French villages, so beautiful and contented in times of peace, were reduced to mere heaps of ruins.

rains caused a flood which washed away bridges upon which the French depended for their supplies. The Germans rushed reënforcements to that point and the French were forced back with heavy loss, even sacrificing some of the territory that had been gained in the Battle of the Aisne. But the retreat was soon checked, and for nearly a month the armies at that point contented themselves with holding each other rigidly to the line of their trenches.

For a time activity shifted to that part of

Much of the country is a level plain traversed by sluggish rivers. A watcher in the days before the war could see all about him closely built little French villages, separated one from the other by ten to fifteen miles of smiling countryside. The French farmer in the main does not live on his farm as do the Americans. As a result one sees but few farmhouses, but groups of villages surrounded by miles of fertile country. But by

March of 1915 the villages were smouldering heaps of ruined masonry and the fields were scarred in every direction by trenches, and plentifully dotted with the crosses that mark the resting places of the quiet dead.

Early in March the most important battle of the year was fought in and about the little French town of Neuve Chapelle by the British forces. The battle raged for three days, beginning on the tenth, and in it the British lost 12,811 men of whom nearly 2,500 were killed. The German losses were heavier, and as the result of the battle very material gains were made by the British on that part of the battleline. The main point of attack was the closely built stone village which was held by the Germans who, in the ponderous farmhouses and behind the stone walls of the orchard which flanked the village on either side, had established machine guns and heavy batteries of field artillery. The assailants were handicapped from the outset by a heavy mist which persisted throughout the three days of fighting. Sir Douglas Haig and Sir Horace Smith-Dorrien, two British leaders destined to win great reputations during the course of the war, led the attack. For the first time in serious fighting on this section of the

Graves marked with bottles

battleline the picturesque East Indian troops of Great Britain were brought into action and conducted themselves with great gallantry. In numbers engaged and in losses the battle of Neuve Chapelle closely resembled that of Waterloo. But Waterloo was the turning point of a war —Neuve Chapelle only an incident in an interminable deadlock.

As was the case with so much of the fighting in France, this attack was made not so much because of any special strategic value attaching to the ground immediately fought for, but for its effect on the campaign in the East. In eastern Prussia at this moment the Russians were just beginning to recover from the crushing blow delivered by Von Hindenburg at the Masurian Lakes and had themselves again resumed the offensive. Accordingly the French and the British on the western battleline were attacking at every point in order that they might keep the Germans in their front so busily engaged that there would be no possibility of detaching forces to be sent to meet the Russian onslaught. Hence the battle at Neuve Chapelle and the attacks that were being made almost simultaneously by the French troops at Arras and in the Champagne country.

The end of a faithful friend

Uhlan patrol ambushed by English machine gun

By the second year of the war the supreme importance of the artillery had become evident, and the Teutonic allies were bitterly complaining that the enormous supply of ammunition from the United States was the one thing that delayed their certain victory.

It was near Neuve Chapelle that the forces of the Allies began first to see evidences of the care with which the Germans had prepared for a long sojourn in France and had constructed green boughs and shrubbery so that they might escape the attention of the enemy's aeroplanes. In these places the men took refuge when not actually engaged on duty in the open trench. They were well furnished, usually with furniture made by the men, but often with more luxurious fittings secured by raiding neighboring chateaux of which there were many in that country. Many had pianos, and not a few were decorated with

Wounded soldiers in the American hospital at Saignton, England

their trenches not merely for safety, but with an eye to getting at least a small amount of comfort out of the situation. Miles of the trenches, especially in swampy regions, were lined with concrete. The one difficulty about this, as some of the captives remarked, was that while the water could not seep in from the adjacent swampy soil, when it rained in there was no way of getting it out. After a while they constructed hand pumps, and whole companies would be employed in baling out the trenches as sailors desperately man the pumps on a sinking ship.

Some of the trenches had two stories, and attached to some were rest houses built of concrete wholly underground, proof against falling shells and concealed on the surface by good pictures which formed part of the army's loot.

The country called the Champagne country in which occurred much of the desultory fighting of the first half of 1915, which was so largely without definite result, is a vast plain, undulating somewhat like what we call rolling prairies and with scarcely a hill higher than 200 feet. The official "British observer," describing the character of the fighting done in this section, says of it:

"Every day an attack is made on a trench, on the edge of one of the little woods or to gain ground in one of them; every day the ground gained has to be transformed so as to give protection to its new occupants and means of access to their supports; every night, and on many days, the enemy's counter-attacks have to be repulsed.

"Each attack has to be prepared by a violent and accurate artillery fire; it may be said that a trench has to be morally captured by gun fire before it can be actually seized by

Hot broth for the wounded soldiers. A British Red Cross kitchen ambulance issuing strengthening drinks to men who are on their way to the base hospitals

the infantry. Once in the new trench, the men have to work with their intrenching tools, without exposing themselves, and wait for a counter-attack, doing what damage they can to the enemy with hand grenades and machine guns. Thus the amount of rifle fire is very small; it is a war of explosives and bayonets.

"Looking at the battle at a distance of about 2,000 yards from the enemy's line, the

stillness of what one sees is in marked contrast to the turmoil of shells passing overhead. The only movement is the cloud of smoke and earth that marks the burst of a shell. Here and there long white lines are visible, when a trench has brought the chalky subsoil up to the top, but the number of trenches seen is very small compared to the number that exists, for one cannot see into the valleys, and the top of the ground is an unhealthy place to choose for seating a trench. The woods are pointed out, with the names given them by the soldiers, but it needs field-glasses to see the few stumps that remain in those where the artillery has done its work. And then a telephone message arrives, saying that the enemy are threatening a counter-attack at a certain point, and three minutes later there is a redoubled whistling of shells. At first one cannot see the result of this fire—the guns are searching the low ground where the enemy's reserves are preparing for the movement, but a little later the ground in front of the threatened trench becomes alive with shell bursts, for the searching has given place to the building up of a wall of fire through which it is impossible for the foe to pass without enormous loss."

Through much of the spring a great battle raged incessantly in that part of the works in the neighborhood of Neuville and Écurie just north of Arras, called the Labyrinth. This network of trenches built by the Germans seemed to be absolutely impregnable. For intricacy, skill of design, and defensive power the works were without parallel in the history of war. While the French army had been menacing it for months the determined attack by which this veritable hornet's nest was cleared of its defenders began in the early part of May, and lasted until the middle of June. Like the Battle of Ypres, the Battle of the Labyrinth was now lost, then won, then lost again by the defenders. Its story would make a volume in itself and is hardly to be told with

"I always had a fairly accurate sense of direction; but, standing in many places in this giant battlefield, it was impossible for me to say where were the Germans and where the French, so completely was I turned around

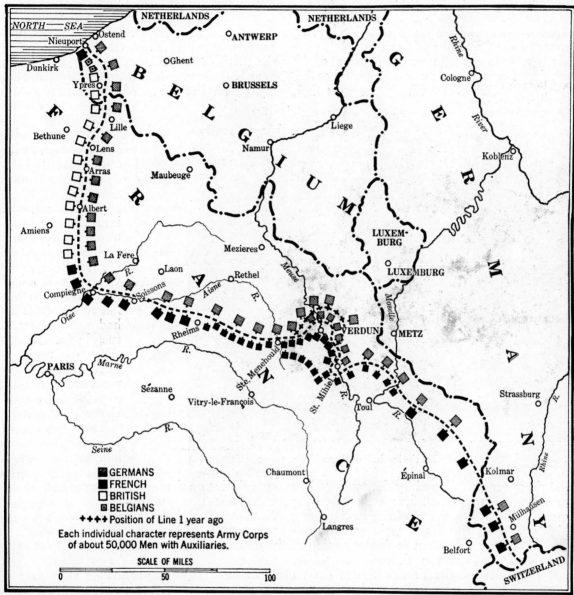

The western front, early summer, 1916. Spring in the western theatre of war again, as was the case in 1915, found the initiative in the hands of the Germans. They desired, first, to capture the French position of Verdun, which controls the line of the Meuse River. The French, however, resolutely refused to be driven back and, in the first weeks after the launching of the great German attack at Verdun, managed to make good their ground. To the hammering of the most powerful heavy artillery ever brought into action, and the persistent assaults of the machine-like German infantry the French with equal persistence opposed their own artillery and veteran troops. The French watchword was "They Shall Not Pass," and they made it good

complete accuracy until the war is ended. An American journalist present during the battle, says of the complicated character of the positions:

on account of the constant zigzag of the trench lines. Sometimes, when I was positive that a furious cannonade coming from a certain position was German, it turned out to be

French. At other times, when I thought I was safely going in the direction of the French, I was hauled back by officers who told me I was heading directly into the German line of fire. I sometimes felt that the German lines were on three sides, and often I was quite correct. On the other hand, the French lines often almost completely surrounded the German positions.

"One could not tell from the nearness of the artillery fire whether it was from friend or foe. Artillery makes three different noises: first,

Copyright by International News Service

What the howitzers did to a Namur turret

the sharp report followed by detonations like thunder, when the shell first leaves the gun; second, the rushing sound of the shell passing high overhead; third, the shrill whistle, followed by the crash when it finally explodes. In the Labyrinth the detonations which usually indicated the French fire might be from the German batteries stationed quite near us, but where they could not get the range on us, and firing at a section of the French lines some miles away. I finally determined that when a battery fired fast it was French; for the German fire is becoming more intermittent every day."

During the month that the fighting was in progress in Champagne more than half a million men were in action on either side.

Hardly had the echoes of this conflict died away when the Germans in their turn launched their great offensive in the west in the second battle of Ypres. They struck that section of the British line which was held by the Canadians linked up with the French. It was here that the men from Great Britain's most important American colony made their reputation as possibly the best fighters in the British Army. They were all new hands. War had never come to that fortunate country which lies north of the United States, beyond a border which is maintained without forts, without garrisons, without even men-of-war on the Great Lakes. After a scant six months of training in the great camps around London these Colonials took the field and sustained the attacks of the German forces like veterans. They had, furthermore, to sustain for the first time two new and terrifying engines of warfare—the asphyxiating gas and the curtain of fire.

The use of a suffocating gas in warfare had been anticipated for years by writers speculating on the new horrors which what we call civilization would bring to modern war. Novelists had long been describing it as a weapon which could not be met, and which would therefore make war impossible because of its very deadliness. The Chinese, who have had a habit of preceding us in many inventions, applied its principle in a small way with the bombs they called "Stink Pots." But the Germans first reduced the use of gas to something like a science, and the British, after a very brief period of heated denunciation of the device as inhuman and barbaric, hastily adopted it for their own use. The gas, which is a product of chlorine, is of very heavy specific gravity, forming, when liberated from the receptacles in which it is carried to the front, a sort of greenish-yellow vapor

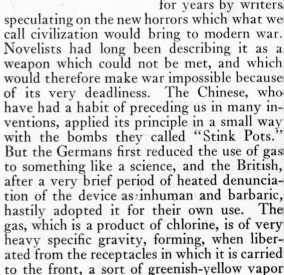

which lies close to the ground. As there is no means of propelling it artificially, except when it is used in exploding shells, it can only be used when there is a favorable wind which will carry it toward the enemy's trenches. Given such a wind and reasonable good fortune it forms a most serviceable curtain for the advance of troops. For the gas not only is dense enough to conceal the lines advancing behind it, but if carried into a trench will almost instantly put its defenders out of action. Once inhaled it causes the most frightful agony, and if death does not occur to the victim it leaves him crippled and subject to all sorts of bodily distress in after life. Very quickly, however, upon the appearance of chlorine gas as a factor in war inventors produced a respirator which serves as an almost complete defence. It has the appearance of a cloth hood pierced for the soldier's eyes, but containing in the mouthpiece fabrics prepared chemically which take from the gas all its deadly qualities as the soldier breathes. The men thus accoutred are of a weird and ghastly appearance with no human features apparent save two huge and staring goggle eyes. They look not unlike the apparitions which, under the title of the Ku Klux Klan, in the days of Reconstruction were used to terrify the negroes of the South into subjection.

The chief difficulty involved in the use of the curtain of gas was that a shift in the wind might turn it back upon the troops following it and destroy them. The curtain of fire, though available only to clear a way for twenty or thirty feet, was not subject at least to this disadvantage. Projected for that distance or more from tubes held in the hands of a line of advancing soldiers, this fiery scourge could neither be evaded nor sustained.

An English correspondent who witnessed at Ypres the effect of this new and untried weapon upon soldiers who not only had not encountered it before, but who had never even heard of it as a possibility, gives this account of its effect upon these troops:

"The strong northeast wind, which was blowing from the enemy's lines across the French trenches, became charged with a sickening, suffocating odor which was recognized as proceeding from some form of poi-

Copyright by International News Service

Wreckage at Namur—hitherto considered practically impregnable

sonous gas. The smoke moved like a vivid green wall some four feet in height for several hundred yards, extending to within 200 yards of the extreme left of our lines. Gradually it rose higher and obscured the view from the level. . . .

"Soon strange cries were heard, and through the green mist, now growing thinner and patchy, there came a mass of dazed, reeling men who fell as they passed through our ranks. The greater number were unwounded, but they bore upon their faces the marks of agony.

"The retiring men were among the first soldiers of the world whose *sang-froid* and courage have been proverbial throughout the war. All were reeling through us and round us like drunken men."

The suffering endured by the victims of these two new military weapons caused bitter protest at the time and led to an agitation, which will probably survive the war, for the adoption of an international agreement after the war shall be over to prohibit both as inhuman and barbaric. But the course of this war has demonstrated that international agreements are but of little service when once the guns get into action. It is more probable that the comparatively slight military service accomplished by either the gas or the fire will lead to the military abandonment of both. After the first two or three battles,

Steel turret for trench use devised by Germans. The French advance in Champagne resulted in the capture of several steel turrets like the one in the photograph. They were made of three-inch plate, could be revolved, and each held a 50-millimetre gun and three gunners

in which the element of surprise and novelty gave to these weapons an especial frightfulness, it is not recorded that their use ever produced any decisive advantage to the side employing them.

In May Ypres and the Yser River became once more the battleground. The Germans this time forced the fighting, and their purpose was clearly to reopen the campaign for Calais which had so signally failed in the fall. There was savage fighting in the water-logged country intersected by sluggish canals which attacking parties sometimes swam under fire, at other times crossed on rude rafts in the face of a storm of bullets against which it seemed that no life could endure. In the

end it all came to nothing. By this time the British Army so slowly raised and so arduously drilled on the plain of Salisbury had come to be a war machine worth reckoning with. Within the safety zone of the English Channel, fenced off from hostile craft by a picket line of destroyers and scouts at either end, the gray transports which so lately had been gay transatlantic liners were plying back and forth dropping on the soil of France at each trip 2,000 or more soldiers—no longer a mere mob, but men trained in every art of war save the ultimate one of inflicting and defying death. Months before Kitchener had said, "I don't know when this war will end, but it will begin in May." May was now here and the British Army had begun to be an effective machine.

While the fighting was in progress about Ypres the Germans were making a determined effort to capture Dunkirk on the coast of the North Sea. This would have served somewhat as a consolation prize for their failure to secure Calais. They had indeed captured Zeebrugge, the port of the city of Bruges. From this town they expelled all its inhabitants and converted it into a naval base, which was unsatisfactory because of the shallowness of the harbor. But their ambitions were still centred upon either Dunkirk or Calais. The latter began to be the target for shells dropped from Zeppelins and Taubes, and about the middle of May a bombardment was begun of the town from a battery, the location of which never was discovered. Aeroplanes hovering above the city directed the fire of the battery, which was very accurate. As at the time the most advanced line of the German entrenchments was some twenty miles east of the city the shells must have been fired from a point of even greater distance. It was believed that the battery was a fixed one of great guns erected upon concrete foundations near Dixmude.

More vigorous and persistent, however, was the bombardment of Ypres. Prior to the war this was one of the most beautiful ancient

Flemish cities in a land full of artistic towns. But lying as it did for some time between the Allied and the German line and occupied in turn by either belligerent, it suffered cruelly. Its grand square, or Place de la Ville, had long been one of the show places of Europe. One side was formed by the famous Cloth Hall, built at a time when trades unions were accustomed to house their places of business in buildings on which no artistic effort was spared, and on another by the Gothic cathedral dating from the thirteenth century. Both were practically demolished. The town itself was depopulated, its people fleeing farther into France from the continuous rain of shells. The town

The new model French soldier. Besides his rifle and regular equipment he carries the bag at his side with extra cartridges and three grenades

was the object of almost constant German counter-attacks without success. The west bank of the Ypres Canal, on which the Allies had established themselves, was another point of constant fighting beginning as early as the 22d of April when the Allies were driven from it with a loss of 6,000 prisoners and thirty-five guns. By the 2d of May the German General Staff admitted a loss of 12,000 dead in the Battle of Ypres.

By this time the diplomatic representatives of both sides were making fierce accusations and counter-accusations as to the character of warfare employed by their enemies. Both had by this time come to use asphyxiating gases both in shells and hand grenades. The French employed

itself had no particular strategic or defensive value. It suffered merely because it lay in the very middle of the country for which the enemies were so savagely fighting. That fighting was continuous for months. Its chronology presents a monotonous series of successes and repulses, attacks and counter-attacks on either side. Hill 60, taken early in the action by the British,

a device for spraying flaming liquids on the German trenches, declaring in response to the criticisms of humane observers that it was done by way of reprisal. To the northeast of Ypres on one occasion the Germans before attacking the British rolled a huge cloud of asphyxiating gas toward their lines, the volume of fumes being forty feet high along a six-

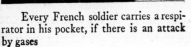
Every French soldier carries a respirator in his pocket, if there is an attack by gases

Scene in the first-line trenches, where papers, particularly illustrated ones, are much in demand

mile front. Imagination refuses to conceive the emotions of the defenders who watched this slow-moving, death-dealing cloud rolling mysteriously down upon them. But the

extended farther and farther to either sid of that little city. The fighting extended t Lens, to Nieuport, to Arras, to Lorett Heights, to Souchez, and Carency. A through Franc to the west (Rheims th guns were roa ing and th charges an counter charges bein delivered dail But the sprin passed int summer an the summe into autum with no m; terial advar tage derived b either party It no longe could be sai that such deadlock w; equivalent t German defea for now the tas of advancin becameobv ously incun bent upon th Allies. The had blocke the triumphar march of Ge many upo Paris. To th; extent the were victor ous. But no their necessar task was th expulsion o the invader from Franc and from Be gium. So lon as the Germar held all of th

A bit of warm work near Ypres

British report of the action declares that because of the use of the then newly invented respirators comparatively few deaths resulted.

As the weeks rolled on the Battle of Ypres

latter state and a great part of the economicall rich section of northern France they held th whip hand. The horrors of war had not ye extended beyond the German frontier. Froi the enemy country they held huge sums c

One of Germany's "Busy Berthas"

oney were extorted in the way of fines and voluntary tribute laid upon municipalities. he mines were worked by the compulsory bor of French and Belgians and for the sole benefit of the invaders. The fields, too, were tilled by the compulsory toil of the peasants in order that their product might help to make up the shortage in foodstuffs in Ger-

War and art at Ypres

many due to the British blockade. It was clear that while such a situation existed any negotiations for peace would be conducted with Germany holding the great advantage. Before such negotiations could be begun the invaders must be driven back to their own territory. Every day during which they successfully resisted the efforts of the British and French to thus expel them had to be counted a day won for the invaders.

Desultory fighting without material results occupied the armies in Flanders through-

there was much dissatisfaction with Sir John French who had hitherto been the idol of the British Army and people. His reserves had not been brought up, and the advance upon Lens was not pushed. The German lines had not been pierced, although they were weakened by sending great masses of troops to the Russian front. Probably as a result of this failure General French was transferred to other activities and General Sir Douglas Haig succeeded him as commander-in-chief of the British in France and Belgium. The

A German motor convoy destroyed by French Dragoons in the Forest of Villiers-Cotteret

out the summer. There were steady rumors that a great drive by the Allies was to be expected. But Great Britain was still palpably unprepared. The Battle of Neuve Chapelle, in which according to Lloyd George as much ammunition had been expended as during the whole Boer War, had shown how vital to success artillery ammunition, in quantities hitherto undreamed of, was. Accordingly activities halted until September. Then a great drive was undertaken by the Allies. The French attacked along a fifteen-mile front in Champagne and the English captured Loos and for a time seemed on the verge of taking Lens. But although a victory the action at Loos resulted in so small a part of what might have been expected of it that

spring drive which had been promised had become an autumn drive and that had culminated in failure. From this time until the summer of 1916 there was no further serious effort to oust the Germans from their foothold in the west.

That period was needed by the Allies for the organization and great extension of their facilities for making ammunition, and by the British especially for the creation of a sufficient army by enforced service. Two facts have been demonstrated by this war. Artillery and ammunition in quantities never before dreamed of form the backbone of modern military tactics. The Allies would have been annihilated in the second year of the war had it not been for the munitions

Returning through the mud to duty in the drowned trenches

factories of the United States. Germany would have been beaten had not her first dash given her control of the iron and coal deposits of France and Belgium and the metal works of the latter country. As for the armies it has been demonstrated to all nations that universal military service is the price of national safety. Perhaps the most remarkable feature of the whole international broil is that in the years preceding 1914 France and England did not see what was coming. Certainly Germany never made any bones about rattling her sword in its scabbard and proclaiming her ambitions.

Effect of French artillery fire on German positions before Verdun. The terrible tornado of explosives that the French let loose on their enemies before storming their positions sweeps the earth clear of vegetation and of life where not protected by trenches

The German attack on Soissons. The smoke on the left indicates French artillery answering the German shell which is shown bursting. The river is the Aisne

CHRONOLOGY OF PERIOD TREATED IN CHAPTER VI

October 30. Belgians flood lower valley of the Yser River and compel Germans to withdraw.

October 31. Germans heavily reënforced along the Yser.

November 2. Allies take Ramscapelle with the bayonet.

November 4. Germans losing along the Yser. Three days' heavy fighting around Ypres.

November 8. Belgians gain at Dixmude and Ypres.

November 11. Germans capture Dixmude, cross the Yser Canal, and drive Allies out of St. Eloi.

November 15. Germans complete defensive line from the North Sea to the Rhine.

November 19. Fighting in Flanders slackens, troops go into winter quarters.

December 1. Germans prepare for new dash toward the sea. Winter conditions in Flanders very severe.

December 3. Germans take offensive between Ypres and Dixmude. They lose heavily trying to cross the Yser on rafts.

December 7. Allies begin a general offensive movement.

December 22. Germans claim that the Allies' advance pressed since the 7th has failed.

December 27. Germans begin preparations for the defence of Antwerp, fearing Allied advance.

January 3. French gain near Rheims and San Mihiel.

January 8. Allies gain north of Soissons and Rheims.

January 13. Germans, reënforced, win victory at Soissons, forcing French to abandon five miles of trenches and to cross the Aisne, leaving guns and wounded. Fourteen guns and 3,150 prisoners taken by the Germans under the eyes of the Kaiser.

January 21. Germans repulsed in the Ardenne Woods by French and Belgians. French retake trenches at Notre Dame de Lorette.

February 5. Allies undertake a strong offensive in Belgium.

February 16. French gain in Champagne.

March 2. British gain near La Bassee.

March 4. Germans for the first time use liquid fire against French advancing in Malancourt Woods.

March 11. British capture Neuve Chapelle. German loss estimated by the British at 18,000.

March 15. British and French prepare for a general offensive.

April 5. German gains in the Argonne Forest and in the Forest of Le Pretre, bombardment of Rheims continues. It is reported that one-third of the houses have been destroyed and another third damaged. The Cathedral still suffering.

April 19. The British line south of Ypres has been pushed forward three miles.

April 22. Germans drive the Allies back at Ypres taking 6,000 prisoners. The fiercest fighting of the war in the west is raging, about this position for the next ten days.

May 12. Severe fighting on the whole front from Ypres to Arras, the Allies taking the offensive.

June 2. Battle of the Labyrinth begins.

June 22. Official announcement of the capture of the Labyrinth by the French.

July 2. In the western part of the Argonne the German army under the Crown Prince begins an offensive destined to last for many months without material effect.

BRITISH SHIP IN ACTION IN THE DARDANELLES

Turkish warships in the mouth of the Golden Horn. The ship at the left is the *Breslau*, which was transferred to the Turkish Navy after its escape from the British and French Fleets

CHAPTER VII

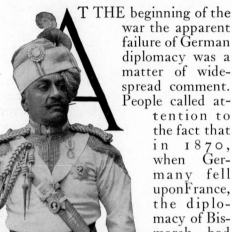

Copyright by Stuart

AT THE beginning of the war the apparent failure of German diplomacy was a matter of wide-spread comment. People called attention to the fact that in 1870, when Germany fell uponFrance, the diplomacy of Bismarck had been such that the war was absolutely isolated and the two belligerents left to deal with each other as their respective military strength permitted. But there was no Bismarck in 1914. When Germany had thought to do battle with Russia, France, Servia, and Belgium at the utmost, having Austria-Hungary for her ally, she found that her foreign office had so concocted affairs that England was at once drawn into the war as her enemy; that Japan, in the far-off Asiatic waters, became her foe; and that Italy which she supposed would surely be her ally, or at least neutral, declared war on Austria-Hungary and to that extent became the foe of Germany, though, curiously enough, Italy did not actually declare war on Germany until the war had lasted more than two years.

However, while this indictment of German diplomacy seemed a conclusive one, there was one point, overlooked by the observing world at the beginning of the war, in which the German diplomats were wholly successful.

This was in Turkey, and the success early won there extended in a great degree to the other Balkan States. The process of winning the Turks to the German side had begun long before the shadow of this war had been cast upon the face of Europe. For decades England had been the dominant power at Constantinople, and the British Ambassador to that capital had been in effect its ruler.

The diplomacy by which British influence at Constantinople was undermined was set on foot by Emperor William himself, who in 1889 visited Constantinople and held an interview with the Sultan Abdul Hamid. Beginning with that acquaintance between the two almost autocratic rulers German influence in the Turkish dominions developed rapidly. German immigrants established colonies in Asia Minor and Syria. German banks were established in Constantinople, and German capitalists, backed by their government, secured railway concessions in the Turkish provinces. Abdul Hamid tottered to a fall and final exile, but the "Young Turk" movement which overthrew him was fomented by German influence and its strategy directed by German diplomats. The ruling families of Turkey were encouraged to send their sons to Berlin to get their military education, while General von der Goltz was sent to Germanize the Turkish army.

In 1898 the Kaiser paid a second visit to Constantinople in the course of his picturesque pilgrimage to Jerusalem. Immediately thereafter Germany secured a concession for the Bagdad railway, extending through Anatolia and Syria down the valleys of the Tigris and the Euphrates to the Persian Gulf. This was a direct challenge to Great Britain, menacing as it did her control of the route to India. Astute German political agents accompanied the surveyors of the railroad line and spread among the people of those countries the most

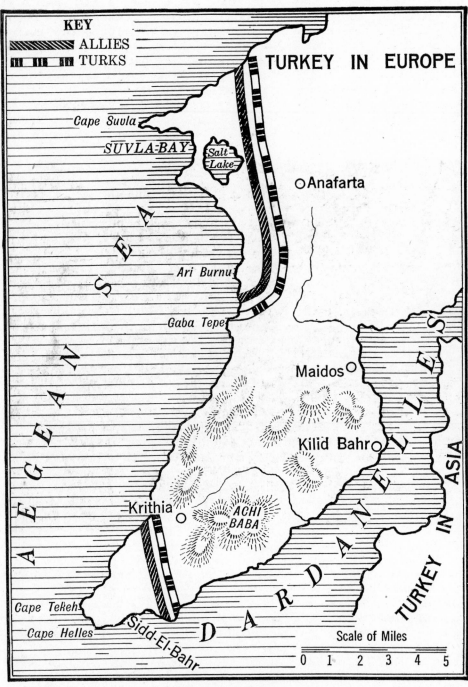

The Gallipoli Peninsula

a holy war on the Christian dogs of Europe. Isolated as they were from any knowledge of the world, the simple tribesmen of the Turkish dominion believed these fables and were ready to follow the leaders of the "Young Turk" party who had long before been won over to the German cause by more material methods.

Accordingly the war had hardly begun when incidents in the inner circles of Turkish diplomacy, and pro-German outbreaks in the Constantinople streets indicated that the sympathies of that nation would be with Germany. The usual proclamation of neutrality was issued by the Sublime Porte and the mobilization of the army was ordered. The Dardanelles were closed to all ships and barred by rows of mines. For nearly two months a succession of petty but none the less significant incidents caused European observers to feel certain that Turkey would ultimately align herself with the Teutonic allies, but with characteristic procrastination the Sublime Porte held off any definite declaration

picturesque and at the same time ridiculous stories of the character of the German people and their ruler. Pictures of William II in full Turkish costume brandishing a scimitar were widely distributed, and the story told that he and the entire German people had become converts to Mohammedanism and would in conjunction with his brother the Sultan wage

Early in August there had been a curious incident which intensified this conviction. Two German ships of war, the *Goeben* and the *Breslau*, the former a powerful modern battle-cruiser, were apparently trapped by a superior British fleet in the harbor of Genoa. To the amazement of the naval world they steamed boldly out of that harbor and without attack from the British made their way around the end of the Italian peninsula and into the

a purchase was in itself a gross breach of neutrality and Great Britain made a determined protest. But the diplomatic correspondence on the subject prolonged by the proverbial procrastination of the Turks dragged on for weeks until it was forgotten in the declaration of war.

That declaration was hastened by the actual commencement of hostilities by the Turks who on October 29, 1914, bombarded

The Sultan leaving his carriage

Dardanelles. It was discovered later that they had in some way obtained possession of the secret code of British naval signals and had tricked the British commander, Admiral Troubridge, by its use. But even so the British fleet pursuing them had every reason to believe that the blunder could be rectified. At the time they took refuge in the Dardanelles Turkey was still at peace with all belligerent nations. Under international law it was her duty to compel the belligerent ships taking sanctuary in her waters to leave them within twenty-four hours, but day followed day without action until on the 13th of August the German cruisers displayed the Turkish flag and announcement was made that they had been purchased by Turkey. Such

Odessa from the sea, and by the Russian fleet which on the same day attacked the Ottoman fleet in the Black Sea. The formal declaration followed on November 5th, England and France simultaneously joining Russia in that action.

The fighting force brought into the field against the Allies by this conclusion was one not to be scorned. The world has looked contemptuously upon the Turk in industry, progress, and his relations to modern thought, but no one of general information ever questioned his fighting ability. At the moment that the European war broke out the Turks were all veterans. They had been fighting steadily in the Balkans for years. They are fatalists in character and heedless of life in

A view of Gaba Tepe

their struggles against even superior forces. At this moment, moreover, they had been subjected as never before to the rigid discipline of a modern army under German leaders. They had always known how to fight, but had not known how to get the greatest advantages out of coöperation and how to care for themselves in camp and field. The Germans, too, had equipped them with the most modern arms and munitions. Accordingly the Turks brought to the Teutonic allies immediately an effective force of more than a million men, with the reserve power which inheres in a nation of 17,000,000 people.

Financially, however, they brought only a heavy burden, for there was nothing in the Turkish treasury, and the expenses of the Turkish campaigns had to be met from the German war chest.

Morally, however, the Turkish aid was perhaps greater than materially. To begin with it instantly put Great Britain on guard in Egypt and the Soudan. These Mohammedan countries had been held by Great Britain under a protectorate. Egypt, ruled nominally by a Sultan, was practically under British domination. How far, however, the puppet Sultan and the people who were tied to Turkey by the bond of a common religion could be trusted in this emergency was a matter of grave import to the British Government. No outbreak, however, occurred, but the British thought it expedient to declare formally a British protectorate of the country. Like action was taken with reference to the Island of Cyprus.

It became apparent immediately upon the declaration of war by Turkey that, at German incentive, the Suez Canal would be the immediate objective of the Turkish armies. Troops were instantly sent into Asia Minor, and the tribesmen of that territory under the suze-

Australian troops taking a swim at Alexandria before their transport leaves for the Dardanelles

Street scene in the village of Gallipoli

ainty of the Sultan were encouraged to put their armies into the field and attack the infidels at every point. The prolonged and savage fighting in Asia Minor, in Persia, and the Sinai Peninsula cannot be described in any detail here. Several times the canal was menaced, but in the end all the efforts for its seizure or destruction proved futile. The British landed heavy bodies of troops drawn largely from India on the Mediterranean and Red Sea coast while the Russians entered Asia Minor from the Black Sea, taking the enemies of the Allies in the rear. The fighting was vigorous but inconclusive. Only once was the canal put in serious jeopardy. The efforts of the Porte to have the tribesmen declare a holy war were futile, and the sanguinary horrors of that sort of conflict were happily averted. The story of the fighting in Syria, Palestine, and the countries bordering on the Mediterranean were curiously reminiscent of the Hebrew scriptures with their continual references to places and provinces mentioned in the Old Testament.

But while this desultory and inconclusive warfare was being waged in Asia Minor the British were preparing for a stroke at the Turkish power, which, had it been

successful, would have ended the menace of the Turco-German alliance, would have destroyed all Turkish influence in either Europe or Asia, and would have appreciably hastened the end of the war. Instead of doing any of these things, however, it failed and failed disastrously.

Constantinople, as is well known, lies just off the sea of Marmora and is reached from the Mediterranean by the narrow strait known as the Dardanelles. During the period of modern European history sovereignty over this strait has been conceded to the Turkish empire.

The British now determined to break the

One of the British transports off Gallipoli

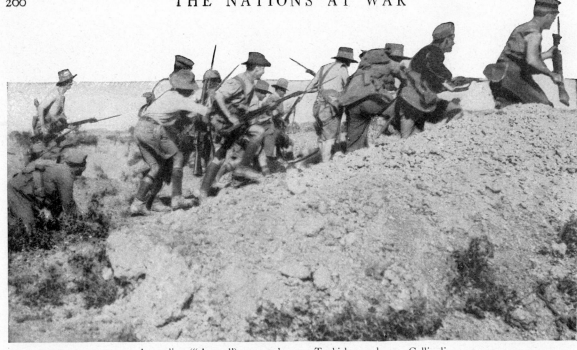

Australian ("Anzac") troops charge a Turkish trench near Gallipoli

Dardanelles barrier. They blundered at the outset by underestimating its strength. The forts along the precipitous sides of the narrow waterway were no longer merely the works of antiquated masonry which for centuries had guarded the strait. Under the direction of skilled German engineers powerful earth works had been erected and equipped with the most modern weapons of precision and power that Krupp's works could produce. They were manned by Turkish soldiers, now drilled into a state of the highest efficiency by German drill masters, while German artillerists directed the fire that was concentrated upon the attacking ships.

The Allies made their initial blunder by proceeding with the utmost deliberation with all their preparations for an attack upon this stronghold. There is every reason to believe that had that attack been delivered in force, both military and naval, in the last months of 1914 it might have succeeded. At that time the effect of German organizing ability had not yet been manifest among the

A small portion of the stores at Lancashire landing, near Sedd-el-Bahr

British troops land at the Dardanelles and gain firm footing

Turkish troops, nor had many of the forts then been equipped with German artillery. But in November of that year the Allies did the worst possible thing by giving evidence of their intention to attack the straits by beginning a desultory bombardment of the forts. To this warning was soon added the news that a great naval expedition was being fitted out by both England and France. Thereupon naturally the Turks spurred on to action by their German leaders began feverish endeavors to put the threatened point in the highest state of defence.

When the Allies actually moved they blun-

dered again. It seems probable that a joint military and naval expedition striking simultaneously so that the enemy's forts would have been engaged both on the landward and the seaward side might have succeeded. Instead of it, the first attack was made wholly by the navy. What was probably the most powerful fleet ever brought

A short rest at Suvla Bay

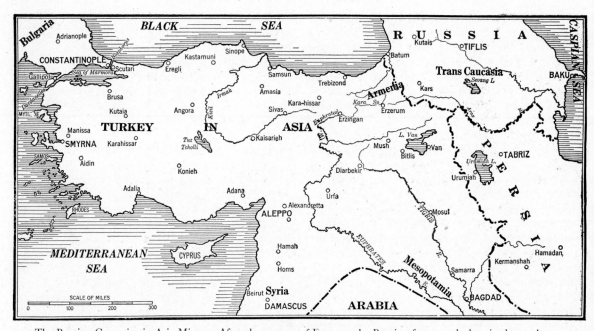

The Russian Campaign in Asia Minor. After the capture of Erzerum the Russian forces pushed on in three columns, one toward Trebizond, the second toward Erzingan and Sivas, where the main Turkish army had its base, and the third column southward to Mush and Bitlis. The capture of Erzerum and the advance into Asia Minor enabled the Russians to capture Kermanshah, in Persia, and to turn westward toward Bagdad, with the aim of coöperating with the British in Mesopatamia

into action composed of more than fifty British and French ships appeared at the entrance to the Dardanelles late in February. The strait itself is about forty-two miles long, very tortuous in its course, and varying in width from one to four miles. The channel was of course blocked at the outset by Turkish mines. The defences at the Ægean entrance were antiquated and quite readily silenced by the assailants. First among the attacking fleet was the famous super-dreadnought *Queen Elizabeth*, carrying eight 15-inch guns in her primary battery with a range far exceeding that of any ordnance mounted in the Turkish batteries, so that she could easily lie at a point thoroughly safe from any fire from the enemy, sheltered by intervening hills, and drop her 15-inch shells into the enemy's works. One of these shells discharged 20,000 shrapnel bullets. Backed by such ships as the *Agamemnon*, *Irresistible*, and the French *Gaulois*, she began the bombardment at a range of from 11,000 to 12,000 yards, and in less than an hour the forts at Kumkale and Sedd-el-Bahr were reduced to such a degree of impotence that the smaller vessels could run in and finish the work. This engagement took place on March 5th, and the success of the British was so complete that they felt confident that the conquest of the

straits from end to end would be effected with equal ease. This hope, however, proved illusory. On March 18th the allied fleet entered the straits with the purpose of pressing through and silencing the forts on either side as they progressed. But they found that forts and batteries they supposed were silenced suddenly sprang into new life and poured upon them a savage and well-directed fire. Trawlers and destroyers had been sent ahead to sweep the strait of mines, but the battle had hardly been in progress two hours when the *Bouvet*, the largest of the French battleships on the scene, struck a mine. Sinking by the stern as she rapidly began to do, she attracted the attention of the Turkish gunners who concentrated upon her a fierce fire. Badly cut to pieces and with the operation of her machinery abruptly stopped, the *Bouvet* sunk while surrounded by torpedo boats and destroyers striving to save her crew. Only a few could be rescued. Shortly thereafter the *Irresistible*, a British pre-dreadnought and the *Ocean* of the same class, also went down, but swift action by destroyers saved most of their personnel. The British had thought the Turkish tiger was sleeping, but it had savagely used its teeth and claws.

The complete failure of the allied fleet in the Dardanelles was a bitter disappointment to its champions, particularly to those in England where it had been believed that the British navy was equal to any task that might be set it. But it may be said that this war has demonstrated that a fleet alone can never be effective against land fortifications. Naval authorities of both allied nations insisted that the passage of the straits was not impossible, but coupled their insistence with the conclusion that such a passage would be valueless unless accompanied by a land force to take possession of the defences which the ships would put out of action.

Accordingly while the allied fleets, anchoring out of danger, continued a desultory bombardment of the forts, a great military expedition was organized in Egypt under the command of Sir Ian Hamilton. Fifty thousand men, both French and British, reached the Gallipoli Peninsula early in April. The Turks were well warned by this time and were feverishly preparing for defence. They were ably seconded in their efforts by the British, who, when they came to unload their transports, found that the various units and their supplies had been so badly mixed on embarking that it was impossible to unload them

with any efficiency. The whole fleet had to return to Egypt, and after rearrangement returned and began its landing on April 25th. By this time the Turks had rushed troops into the Gallipoli Peninsula until they outnumbered the invaders easily four to one. At every point where the typography of the shore lent itself to a successful landing the Turks were strongly intrenched, their earthworks and their batteries masked so that from the ships there seemed no serious obstacle to taking possession of the country. The British troops were wholly without experience in war, the vast majority of them being men who six months before had been leading a peaceful life in Australia and New Zealand, five thousand miles away. Their officers were equally inexperienced. The first landing was made at a point, Gaba Tepe, a bay on the Ægean side of the peninsula away from the Dardanelles. The landing was begun about 3 A. M. while it was still dark, the men being placed in small boats which were towed by the battleships and destroyers as near to the shore as the draught of water would permit. About a half a mile from shore the boats cast off and made their way

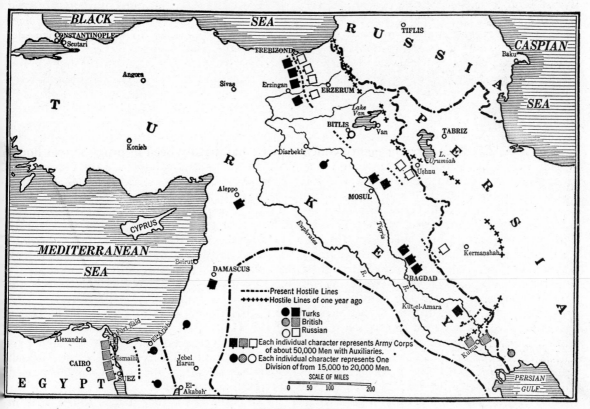

The Turk in Asia

toward the beach. In that darkest hour that precedes the dawn the watchers on the ships could not tell whether their fellows were approaching a deserted coast or whether in that blackness there lurked a powerful force of the enemy ready to greet them with rifle shots and machine guns. Suddenly they saw an alarm light flash on the shore and signal for a moment or two, when there burst out a rapid fire of rifles that told to the men still on the ships that their comrades would have

"From them we learned what had happened in those first wild moments. All the tows had almost reached the beach, when a party of Turks intrenched almost on the shore opened up a terrible fusillade from rifles and also from a Maxim. Fortunately most of the bullets went high, but,

At the Dardanelles

to fight their way to a foothold on the beach. A correspondent of the London *Times* tells in graphic phrase the story of this first effort of the British forces to establish themselves on Turkish territory:

"The first authentic news we received came with the return of our boats. A steam pinnace came alongside with two recumbent forms on her deck and a small figure, pale but cheerful, and waving his hand astern. They were one of our midshipmen, just sixteen years of age, shot through the stomach, but regarding his injury more as a fitting consummation to a glorious holiday ashore than a wound, and a chief stoker and petty officer, all three wounded by that first burst of musketry which caused many casualties in the boats just as they reached the beach.

nevertheless, many men were hit as they sat huddled together forty or fifty in a boat.

"It was a trying moment, but the Australian volunteers rose as a man to the occasion. They waited neither for orders nor for the boats to reach the beach, but, springing out into the sea, they waded ashore and, forming some sort of a rough line, rushed straight on the flashes of the enemy's rifles. Their magazines were not even charged. So they just went in with cold steel, and I believe I am right in saying that the first Ottoman Turk since the last Crusade received an Anglo-Saxon bayonet in him at five minutes after 5 A. M. on April 25th. It was over in a minute. The Turks in this first trench were bayoneted or ran away, and a Maxim gun was captured."

But the Turks did not long continue to

run, nor did they run far. The braggadocio of British journalists in the early days of the campaign on the Gallipoli Peninsula sounds merely laughable when read in the light of the events of that disastrous enterprise. All along the promontory from the Bulair Isthmus to the toe of the boot to which that bit of land is sometimes compared, the landing was pushed, with gallantry it is true, but against savage opposition. The country lent itself readily to defence, for steep bluffs

ground, but on the 26th actually charged the invaders while their snipers tried to pick off the officers and men on the decks of the ships a mile or more away. The British tried some curious expedients to deceive the enemy and to smuggle additional forces ashore unseen. At one point on the peninsula a big herd of donkeys with dummy baggage was put ashore in the hope of attracting the Turkish attention to that spot while a large detachment of troops was being landed

Ambulance wagon passing through the great gully at Helles

rose directly from the beach and the tableland above was so broken with ridges, valleys, bluffs, and sand pits that the enemy's snipers and machine-gun batteries could find cover on every hand. The landing operations were conducted at three points, and from the ships lying two miles or more out a heavy and continuous fire was poured upon the land occupied by the Turks. Every kind of shell was dropped upon their works from the 15-inch shrapnel of the *Queen Elizabeth* down to the little one-pounders which made up in numbers what they lacked in size. But the Turks, fighting with their customary gallantry, not only held their

at another. Again a big merchant liner, filled with troops who were kept under hatches, was allowed to drift, apparently helplessly, toward the beach. She was obviously not a ship of war and was apparently abandoned, so that the Turkish batteries let her run aground without attack. The idea had been that as soon as she was actually beached great doors that had been cut in her sides would be flung open and the men rushed ashore without the need of boats or exposure to fire other than briefly. Unluckily she stranded at a point where there was deep water between her and the beach. This made it necessary to bring up a lighter to ford the men across. Naturally this attracted the attention of the Turks, who instantly directed a perfect tornado of rifle and machine-gun fire on the men as they showed themselves. Disembarkation under these conditions meant certain death, and as it was apparent the Turks had no heavy artillery at that point with which to demolish the ship, any further action on the part of the two thousand men aboard was stopped for the time. So the men aboard lay between decks all day while the clatter of bullets rattled against her sides and the battleships round about kept up a fierce fire on the

fired and the green bird promptly fell to the earth, dropping his rifle. Its hands, face, and rifle were painted green and its clothing was of the same color, but of a darker shade. The bag was as heartily cheered by the men as if it were a Turkish regiment, for that particular sniper had been an undoubted terror. On another part of the field a pretty harem lady sniper was after considerable effort rounded up and brought into the British lines. She cried and struggled, pointing pitifully to another part of the bush from whence she had been brought. At length a detachment of men allowed her to lead the

The wreck of H. M. S. *Loma* which ran aground in a southwest gale. A shell from the enemy battery is seen striking the water close to the wreck. The telescope on the right is that of an observer who is trying to spot the enemy battery which is firing

neighboring coast to prevent the Turks from bringing batteries into action. Under the cover of darkness the troops finally got ashore with but little loss.

Very early in this campaign the invaders came to have a very high respect for the Turkish "sniper." Some of the stories of the devices adopted by these sharpshooters for escaping attention while striking down their enemies are most picturesque. A writer in the *Fortnightly Review* tells these two:

"A captain of a London territorial regiment happened to look back after his men had passed a solitary tree on the field when he noticed something moving on it. It looked like a green bird. He took aim and

way to the spot indicated, and here they found her child in a dugout tastefully furnished. In a corner was a pile of identification disks probably taken systematically from the necks of dead soldiers, and an almost endless supply of ammunition. Carefully hidden away was her yashmak (veil) which the men allowed her to take away."

While the British were landing on the European side of the Dardanelles the French under General D'Amade also landed on the Asiatic side and established themselves firmly. Their first attack was on the fort at Kum Kale which they took. But thereafter for months, though there was continued fighting, and both the British and French troops were repeatedly reënforced, the effort to push up the peninsula and the mainland toward the narrows was but a distressing record of continued reverses. In fact, it was but a few weeks after the landing was complete before the military authorities of the allied governments began to understand that the problem likely to be forced upon them was not how they should get to Constantinople, but rather how they should get their men off the peninsula and to safety. There was no lack of gallantry on the part of the invading forces, but they were enormously outnumbered. Though they were supplied

peoples. It might not come, but even so it was of vital importance that no admission of a great disaster should be made public at that critical moment.

In August, 1915, following a visit to Egypt of Lord Kitchener a new expedition of 50,000 men to join in the Gallipoli attack was embarked at a port on the Island of Lemnos and moved to Suvla Bay near the head of the Gallipoli Peninsula. This time there had been no blundering in the embarkation while the attention of the Turks had been successfully diverted from the landing point by feints made by other forces in other direc-

Greatest care was taken with the drinking water of the allied troops at the Dardanelles. It was filtered and immediately placed in cans

with every possible engine of war, the stubbornness of the resistance they encountered was such that their expedition was actually abandoned before they reached the first line of the Turkish defence of Constantinople.

The spring and summer of 1915 was a period full of discouragement to the Allies. Everywhere they were fighting defensive battles, nowhere could they point to a more inspiriting success than merely holding the enemy in check. Great Britain had not yet successfully grappled with the conscription issue, and the troops which had been raised by voluntary enlistment had not yet become really effective. Some great success was most desirable to stimulate the enthusiasm and reawaken the confidence of the allied

tions. Accordingly they were put ashore without serious opposition at a point called Ari Burnu, but which the soldiers promptly named Anzac Bay, that name being derived from the initials of the words by which the troops engaged in the expedition were known —"Australia and New Zealand Army Corps." With this foothold it was hoped that the Turkish main force on the peninsula might be attacked simultaneously front and rear and thus overwhelmed. Admirable as the plan seemed it was destined to failure. There followed twelve days of uninterrupted fighting in which the losses were heavier than at any other period of the Dardanelles campaign. And yet nothing came of this at all except the definite check of the British,

With the failure of this effort to destroy the Turkish defences, which became apparent by the middle of October, any further serious attempt on the part of the British to carry out their original plan of campaign against Constantinople was abandoned. The presence of defeat was too obvious. The offensive was dropped and all military minds in the general staff of the Allies were concentrated on the problem how to get the army, which by this time numbered 200,000 men or more, out of the peninsula. Here for the

the first week of January, 1916, all had left the peninsula. The French, who had held the Asiatic mainland, were withdrawn at about the same moment.

No single operation of the great war resulted so disastrously to the Allies as the Dardanelles expedition. It had been mismanaged from the first, and the ultimate failure was made all the more bitter to Eng-

British batteries at work at the Dardanelles

first time the Turks, notwithstanding their German leadership, showed inefficiency. They had been magnificent in defence. While it was true that they had the advantage of overwhelming numbers, they defended their country successfully against a powerful attacking force on land and a naval force of absolutely unprecedented strength. But now they let slip the game that was fairly within their grasp. For some reason they could not be led into any effective attack upon the British forces which were really at their mercy. Instead they kept up a merely desultory assault upon the British outposts, while with most admirable skill Sir Ian Hamilton gradually withdrew his forces until by

land because the record showed so many points at which military miscalculations or mere stupidity explained that failure. The price paid was a loss reported officially up to December 11, 1915, of 112,921 men. Moreover, there were up to that time 96,683 men admitted to the Allies' hospitals. Six battleships, one of them French, were lost in the course of the naval operations. The number of men invalided to the hospitals was abnormal in the course of this war, during which the most scientific systems of sanitation had kept the mere cases of sickness down to a minimum never before maintained in large military operations. But the conditions of fighting were such as to break down the constitutions of the men. The water supply was utterly inadequate. All water had to be brought by ship, landed in water bags, and carried on mule back to the various camps. General Hamilton reported that in the battle of August 10th he dared not order his reserves into action because of their sufferings from thirst.

"At Anzac," he said, "when the mules

fortune in attack. There has seldom been so extraordinary an achievement as the withdrawal of the British force from Suvla and Anzac with practically no loss whatsoever. General Hamilton in advance estimated his probable casualties at 50 per cent.; they were in fact three killed and five wounded out of more than 70,000 men withdrawn. The withdrawal was effected in two nights

View of the landing camp pitched by the Allies at the Dardanelles

with water bags arrived at the front, the men would rush up to them in swarms just to lick the moisture that exuded through the canvas bags." At other points lighters carrying the water from the ships to the shore grounded some distance out and the men had to swim to them to fill their water bottles.

Notwithstanding all these difficulties General Hamilton was bitterly aggrieved by the order to retire. He felt that arduous as was the task its performance was still not hopeless and with reënforcements and pertinacity he might still carry the day. But his orders were imperative, and his good fortune in retreat made up to some degree for his mis-

and conducted so quietly and with such astute measures for the deception of the Turks that the latter were lulled to security and hardly awakened to the fact that their enemy was stealing away before the entire British expedition was again on its ships.

So ended the Dardanelles expedition. It accomplished nothing for its projectors, but its failure had no material effect on the progress of the war. It is true that some 300,000 Turks were set free to join in the attack on the Suez Canal. How little they accomplished in that direction was soon to be shown.

While the British and French were pushing their Dardanelles expedition with a gallantry worthy of a better outcome the Russians were advancing into Asia Minor from the east and the British from the west, while the Turkish forces between them were putting up a magnificent fight on both fronts with a degree of success that even at the end of the second year of the war left the question of domination in Asia Minor still undetermined. The Russians and the Turks were on the offensive, the British strictly on the defensive, for their one task was to defend the Suez Canal. What the Russians sought first was the capture of the town of Erzerum, a town in Armenia just southeast of the Russian border.

and though railroads were unavailable and the country most difficult to cover, penetrated far into the interior. The Russian Grand Duke Nicholas who had suddenly and mysteriously disappeared from around Galicia, where he had been in command of the Russian armies during their first advance into that country, appeared in the Caucasus in the middle of February, 1915. His appearance there was an amazement to the military world as well as to the defenders of that town, for the campaign had been undertaken in the dead of winter, the converging columns of Russians advancing through a tangle of

Troops landing at the Dardanelles

sian border. This ancient fortress on the Turkish road to India, and on the Russian road through Asia Minor to Constantinople, has long been a strategic point for which the Russians and Turks have struggled. Since the beginning of the last century this warfare has taken the shape of endless riot, massacre, and border warfare between the Christian Armenians and the Kurds who yield allegiance to the Crescent. The Christian world has long sorrowed for the sufferings of the Armenians, but has been able to accomplish nothing for the amelioration of their lot because of the international politics involved in that situation. Perhaps one good that may come of this great war will be the end of this continuing crime which has shocked humanity for half a century.

Scarcely had war between Russia and Turkey been declared when the Russian army crossed the border, overran northern Persia,

mountain passes on wretched dirt roads and without a single railroad. The Black Sea was of course open to the Russians, but the only port connected with Erzerum by a tolerable road was Trebizond which was in the hands of the Turks. With Erzerum taken the next important step in the Russian campaign was the capture of this point on the Black Sea. Accordingly in the summer of 1915 about a third of the Grand Duke's army at Erzerum was dispatched to take Trebizond, while the remainder turned to the southward pursuing the Turks and fighting for control of the roads leading up to the Bagdad railway. It was on the 16th of February that the chief Armenian city had been taken; March 2d they took the fortified city of Bitlis; and on the 18th of April, with the Black Sea fleet coöperating with them, the Russian land forces actually entered Trebizond. This rapid advance, though it affected a comparatively small section of Persia, was of incalculable value to the British for it diverted the attention of the Turks from their attack upon Suez. Notwithstanding the difficult nature of the country in the Sinai Peninsula, where water for the use of the troops had to be hauled, where a railroad had to be built, and where the historic camel held his ground against the modern automobile as a means of transport, the dashing and pertinacious Turks had been able more than once to get across from Palestine to Suez with small bodies of troops. In February, 1915, just as the Grand

months their successes were uninterrupted. By July of 1915 the expedition then under command of General Sir John Nixon was within striking distance of Bagdad. But thereupon misfortune fell heavily upon them. The British had evidently erred as they did at Antwerp, and again at the Dardanelles. They had sent a boy to do a man's job. Attacked at Ctesiphon by an overwhelming Turkish force the expedition was badly beaten and under command of Sir John Townshend forced to retreat some sixty miles to a point called Kut-el-Amara. Here for five months it was held so closely invested

Turk troops at Gallipoli which have held the Allies at bay

Duke was beginning his campaign, a body of Nizams did actually succeed in getting across the desert carrying bridging material and getting a foothold on the south bank of the Canal only to be driven back.

Most important of the British expeditions in Asia Minor was that into Mesopotamia, begun early in the war. The Euphrates and Tigris rivers, uniting in the Shatt-el-Arab, flow through important oil fields belonging to an English company. The war had hardly begun before the importance of oil as a munition of war became apparent, and the British, having taken the port of Basra some distance up the river, undertook an expedition partly for the protection of these oil fields and partly to begin an advance upon Bagdad which was destined to be the terminus of the German railroad south from Constantinople. They were opposed by the Turks from the very first, but for eight

that it could be reached only by aeroplanes. Early in January, 1916, a strong relief column was sent out to its aid. But its path was blocked by superior forces. In the end the beleaguered British were forced by starvation and the exhaustion of all supplies to surrender on April 29, 1916.

The war in the irregular quadrangle, bounded by the Black Sea, the Caspian Sea, the Persian Gulf, the Red Sea, and the Mediterranean, was fought by the troops of four great nations and almost uncounted irregular forces representing various Ottoman tribes. The Shah of Persia early declared himself with the Allies, while the Mohammedans of Egypt and the tribes of India proved to be, if not at heart altogether loyal to Great Britain, at least sufficiently so to give no serious cause for anxiety. Had it been otherwise the situation of the British, particularly in that section, would have been desperate. As it was, with the exception of a single serious defeat at Kut-el-Amara, they suffered no serious reverse, and although mainly on the defensive, saw the second year of the war end with both the Suez Canal and their East Indian possessions apparently free from any further menace. For the Turks the situation was more serious. It appeared that they were to pay dearly for their alliance with the Teutons. The Persians whom they looked upon as allies, and the Arabs whom they regarded as their vas-

sals, threw off their Turkish yoke and sided openly with the Allies. The Syrians, too, revolted against Turkish despotism, and through it all, while the British were content with stubbornly guarding their own, the great Russian armies drove through the Turkish territory, forcing its defenders from one fortified town to another, capturing whole armies with their guns and munitions, and apparently assured of success in their purpose of reducing Turkey in Asia to complete subjection.

Copyright by Newspaper Illustration, Ltd

Heliograph signallers with the Turkish Army

CHRONOLOGY OF PERIOD TREATED IN CHAPTER VII

October 29. Turkey begins war with Russia by bombarding Odessa.

November 5. England and France declare war on Turkey; Russians begin invasion of Armenia.

November 15. British troops land in Basra province and invade Arabia.

November 22. Turks in small numbers reach Suez Canal.

December 23. Turkish army leaves Damascus and marches toward the Suez Canal.

January 9. Turks build railway across Sinai Peninsula to attack Suez.

January 27. The British defeat the Turks near El Kantara.

February 3. Turks, while trying to cross the Canal, are routed with heavy loss, many drowned in the Canal.

February 28. Turks withdraw from the Sinai Peninsula and abandon the attack on the Canal.

March 26. Turks massacring native Christians in various parts of Persia and Armenia. United States Ambassador Morgenthau at Constantinople called upon for aid.

February 25. British and French fleets reduce forts at the entrance to the Dardanelles.

February 27. Forty British and French warships penetrate the Dardanelles for fourteen miles.

March 18. End of British successes in the Dardanelles. British battleships *Irresistible* and *Ocean*, and French battleship *Bouvet*, are sunk.

April 30. British land expedition against the Gallipoli Peninsula begun.

July 7. Heavy fighting between the Allies and Turks on the Gallipoli Peninsula. British public begins to doubt the wisdom or the possible success of the expedition.

July 24. British report successes in southern Arabia.

August 2. Australians and New Zealanders take important points in the Dardanelles.

August 25. Allies advancing along a twelve-mile front on the Gallipoli Peninsula.

August 31. Germans claim the British have lost 50,000 men in the Dardanelles since August 6th.

September 16. Official British figures show British casualties at the Dardanelles up to August 21st to reach 87,600

September. 23. French and British reënforcements to the number of 110,000 sent to the Dardanelles.

October 15. British report 96,899 men lost at the Dardanelles

October 19. Major-General Monro succeeds General Sir Ian Hamilton as British commander in Gallipoli.

November 24. British fall back when within 18 miles of Bagdad with loss of 2,000 men. Turks aggressive thereafter.

December 3. British Mesopotamian expedition retires to Kut-el-Amara and is besieged there.

January 9. Allies abandon the Gallipoli Peninsula.

January 16. British relief expedition on the Tigris drives Turks to within six miles of Kut-el-Amara.

February 2. Floods check British relief expedition.

April 29. British surrender ten thousand men and equipment at Kut-el-Amara.

RUSSIAN CAVALRY RETREATING AFTER DEFEAT BY GERMANS

Russian troops passing through Stryj (Galicia) after the capture of Przemyśl

CHAPTER VIII

WARSAW AND AFTER—FAILURE TO DESTROY RUSSIAN ARMY—
THE PROLONGED RUSSIAN RETREAT—THE BEAR TURNS TO BAY
—TRANSFER OF GRAND-DUKE NICHOLAS—GENERALS KUROPATKIN AND
BRUSSILOV LEAD THE NEW DRIVE—RECORD OF RUSSIAN SUCCESSES

Viceroy's body guard

THE fall of Warsaw seemed to mark the culmination of the German successes in the campaign against Russia. It was heralded widely throughout the world as a decisive victory, as indeed it was with one limitation. That is to say, the Germans had been successful in capturing the city which had been their goal during months of hard fighting. They secured possession of the political and industrial capital of Russian Poland. They were able to announce to the world a success which coming after so long a struggle could not fail to impress public opinion with a new respect for the German arms, and to enhance the morale of the German army, which, indeed, at no time during this savage war, has manifested any need for improvement.

But, on the other hand, it was very quickly demonstrated by events following the capture of Warsaw that it was in fact but half a victory. It cannot be too strongly emphasized in any account of this war that the struggle at the end of two years has reached only an inconclusive point, because while cities and fortresses have been taken and lost, while provinces have been reduced to the temporary occupancy of an enemy and again triumphantly rescued by their defenders, there has not been one instance, save perhaps that of Servia, in which any considerable army of any belligerent has been destroyed. Even the Belgian army, weak as it was in the face of the German aggressor, still existed as an effective fighting unit two years after the first fort fell at Liége, and in August, 1916, a fragment of the Servian army was in the field. Von Kluck's advance upon Paris was indeed checked before that city became his prize. But even had he succeeded in his object, French strategy had already made ample preparations for the escape of the French army, and with that army in being the defence of the nation would have continued even though the German flag floated over the French capital. In our own Civil War while Richmond was the prize for which Grant's army strove for more than two years, its capture would not have ended the war. Had not Lee clung to Richmond until his army was cut to pieces exhausted, and on the verge of starvation, that war might well have been prolonged another year. It was the destruction of the armies of the Confederacy, not the capture of its capital, that brought peace.

So in occupying Warsaw, without destroying the Russian army which had defended it, General von Hindenburg failed of complete success. Though the Russians were in fact beaten, they nevertheless were withdrawn from the lost capital by the Grand Duke Nicholas with consummate military skill and without serious shock to their morale.

In the midst of their exultation over the capture of Warsaw the Germans did not lose sight of the fact that with the Russian army still in existence their victory was incomplete. Von Hindenburg pressed on rapidly in pursuit of the retreating Russians. It was his hope and the hope then of the German people that if this army could be overtaken and annihilated Russia would be willing to negotiate a separate peace and leave the French and English to their fate. It has been demonstrated later that this was but a futile aspiration. Even had the armies of the Grand Duke Alexieff been annihilated the spirit of the Russian Government contemplated no such retreat from the conflict, and the patient ox-like Russian peasant had

city and slipped out of his clutches. The Germans followed swiftly and pertinaciously. In some quarters it was believed that this retirement of the Russians in the direction of Petrograd was in fact a ruse intended to lure their enemies farther into Russian territory where the great distances and the abominable roads would make their movements difficult, while fresh Russian troops

Copyright by Underwood & Underwood

German Zeppelin inspecting Warsaw

no thought in his mind of refusing to obey the orders of his superiors though they carried him to the field of carnage. But as a matter of fact the Russian army was in no real danger of destruction. Alexieff had prepared many positions back of Warsaw to which now his army retreated and checked for a time the Teutons in their advance. One by one these positions were taken by the invaders. At Vilna, well within Russian territory, Von Hindenburg failed only narrowly of bagging a large force that had taken refuge in that fortress. He had surrounded it all save for a narrow gap of a few miles only, when the Russians wisely abandoned the

with their store of munitions renewed would be able to cut them off from communication with their base.

The German press and sympathizers on the other hand were exultant over the Russian retreat and noisily claimed that within a few weeks the German armies would be in Petrograd. But, as in so many instances in this war, the triumphant pursuing army seemed to suffer more than the one in retreat. Kovno and Grodno, important Russian fortified points, were indeed taken by the invaders, while Von Mackensen, commanding the southern end of the German lines, took Brest-Litowsk, the greatest intrenched camp in all Russia. Here he hoped to secure great quantities of munitions, but in this he was disappointed, for by this time the Russian armies had not enough munitions for use, and certainly none for storage. Moreover, like his colleague, Von Hindenburg to the north, he had failed to catch the defending army which slipped away and continued its rear-guard fighting until by the end of shells, and munitions of war from the busy factories of Japan. The Russian forces had suffered from a dearth of skilled artillerists, but during this slow retreat men had been trained to the use of the great guns, and more and more the artillery came to be an efficient aid to the hundreds of thousands of untrained common soldiers whom the great empire of the north had been able to put into

Prince Leopold of Bavaria, the conqueror of Warsaw, riding at the head of his staff along one of the principal streets of the ancient Polish capital

October the Germans had penetrated that part of Russia almost to the Pripet River. The long German line then stretched from the Baltic Sea to the Carpathian Mountains. All of Russian Poland lay behind it and bending out to the westward it included in its bow thousands of square miles of the territory of Russia proper. But here it stuck. Further advance appeared impossible. The great bear that had been walking backward had turned with teeth and claw to bay. The trains of the Trans-Siberian Railroad had been rolling westward from the Pacific bringing new supplies of cannon, the field. When winter fell Russia began again preparations to take the offensive.

At this time the Grand Duke Nicholas was recalled from command probably for political reasons and the Czar in person took his place as nominal commander of the Russian armies in Poland and Galicia. Actually Generals Brussilov and Kuropatkin directed the movements of the Russian armies in the south and north respectively. Nicholas meantime in Asia Minor, by his swift descent upon Erzeroum and Trebizond, gave convincing proof that it was for no lack of soldierly qualities or skilled generalship that

Russian troops retreating from Przemysl at the approach of the Austro-German forces

he had been transferred. His activity in that region indeed kept the Germans so busy that they had no time to push an offensive campaign in Russia. The winter was not, however, wholly inactive. In the west the armies settled down in the trenches merely keeping watch of each other without material effort to gain ground. But in the east the hostile forces swept backward and forward passing over the same ground time and again so that in the reports of their operations we find the same town held by both belliger-

ents two or three times in the course of a month. It was a melancholy and agonizing experience for the people residing in the theatre of war. Early in the struggle the Jews whom for one reason or another the Russians suspected of disloyalty were expelled altogether from that section. More than a million five hundred thousand were thus driven from their homes without resources to seek a living elsewhere. But the barbarism of the war did not fall upon these hapless Hebrews alone, for when the Ger-

Austrians burying Russian dead in Galicia. Note the rough wooden cross ready for erection

mans began to march into Russian territory the retreating Russians adopted the method which caused the downfall of Napoleon a century before. The country was thoroughly devastated, railroads were torn up, factories and stores destroyed, such crops as were standing were thrown down and made unavailable as much to the people of the country as to the invader. Three million features of this war has been the enormous use of motor cars for military purposes. But in Russia the automobile had never been the popular plaything or the useful adjunct to industry which it had been in western Europe. During the very first campaign the skilled men in the Russian army of the quality necessary for operating automobiles efficiently were put out of action. British, French,

A hasty meal by the wayside in Russia. Soldiers receiving food from a camp kitchen of the portable type. The Russian commissary is much less complicated than that of the Germans because the Russian is content with simple food

civilians fled to the interior of Russia with no idea as to what they might do there, but hoping for some chance of saving their lives. The country thus laid waste comprised a strip nearly three hundred miles wide and eight hundred miles long—an empire equal practically in extent to that comprised between Boston and Detroit with Albany and Buffalo on the north and Pittsburg and Philadelphia on the south as boundary points. During the winter the main task of the Russian armies was to refit and to prepare for a great advance in the spring. Their transportation system had broken down badly. One of the most striking Belgian, and even Japanese military automobilists and aviators were sent to take charge of the armored motors and aeroplanes. By way of recompense for this Russia sent six army corps of her surplus troops to France who entered that country by way of Marseilles, creating a tremendous sensation in military circles. Even with this addition to its expert services Russia was still handicapped by lack of aircraft and observers. For this reason the early spring months were devoted to feeling out the enemy's lines in preparation for the great offensive to come later. But these smaller battles, making up indeed a very considerable record of their

German artillery advancing on Warsaw

own for the numbers engaged and the numbers sacrificed, had no effect on the progress of the war. Indeed the Russians themselves at that time, though planning for a spring offensive, apprehended that the Germans might take the lead with a drive on Petrograd. As it turned out the Germans had tried to crack so hard a nut at Verdun that they had no mind nor men wherewith to undertake an offensive elsewhere.

June 1, 1916, the great Russian army of not less than 1,500,000 men stepped forward unitedly in an attack upon the German line. That line extended from the front of Riga on the Baltic Sea almost directly south to Czernowitz in Austria-Hungary. The fighting was heaviest on the southern half of the line on which lay the cities which more than once had been the object of savage fighting, Pinsk, Dubno, and Tarnopol. Here the forces opposed to the Russians were mainly Austrians, only two out of ten army corps being German. The success of the Russians was immediate and continuous. The Austrian lines were rolled back day after day and prisoners by the thousands were taken. Checked for a time on the River Stokhod, they shifted the attack to the south and captured the considerable Hungarian city of Czernowitz. The fortresses at Dubno and Lutsk

German transports in the campaign against Warsaw

Photo by Paul Thompson

German troops under General von Hindenburg on the march toward Warsaw

which had been lost in the preceding summer were retaken, and by the latter part of June it appeared that the entire Austrian line was to be swept away in one vast indiscriminate rout. The number of prisoners taken before the end of June exceeded 200,000. Guns, ammunition, and supplies of every sort were a rich prize to the Russians who without manufactures of their own found every captured cannon precious booty. Before the 1st of July the crests of the Carpathians saw again the standards of Russian regiments of which they had been cleared a year before.

A correspondent of the London *Times* accompanied General Brussilov's columns on their successful drive into the province of Bukovina. He declared the Russian spirit and dash to be almost incredible. At various points they were fighting against odds sometimes of three to one. By direction of their officers they were sparing of their munitions. The new Russian rifle was equipped with a thirty-inch bayonet fixed to the muzzle of the weapon and never taken off. With this in the main they charged their enemy and drove him from his trenches. Many military authorities have given expression to their appreciation of the extraordinary gallantry of the Russian infantry. They had to go against

Russians captured at Prasznysz

which always preceded such an attack in the western theatre of war. None the less the Russian peasant, dull and uncomprehending as he is supposed to be, responded even cheerfully to the appeals of his officers and with almost Oriental fatalism rushed into the face of apparent certain death until victory was assured. That Russia exceeded any of the other belligerents, perhaps any two combined, in the number of men capable of bearing arms was known at the beginning of the

Copyright by Underwood & Underwood

Russian Black Sea troops going into action

trenches and barbed-wire entanglements without the aid of the heavy artillery preparation war. But that in so brief a space of time these farmers and peasants could be drilled

Copyright by Underwood & Underwood

How the Russians retreated in haste before the great German advance and disciplined until they formed a coherent fighting force with the quality of veterans amazed the military world.

"The only thing," said a German officer once speaking of the Russian soldiers in attack, "you can do is to slaughter them and pray that you will have ammunition enough to keep it up." Wartime observers speaking of the Russian soldier seem always to treat of him in the mass. They lay stress on the individual resourcefulness and dogged pertinacity of the English "Tommy." The French "poilu" they find gay, gallant, dashing in bravery though with a lack of pertinacity. The Italian manifests great ferocity but is easily discouraged. The German will go anywhere his officers will lead him— but he must be led. Discipline has driven individual initiative out of the German head.

The King, Queen, and Crown Prince of Roumania. Roumania's entrance into the war on the side of the Allies and her spectacular invasion of Transylvania in September, 1916, were the outcome of two years' negotiations

The importance of Vilna. This bridge over the River Vilna is the only bridge in a radius of 100 miles that is strong enough to bear the heavy artillery which is so strong an element of German military power

But when the first-hand observers come to speak of the Russians, they tell of their bovine patience and fatalism but lay chief stress upon their infinitude of numbers— their slow-moving, terrifying, irresistible mass. The French leap to the charge like an avalanche. The Russians advance like a resistless glacier. You think of them in

indomitable will—a real man of blood and iron this, best worthy of that title in Prussia since Bismarck. Nor could there be any thought of sending German regiments from France to the hard-pressed Austrians. There Verdun was holding the Teutonic foe in play with a vengeance. Of little strategic value in itself, this French fortress had enlisted

Copyright by Underwood & Underwood

A field of bayonets on the Polish frontier

lines ten or twelve deep, line after line, and all with the fearlessness that fatalism alone breeds.

All the way from Riga to the Roumanian line this remorseless pressure was being applied to the Teutonic lines. It was most savage in the south where the troops of General Brussilov were in contact with the Austrians. There could at this time be no reënforcement of the troops of Francis Joseph from the German lines, for in the north Kuropatkin was pressing hotly on grizzled old Von Hindenburg, who stood savagely at bay while the population of Berlin was childishly driving nails into his wooden effigy in token of admiration for his

the bloody efforts of France and Germany in a struggle which had already endured for months, and in fact outlasted the second year of the war. Its reduction and its defence had become a matter of pride, a fetish, a religious obsession almost to the two warring foes. "If we take Verdun we win the war," said the Germans, though no military strategist has been able to point out the reason for such a belief. "They shall not pass!" was the French cry when the assault on Verdun was mentioned, and the French made their contention good. Moreover, they held so many of the Teutons in the salient of St. Mihiel and the hills about Verdun that the endangered Austrians cried in vain for aid from that section. It was becoming apparent to the onlooking world that at last the Allied campaign was being urged offensively along all the fronts at once as though directed by a single master mind.

It was, indeed, in the very course of perfecting that coherence of action among the Allies that Great Britain lost her greatest

of Lord Kitchener's death nothing is known nor was his body ever recovered.

More than any man in England at the outset of the war, Kitchener foresaw its proportions and duration. Three years he thought would be its least duration, and, being entrusted with building up the British army, he built it with a view to a long-drawn

Serbian infantrymen arrive in Warsaw in time to check the German attack

military figure of modern times, Field Marshal Lord Horatio Herbert Kitchener, British Secretary for War, "K of K." as the man in the street loved to call him in abbreviation of his earlier title Lord Kitchener of Khartoum. It was illustrative of the far-spread nature of this war that this soldier whose fame had been won in South Africa should meet death in the icy seas off the Orkneys while en route for Petrograd to consult about Russian operations in Poland and Galicia. His ship, the British cruiser *Hampshire*, struck a mine June 5th, and went down with all on board except a warrant officer and eleven seamen, who were picked up later on a raft nearly dead from exposure. Of the precise manner

struggle. The impatient public, and a part of the press, attacked him vehemently for deliberation, for stubbornly refusing to rush half-trained troops to the front, for putting solid organization and adequate equipment ahead of action in the field. But he beat down opposition and attack and before his death saw his policy on the threshold of success and already commanding universal approval. It was, doubtless, a tribute to his influence, not only in Britain but in all the allied countries, that the plan of joint and simultaneous offensive by all the powers which he had started for Petrograd to urge, was followed vigorously after his death.

In the two months of the Russian drive

Resting among the dead. Austro-Hungarian soldiers detailed to clear the field after a battle sit down on a hillside for a brief rest, while the dead Russians lie all around them

ume and steady continuation of his artillery fire told convincingly of the Russian recognition of their blunder of the year before when they tried to carry this same territory with an insufficient supply of ammunition. But he followed his artillery attack not only with infantry assaults, but with cavalry raids that turned his enemy's flanks, menaced his communications, and left to his shattered legions no time for rest or for repairs. The extended field wherein Brussilov commanded was as full of change as a kaleidoscope. It was the very antithesis of the area of battle in France and in Flanders.

The Austrian provinces which felt most heavily the force of the Russian rally and advance are known as Galicia and Bukovina. Virtually they are a single geographical region cut off from the rest of Austria and Hungary by the high walls of the Carpathian Mountains. Their population contains many Slavs, Czechs, Poles, and Cervaks, and it was a significant fact that among the prisoners taken by the Russians were very few of these nationalities. The reason

that preceded the second anniversary of the outbreak of the war, the forces of the Czar carried all before them along that section of the line which was selected for an advance. General Brussilov had been a cavalry leader in the earlier days of service, and in pushing back the Teutons in this campaign brought that arm of the service into active play, almost for the first time in this war which had been fought mainly by artillery and infantry. His movements were swift and unexpected. He employed to the fullest the now established tactics of first overwhelming his enemy's trenches with floods of shell and shrapnel. The vol-

Hundreds of Russians in one grave. A corner of a great trench dug on a battlefield in Galicia, wherein large numbers of Russians were buried together

for their absence seems to have been that because of their manifest sympathy for their brother Slavs in the Russian armies, they were sent away from that battle front as untrustworthy. The troops of which they formed a great part were employed on the Italian front, because between them and the Italians was no racial sympathy.

Czernowitz, the capital of Bukovina, fell into Russian occupation June 16, 1916. Though a considerable city it is singularly isolated from the world beyond the Car-

ress in that section of Hungary was unchecked. The River Pruth was crossed with the Austrians flying in dismay. Kolomea, a notable railroad centre, was taken. Kuropatkin in the north was pushing back Von Hindenburg as successfully as Brussilov in the south. Yet it was the successes of the latter that rendered possible the advance of the former, for the whole Teutonic line, extending from north to south, rested like a balanced pole upon the Austrian armies in Galicia. As fast as Brussilov pushed

Field gun overturned by a shell. Russian artillerymen endeavoring to right a gun capsized by a terrific explosion

pathians, being reached by a single railroad only. This railroad the Russians cut early in the siege, not only isolating the city, but cutting off the only practical line of retreat for its defenders. They might indeed flee through the steep and narrow Carpathian passes pursued by Cossacks, but in the end they determined to surrender and join the rapidly growing colony of captive Austrians within the Russian lines. It is interesting, by the way, to note that, including this garrison of Czernowitz, the forces under General Brussilov took during their nine weeks' campaign in Galicia and Bukovina 358,000 officers and men, 405 cannon, 1,326 machine guns, and a vast amount of other material of war.

After the fall of Czernowitz Russian prog-

back the latter, or weakened them by his constant attacks, the pole would necessarily be drawn to the westward lest it fall altogether. When the second year of the war ended the Russians were once more within striking distance of Lemberg, an Austrian city of enormous strategical value, from which they had been driven a year before.

Austria was now in a dire state. The territory she had lost was not material to the progress of the war, but her losses in men and material threatened her with complete collapse. Her own reserves were exhausted. Her military authorities in June vainly appealed to the government for authority to call into active service men of the class between fifty-six and sixty years of age. She could hope nothing more from Germany, for

Result of bombs dropped in Warsaw by German aviators

by this time the great Allied offen sive on the western front had begun and the Germans were even check ing their attack on Verdun to mee this new menace. In the south Austria had to meet the steady pres sure of the Italians, who, long held in check by the precipitous barrie of the Dolomites, had by this time learned to negotiate those mountair passes and were threatening Gor izia, the gate to Trieste. Moreover late in July it became apparent that the Allies were not going to leave Servia to her fate. The shattered army of that nation, having been reorganized on the Island of Corfu its wounds bound up, its depleted ranks filled, its equipment renewed had been transferred to Salonika There, too, were gathering British French, and Italian troops so that by the 1st of August, the beginning of the third year of the war, not less than 600,000 Allied troops were ready to begin the great drive through Servia to the Hungariar frontier.

Never in the course of the war had the outlook been so black for the Dual Monarchy and for the Teutonic alliance as then. There were constant rumors that Hun gary would split away from Austria

Ten thousand Russian prisoners in one column captured in one of the battles in Galicia

dismember the Dual Monarchy, and
sue for a separate and independent
peace. Again it was suggested that
both Austria and Hungary might
sue for peace leaving Germany to
continue the conflict. Both rumors
were scouted at both Vienna and
Berlin, and the year ended without
either being given substance. But
the situation was unquestionably
one of the gravest import to the
Central Powers. With all her wonderful sacrifices of treasure and of
men Imperial Germany could not
always go on upholding weak and
inefficient allies. But for military
commanders, and tens of thousands
of men sent into Galicia, Austria
would have been crippled by the
first Russian drive, and obliterated
by the second. But even the amazing resourcefulness and self-sacrifice
of the German nation did not seem
able to keep this record up long.

The persistency with which the
Russians returned to the attack after
two great and far reaching defeats
caused the admiration of all the
military world. Not the officers
alone, but the troops in the ranks
manifested this constant aversion to
any admission of defeat. On the
retreat from Warsaw the correspondent of the London *Times*

Copyright by Underwood & Underwood

Famous church of Roketno, near Warsaw, destroyed by artillery fighting
between Russians and Germans

Russian prisoners at Döberitz, near Berlin

GENERAL ALEXEI A. BRUSSILOV

Commander of the Russian drive against the Austrians in southern Russia, Bukovina, and Galicia which heralded the concerted offensive of the Allies on the eastern, western and southern fronts in the summer of 1916

thought to test the fighting spirit of all of the retreating Russian soldiers. He describes the interview thus:

At one point in the road I stopped the motor to talk with the soldiers of the Thirty-fifth Corps, the last unit of which had just crossed the river that morning and had been badly dusted. The colonel of the regiment was sitting on his horse in the middle of a field with notebook in hand checking up his losses. The soldiers of his command were lying along the grassy bank by the roadside, many of them falling asleep the moment they sat down. A field kitchen was halted in the road, and the few soldiers that were not asleep were lining up to get what was perhaps their first ration since the night before. Many were in bloody bandages and all worn and haggard. "Here," I thought, "one will find the morale of the Russians at its lowest ebb. These men have been fighting for days and have lost." So I called up a great strapping private soldier. Wearily he got to

his feet and came over to the side of the motor. His face was gray with fatigue and his eyes glassy for want of rest. "How do you feel now about the war?" I asked him. "Do you want peace?" He looked at me in a dazed kind of way and replied as he shuffled his feet uneasily: "We are all very tired." "But, still, what do you want to do about the war?" I persisted. The Russians are not quick to reply to questions under any circumstances. For a long time the tired soldier looked at me, and then for the second time he said: "I am very tired. We are all very tired." "Well, then," I said, "do you want to make peace and leave the Germans in possession of Warsaw?" For a long time he stood in the hot afternoon sun looking at the dust in the road and then replied: "I am very tired. So are we all. The Germans are taking Warsaw to-day. This is not as it should be. I think I am a better soldier than the German. With rifles and shells we can always beat him. It is not right that we should give up Warsaw." He paused for a moment and then looked up with his eyes flashing as he finished in one quick burst "Never! I am tired, but I want to go back and fight some more. We cannot leave the Germans in Warsaw."

Whether or not this soldier was the type of the Russian under arms can only be conjectured from the fact that a very few weeks after this defeat the Russian army gathered itself together and began again its march to the westward, a march that had not ended when the second year of the war reached its close.

Polish farmhouse fired by retreating Russians

A device of the highly efficient Russian Commissary department. Cattle being driven to the Russian army when it was in Galicia. Beef in this form requires no wagons for carriage and after it is used leaves no "empties" to be brought back

CHRONOLOGY OF PERIOD TREATED IN CHAPTER VIII

(After the fall of Warsaw, on August 5, 1915, there was a steady retreat on the part of the Russians until mid-winter; then the belligerents rested on their arms until the commencement of Brussilov's counter offensive beginning in June, 1916. During this period of comparative inaction there were but few events of sufficient importance to chronicle.)

August 10-12. Rapid advance of the Germans along the Bug River to Sledice sixty miles east of Warsaw.

August 16. Russian line broken at Bialystok with evacuation of the town.

August 17. Kovoro occupied by Germans.

August 25. Brest-Litowsk taken by Germans.

September 2. House-to-house fighting in Gorodno, which is taken by the Germans.

September 1-10. Russian turns at Tarnopol and Trembowla and captures 33,000 Austrians and fifty machine guns.

September 15. Tinsk occupied by Germans.

September 18. Vilna falls and Russian army narrowly escapes.

September 23. Russians reoccupy Lutsk.

October 18. Germans attempt to envelop Riga.

November 10. Russians relieve Riga.

November 20. Russians successful on the River Styr.

December 11. Russians attacking in Volhynia.

December 28. Russians attack fiercely on the Dneister, marking the beginning of renewed fighting in that section.

January 2, 1916. Russians advancing on Czernowitz.

January 12. Russians resume offensive in Bukovina.

January 20. Russians still advancing in Czernowitz.

February 8. Russians active at Tarnopol.

February 11. Russian successes continue in Galicia.

March 19. Germans repulse Russian attacks east of Vilna; nearly ten thousand Russians killed at Lake Narocz.

March 23. Russian armies in Galicia and Bukovina continue to advance. German line pierced in the Riga region.

April 12. Germans repulsed near Pinsk.

April 29. Germans take Russian positions near Lake Narocz with nearly six thousand prisoners.

(*June* 5. The Russian offensive under General Brussilov began on this date with assaults against the Austrian line on a front of 335 miles running south from the Pinsk marshes. It ultimately developed into an assault against the 450-mile front of the Germans north of Pinsk. More than 2,400,000 Teutons were involved of whom 600,000 were put out of action largely by capture. The purpose of the drive was the destruction of the Teutonic armies, not the capture of strategic points. Nevertheless, by August, fully 7,000 square miles of Russian territory had been recovered from the Teutons, and Cossacks had made their way into Hungary through the Carpathian Passes.)

June 5-12. Russian offensive captures 85,000 Austrians, takes Dubno, and invests Czernowitz.

June 14. Russians attack the Austrian centre at Buczacs.

June 17. Russians under General Lechitsky capture Czernowitz.

June 25. Russians clear Bukovina of Austrian defenders.

June 28. Serious Austrian defeat at Kolomea; Russians pass the Stirpa.

July 3. Russians within twenty miles of Lemberg.

July 6. Teuton losses before the Brussilov drive fixed officially at 500,000.

July 7. Russians begin offensive on the Riga front.

July 11. General Kuropatkin attacks Von Hindenburg in the Riga section, penetrating his lines five miles.

July 28. Russians take Brody.

July 29. Report that Austrians are forced to bring Turkish troops to their aid in Hungary.

ALPINE CHASSEURS CHARGE GERMAN LINES ON SKIIS

Conquering the Alps. The Alpini at the foot of the Dolomites

CHAPTER IX

THE WAR IN THE BALKANS—FAILURE OF BRITISH DIPLOMACY—
BULGARIA ENTERS THE WAR—THE BULGAR-TEUTON INVASION OF
SERVIA—DESTRUCTION OF THE SERVIAN ARMY—THE PLAGUE IN
SERVIA—ITALY'S LONG HESITATION—PROGRESS OF ITALIAN
CAMPAIGN—FALL OF GORIZIA—THE COMPLICATED CASE OF GREECE

IN THE last analysis the war which engulfed the most highly civilized nations of Europe sprung from the jealousies and the rival ambitions of the half-civilized peoples who make up the Balkan States—what the diplomatists call the cauldron of Europe. Slav and Magyar and Czech in those mountainous and turbulent regions, in many of which a nomad's rifle is his only law, and a hillside hut of boulders the type of home, struggled for the mastery, and plotted their alliances with the greater powers to the northward, who in turn thought only of swallowing them up. Servia blocked the way of Austria to the Ægean Sea—hence the Austrian attack on that country which precipitated the whole conflict. Servia blocked the German path to Constantinople, and William II, full of his great adventure of making Turkey practically a province of the German empire, lent ready aid to the Austrian assault on Servia if indeed he did not inspire it.

Classed among the Balkan States are Servia, Bulgaria, Roumania, Montenegro, Albania, and Macedonia. The Powers of Europe by solemn treaty had created two additional states, Bosnia and Herzegovina, but Austria had later calmly annexed these two

states to her dominion and the readiness of Germany at the time to back her up to the point of a general war had stifled protest from the other powers. Turkey, the immediate neighbor of the Balkan States, if itself not to be classed as one, entered the war in November, 1914. Greece, whose interests were vitally concerned, managed to stay out of the struggle until after the close of its second year. Her people were strongly in favor of joining the Allies, but the queen, wife of King Constantine, was a Hohenzollern princess, sister of Kaiser Wilhelm, and her influence over her husband long offset public opinion.

From the very first days of the war the diplomatic efforts of the belligerent parties were exerted to the utmost to secure the support of these states. Turkey, as we have seen, was early won over by the Germans. Bulgaria with an army in time of war of about 600,000 men was a prize worth struggling for, but like Turkey, was secured by the Teutons, declaring war in October, 1915. The Bulgarian premier gave a series of plausible reasons for the choice, the chief being dread of Russian aggressions after the war should the Allies be victorious. The real reason, however, seems to have been that at the moment the fortunes of war were strongly on the Teutonic side. The prolonged delay of Great Britain in getting into the war on land had permitted the Teutons to score an almost uninterrupted series of victories which seriously affected the prestige of the Allies among nations still hesitant as to the side with which to cast their lot. It was this that lost Bulgaria to the Allies, and kept Greece so long uncommitted. Though not within the scope of this volume, it may be noted that in August, 1916, after the war had continued more than two years,

Roumania cast her strength with the Allies—for the obvious reason that at that moment their cause looked by far the brighter.

In the earlier days of the war Servia, which had furnished the excuse for the conflict, suffered less than any of the participants. Though promptly invaded by the Austrians her army was adequate for the protection of her territory, and when the growling of the Russian bear in the Passes of the Carpathians forced the Austrians to protect themselves in that quarter, the Serbs in their turn took the offensive and inflicted a crushing

General Sarrail, commander of the Allies in the Balkans

defeat upon the Austrians in the Servian mountains. That victory demonstrated that Austria was incapable of dealing with both Russia and Servia at once, and put an end to further invasion of the latter's territory for some months.

Early in the fall of 1915, however, it became apparent to the diplomats at Berlin and Vienna that if they were to hold Bulgaria even neutral they must prove their ability to pay her price. After the second Balkan war Bulgaria had been despoiled of territory which could be restored only by robbing Servia. But Servia was still unsubdued.

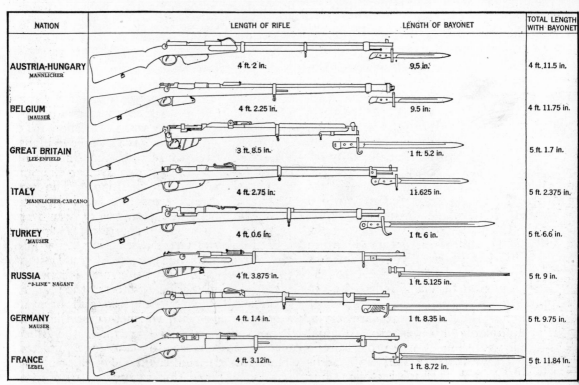

NATION	LENGTH OF RIFLE	LENGTH OF BAYONET	TOTAL LENGTH WITH BAYONET
AUSTRIA-HUNGARY MANNLICHER	4 ft. 2 in.	9.5 in.	4 ft. 11.5 in.
BELGIUM MAUSER	4 ft. 2.25 in.	9.5 in.	4 ft. 11.75 in.
GREAT BRITAIN LEE-ENFIELD	3 ft. 8.5 in.	1 ft. 5.2 in.	5 ft. 1.7 in.
ITALY MANNLICHER-CARCANO	4 ft. 2.75 in.	11.625 in.	5 ft. 2.375 in.
TURKEY MAUSER	4 ft. 0.6 in.	1 ft. 6 in.	5 ft. 6.6 in.
RUSSIA "3-LINE" NAGANT	4 ft. 3.875 in.	1 ft. 5.125 in.	5 ft. 9 in.
GERMANY MAUSER	4 ft. 1.4 in.	1 ft. 8.35 in.	5 ft. 9.75 in.
FRANCE LEBEL	4 ft. 3.12 in.	1 ft. 8.72 in.	5 ft. 11.84 in.

Comparative lengths of rifles and bayonets used in the Great War. The kind of rifle used is indicated under the name of each country

Serbian gun silenced. The Serbian resistance was gallant and stubborn, but they were ill equipped and demoralized by pestilence as well as by superior numbers and equipment

early if Bulgaria was to be influenced this state had to be crushed. Moreover, Germany wanted a direct line to Constantinople. The Allies were menacing Gallipoli, and for its defence guns and munitions must be shipped south from Essen. The campaign in Mesopotamia and the attack on the Suez Canal compelled the establishment of a line of transportation which could not be maintained with the Servian army in being.

It was therefore determined at Berlin to withdraw troops from whatever points could spare them and drive through Servia with the end in view of opening the road to Constantinople. By doing this a rich agricultural country would be opened for the supply of Germany, already feeling the pinch of the British food blockade. Arms, munitions, and reënforcements could be sent to the Turks at Gallipoli and in Asia Minor. Egypt, Persia, and India might be attacked. Bulgaria, Macedonia, Albania, and Turkey would be brought into immediate military touch with Germany, and even Roumania might be won to the Teutonic side.

Accordingly General von Mackensen was recalled from Russia to lead the invading

Servian women burying their dead. Every man, woman, and child in Serbia took some part in the heroic national resistance

Allied camp at Salonika as seen from an aeroplane. This camp is in the rear of the outposts that guard the territory held by the Allies around Salonika. The hills in the distance are heavily fortified

Teuton armies. Early in October he entered Servian territory with a force for which the defenders were no match. Because of the nature of the country reliance was placed largely upon artillery and the wretched Serbs were literally blown out of their land. While the Teutons were advancing from the north, the Bulgars, now at the end of their hesitation, also declared war and pushed in from the east. The Serbians caught between two enemies, and outnumbered at every point, had nothing for it but steady retreat. Belgrade, their capital, fell to the Teuton arms. Nish, their earlier capital, was taken by the Bulgars. Little Montenegro, with its army of 30,000 men, was drawn into the conflict on the Servian side, but was quickly snuffed out

like a candle by the blast of Von Mackensen's guns. By December 1st, practically all of Servia had been subdued and her army driven to the seashore, through Albania, where it rested in hope of aid from the Allies.

That hope was not wholly disappointed although the action of the Allies in viewing from afar the martyrdom of Servia without the extension of a helping hand was one of the tragedies of the war and a blunder as well. When the determination of Germany to crush Servia and bring Bulgaria into the war as an active belligerent became known the question of sending an expedition to their imperilled ally's aid was discussed in the military councils of England and France. The former claim

Roumanians more Latin than Balkan. They claim that Roumania is a Latin community left along the Black Sea and the Danube, and that its people are descendants of Roman legionaries. Their language is essentially Latin. Physically they resemble one type of Italians

rowned upon it. The diplomatic problems ivolved were perplexing. Italy, which had ow declared war upon Austria, was not eager o have Servian power built up, lest that ountry annex Albania upon which the talians themselves had designs. Moreover, n allied expedition to Servia's aid could nly advance through Greek territory from alonika, which the Allies already held in finally won. Early in October the Gulf of Salonika became crowded with transports and merchantmen, flying the flags of all nations but all engaged in transporting troops and munitions for Servian relief. The long, stone quays of the Greek port resounded to the tread of French and English infantry, landed in flat defiance of neutrality but apparently with the warm approval of

rench transports and cavalry horses after disembarkation. This shows a small corner of the great cantonment of French
horses that were poured out of the transports at Salonika

at defiance of the neutral rights of Greece. he statesmen of Great Britain who had gone war because of Germany's violation of the eutrality of Belgium felt naturally nervous out their own continued violation of the eutrality of Greece. However, they deferred these scruples only long enough to make eir expedition for the relief of the Serbs too te to be of service.

It was at the insistence of Premier Briand France and of General Joffre, who crossed e Channel to plead his case, that British nsent to a Servian relief expedition was the Greek people if not that of their king. Up a Greek railroad, about sixty miles, the troops were rushed into Macedonia and to Monastir where they effected a junction with the remnant of the Servian army. In all 200,000 or more Allied troops were thus sent to the southern end of Servia. They attempted no reconquest of the territory taken by the Teutons, but at the end of the war's second year were merely holding their ground—doubtless in part as an object-lesson to Greece and Roumania still hesitating as to the flag under which they would enlist.

Photo by Brown Bros.

Conquering the Alps.   The ascent of the Dolomites

Serbian volunteers who had no rifles. They were mostly old men, and were employed in trench digging. They went with the army when it evacuated Monastir, and being totally unequipped, suffered more than the regular soldiers. Many died by the way

later. Servia would have been saved and these three Balkan States, acting in unison, would have blocked the German march to Constantinople, and have kept Austria so busy with her own defence in the south that the Russians would infallibly have marched without effective opposition through her northern provinces into Germany. As it was the belated activity of the Allies due to Premier Briand and General Joffre was the sole cause of Roumania's accession to the Allied cause, which at the time changed the whole prospect of the war in the Balkan regions. Napoleon said that God was always with the heaviest battalions. However that may be, hesitating neutrals close to the battle zone are always with the side that seems to be winning.

How valuable was that object-lesson was demonstrated in August, 1916, when Roumania came over to the Allies, and King Constantine, his power destroyed, was forced to yield to the war sentiment of his people.

At one time there had been serious criticism of the tactics of the Allies in entering upon the difficult field of Balkan diplomacy and war at all. It was urged, with some reason, that the British might better pour all their troops, as fast as available, into the battlefields of France and Belgium where it seemed that the final issue of the war would be determined. Mainly in order to guard India the British Government repelled this suggestion, fortunately for the Allies. Indeed it would have been more fortunate had there been no such hesitation as was shown in the expedition to the Dardanelles and the abortive effort to aid the Serbs before they were annihilated. For a more decisive front shown in that section in 1915 would have kept Bulgaria neutral, or perhaps brought her to the Allies' side as Roumania came a year

Comparatively little is yet known of the conditions of warfare in the Servian campaigns. The regions were unfamiliar to the average citizen of other lands. The population was sparse, with little association with the outer world, destitute in the main of newspapers or means of making their sufferings known.

An Italian siege gun used to batter down Austrian concrete trenches

Conquering the Alps.   Drawing up a battery of guns during a storm

A cheerful fugitive. At least 70 years old, this man was employed in the transport service. His job was to lead two donkeys aden with shells for field guns

They say the Austrians left the seeds of typhus in Servia—not with malignant purpose, of course, but as a result of insanitary camp and hospital management. It is a fact that when the Servians first retired from Valjevo they left it free of disease. When the fortune of war turned their way, as it did after the first Austrian invasion, they returned to find Valjevo harboring 3,000 Austrian wounded, many suffering from typhus. An account in the London *Times* says:

"In one building, quite a new school, 150 dead Austrians were found in the cellars, and men and cattle were buried indiscriminately in the courtyards adjacent many of them barely covered by a foot of earth. From Valjevo the infection spread like fire,

The war correspondents of English-speaking lands had their attention riveted on the struggle in France, or at the most took a few days from observation of the wrestle for Galicia between Brussilov and Von Hindenburg to run down into Servia and observe what they thought was a mere side action of the war but which was in fact the murder of a nation. Moreover, the censorship was applied in Servia with more rigidity and less intelligence than in any other battle area—though the follies and futilities of the censors were notorious everywhere.

From the information which filtered out from this cauldron of plague and battle it became in time known to the world that in no other section had the horrors of war been so frightful; nowhere else the proportion of wanton sacrifice to cruelty, carelessness, and ignorance so great. The fighting was fierce, but so had it been on other fronts. The attendant barbarities, the destruction of the homes, the devastation of fields, the exile of peaceful folks to meet starvation and death were shocking, but so had they been in Belgium and in Poland. But Servia suffered a martyrdom all her own in the scourge of the plague that swept over the land after the armies of the Teutons and Bulgars had flooded it with blood.

The monument marks where 4,000 Serbs fell in the battle for Monastir in the first Balkan war in 1912. The fighting in November, 1915, passed over the same ground

View of Monastir from a minaret. It is a picturesque old city, the architecture being a strange mixture, with the Turkish influence predominating. The tall, white towers are minarets of mosques

being carried by soldiers returning to their homes and by travelers on the railway. In a few weeks the country had become a seething mass of misery and pestilence.

"The conditions were appalling. The number of patients was beyond all hospital accommodation, and doctors and nurses were dying with their patients. In the Nish Hospital the patients were lying three and four in one bed, with one covering for the whole, while others lay on the floor, and even under the beds. At one time there were 700 patients to 200 beds, with only two doctors, one of them a young Swiss, who very shortly after fell ill. There were no sanitary arrangements. . . .

"And all the time the infection was being carried about by soldiers returning from the army, by peasants wandering at large, and, above all, by the travelers on the railways. The trains were crowded with all sorts of people— peasants in filthy clothes, rags, and goatskins, wandering aimlessly along corridors, looking in vain for accommodation, and all the carriages reeking of naphthalene."

A veteran of two wars in Salonika harbor

In time it may be known, approximately it can never be known certainly, whether weapons of war or disease claimed the more victims in Servia. In July, 1915, it was estimated that more than 100,000 had perished of typhus and cholera. In this moment of dreadful agony the people of the United States responded nobly not only with offerings, but with personal service to the call of distress. The activities of the Red Cross were marvelous. Young men and women, not doctors or students of medicine alone, but youth of all professions who wished to help volunteered for Servian service. This extract from a letter of a clergyman gives some idea of what they had to face:

"They found 1,400 desperately sick and wounded men —Servian soldiers and Austrian prisoners. These had been carried to two dirty tobacco warehouses; 150 of them were lying on mattresses (two and three to a mattress). The rest were on the reeking floor— 1,400 men in stony silence, suffering from gun-shot

Serbian volunteers at roll call. These were some of the many for whom no weapons could be provided, but they were organized to carry supplies. Often they picked up guns of dead comrades and joined the fighting

wounds, shrapnel, and bursting shell. Many were without portions of their bodies; all wounds were infected, not having been dressed since the first rough aid on the battle-field days since.

"But this was not the worst. Lying in filth, unattended and half-starved, germs of the most deadly epidemics were appearing—smallpox, diphtheria, relapsing fever, typhoid, and typhus. Wounded soldiers from the battleline and sick soldiers from the barracks were tottering into the tobacco warehouses, fifty, one hundred, and as high as two hundred and fifty a day.

"The conditions of that pest-camp cannot be told, but this can—that not one of those twelve women and six men faltered or turned back. With a laugh that was nearer a sob, they rolled up their sleeves and bent to their task, making a hospital out of nothing, classifying the unclassable, sawing up boxes for splints, stoking old rusty boilers to secure hot water, performing miracles in the way of operations and cures.

"They were engulfed; they were overwhelmed. Every nurse became a 'lady of the lamp.' They were cooks, sisters, ministering angels, priests, undertakers. Mohammedans, unused to honesty or sympathy in women, reached out feeble hands to touch their garments. Soldiers cut off their prized buttons and officers their stars and chevrons that they might press them into the hand that cooled their brow or dressed the grievous wound."

Human courage, gentleness, and sympathy were never put to a more severe test than in the typhus hospitals of Servia, nor was there ever a more noble response. In this response the United States, too often condemned in Europe as a land of gross materialism, took a leading part.

Italy entered the war by a declaration against Austria—not Germany, on the 23d of May, 1915. Nothing in the campaigns her armies fought was more dramatic than the fight made in her parliament and her public places to drag her into the struggle. Superficially it appeared that she was morally bound to co-

An Italian battleship in Saloniki harbor

Conquering the Alps.   Mass for the Italian troops above the sea

perate with the Teutons. For Italy had long been a member of the Triple Alliance, which bound her to Germany and Austria. But that Alliance was essentially defensive. It provided that all should rally to the defence of any one member that might be attacked from without. It was the claim of those Italians who sought to force the war upon a hesitant Parliament and an unwilling king, that Austria's ultimatum to Servia was in effect an aggression, an incitement to war which no one member of the Alliance had a right to offer without consultation with the others. The plea of the war party in Italy was that Austria was not attacked but was the assailant, and that as a party to a purely defensive agreement Italy was not morally obligated to come to her aid.

A second cause of complaint was that Article VIII of the Triple Alliance bound Austria to refrain from any occupation of Balkan territory without

Old men and boys, side by side, in the Serbian army

agreement with Italy and the payment to her of compensation. Austria, however, invaded Servia without agreement with or even notice to Italy, and though demand for compensation was instantly made the nature and intent of the payment were debated so long by the Austrians that the Italians concluded it would never be paid. Finally the Italian advocates of war contended that Austrian preparations for war upon Russia were in fact a provocation to the latter nation to declare war, and that Italy could not be bound by her agreement

to aid Austria against a Russian attack.

These were the technical arguments employed to force Italy into battle. They were the pleas which Italian statesmen put forward in defence of their action against the criticism of the world. They were bitterly denounced by the Teutonic Allies as being made in bad faith, and indeed they were rather the excuses for, than the true incentives to, the action finally taken by the Italian nation. For Italy, like France, had her lost provinces. Her Alsace-Lorraine are Trent and Triest, the one lying in the Dolomite Alps a scant forty miles north of the Austro-Italian boundary, the latter a noble port at the head of the Adriatic, which has had much to do with the decadence of the maritime glories of Venice, which it faces across that sun-lit sea. For the recovery of these lost provinces the Italian heart has yearned for half a century, and the instant action of the army when war was declared was to plunge into the craggy ranges of the Dolomites in the effort to reclaim "Italia Irredenta," as that region is called in Italy. Moreover, modern Italy has a legacy of hate against the Austrians which no formal Alliance could ever obliterate. Until 1868 the military thrall of Austria was upon the northern provinces of Italy, and Milan and Venice for years lived in sullen resentment as cities held by the enemy. The Italian is an emotional being, and though the Parliament under the control of Giolotti, a strongly

Serbian artillery covering the retreat

end to end. Every po[s]sible dramatic incider[t] was seized upon as [a] rallying point for the wa[r] party. In January th[e] body of Bruno Garibald[i] the grandson of Italy['s] famous liberator, wa[s] brought back fro[m] France where he ha[d] been slain, fightin[g] bravely with the Allie[s]. All Italy went wild wit[h] adoration for the her[o] and applause for th[e] cause in which he ha[d] fallen. His state funera[l] in Rome was a corteg[e] which would have don[e] honor to a king, and th[e] whole city lined the na[r]row and historic way through which it passed. It was the cause equally with the heroic an[d] historic name to which this tribute of a whol[e] nation was paid. From that day there wa[s] no doubt as to the side on which Italy woul[d] land.

It has been asserted that in her final actio[n] Italy was animated by a lust for spoils, b[y] the desire to regain Trent and Triest, b[y] covetousness for Albania, and an intent t[o] make the Adriatic an Italian lake, by a[n] ambition to have a larger slice of the Balka[n]

pro-German statesman, held out for ten long months against war on the Allies' side, an army of orators and pamphleteers stirred up the people to the highest pitch of excitement, and the demonstrations in favor of such action amounted almost to revolution. Gabrielle d'Annunzio, poet and playwright, was a leader in this agitation, traveling from town to town, haranguing the people from the steps of the Roman capitol, and in the grand plaza of St. Peter's, turning out pamphlets as plenteous as the doves of St. Mark's, appealing to all that was emotional in the Italian nature until he had aroused the populace from Messina to Venice to a point that hardly brooked control. After a dissolution of the ministry there followed a campaign which racked the Italian peninsula from

Serbian women, driven from their homes by the Teuton invasion

pie, and a bit of the final slicing of Turkey. Probably that is true. Nations are not unselfish, and statesmen are in duty bound to aid in the aggrandizement of their states. But Italy was not wholly animated by mercenary motives, for she took up the cause of the Allies when in her neighborhood at least it was darkest. The Russians were in full retreat from Galicia when she flung down her gauntlet to Austria. It was the people of Italy, the emotions of Italy, rather than any sordid considerations that rushed her into battle.

French artillery hurried across the Vardar River to aid the Serbs, but too late to avert the catastrophe which overwhelmed Serbia. The tardiness of the French and English in coming to Serbia's assistance resulted in the complete desolation of the brave little country which was overrun by the Teutonic armies

Never had secret diplomacy or the machinations of a cabinet have less to do with calling a nation to arms.

To the non-military mind it seemed that the entry of Italy upon the war ought to have an immediate and decisive effect upon the conflict. The belligerents had been expending their strength for ten months in what seemed at the time to be too fierce a conflict to be long continued. Italy now came to the aid of the Allies with an organized army of 800,000 men, and a male population of military age of about 3,500,000. During the ten months of hesitation every effort had been made to bring the mobilized troops to a high degree of efficiency, but, save for the war in Tripoli against a weak and disorganized enemy, they were without active experience in the field. The Italian navy ranked as superior to the Austrian navy with which it might be expected to come at once into conflict. But its superiority was largely in capital ships, and the Adriatic, in which any naval battle would be fought, was, because of its narrowness, peculiarly favorable to submarines in which Austria was not so greatly outclassed.

The rugged line of Alps, which form Italy's northern border, constitute a protection for Austria, a menace

Serbian camp scene at reveille

to the more southerly nation. For the boundary line gives the crests to Austria. Her troops bent on an invasion would fight downward to the gentle declivities of the Italian foothills. If the Italians on their

has given the territory the name Italia Irredenta or Italy Unredeemed.

Italy struck first, along a five-hundred-mile front. Her armies quickly spread over the Trentino and, on the west, crossed the

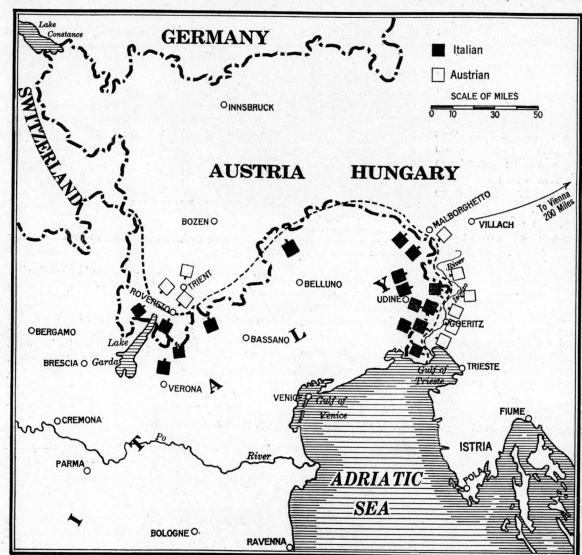

In the Alps the Italian army has had to face the most formidable natural obstacle in Europe

part sought to invade Austria, their columns would have to make their way through narrow passes and tortuous defiles and up precipitous heights to the summit. With all physical conditions against her, however, the Italians had the advantage of conducting their invasion in a land the greater part of whose inhabitants were enthusiastically friendly. For the territory about Trent and Trieste is largely peopled by Italians, whose restive state under the Austrian domination

Isonzo River, and reached Montfalcone within four days of the declaration of war. It seemed for the time as though there were to be no effective resistance by the Austrians, who had indeed been forced by a Russian menace to send to their eastern front an army of 700,000 men who had seen service—men of from thirty-five to forty years who had recently had special training from German officers. With these troops withdrawn the opposition to the Italian advance was necessarily entrusted to troops made up of boys below nineteen and men above forty-five hastily drawn from the threatened territory which was thoroughly permeated with pro-Italian sentiment. As a result the Italian advance for the first two months encountered practically no effective resistance.

The Italian strategy put briefly was:

1. To neutralize the friendly Trentino by capturing or "covering" her defences, and cutting her line of communication with Austria proper.

2. To cover, or capture, Trieste and then move in force in the direction of the Austrian fortress of Klagenfurt and Vienna. The distance of the Austrian capital from the base of Italian operations a week after the war began was little more than that from New York to Providence.

It seemed at first that all this was to be yielded to Italy by default. By the end of July her commanders were satisfied with conditions in the Trentino, and her troops were attacking along the Isonzo from Tarvis to the Adriatic—a front of not less than seventy-five miles. The river itself was a great natural defence for the Austrians. Flowing through narrow gorges, bordered by

War waifs gathered from the snowy trails. Children whose parents were killed or lost during the evacuation of Servia before the advancing German and Bulgarian armies. The one at the left of the photograph had struggled along the Albanian trail for 25 days, without parents or friends, and survived hardships that overcame many adults. The story of the Albanian trail has not been written, but if it ever is it will surpass in horror any of the tragedies of Belgium or Poland

steep cliffs broken only by narrow mountain passes, it had been strengthened by powerful fortresses erected by the Austrians in far-sighted anticipation of trouble with their Italian neighbors. Yet to the amazement of military observers the Italians accomplished the crossing of the river in four separate places. Agile as the mountain chamois, vested with all the reckless daring of the Latin peoples, they proved to be precisely the troops needed for so desperate an enterprise.

Gorizia was the immediate objective and early in August, 1915, the Italian staff announced positively that its capture was a matter of but a few days. Never were military commanders more deceived. Gorizia fell indeed to the Italian arms, but it fell in August, 1916, just a year later. The twelve months between witnessed some of the hardest and most inconclusive fighting that had taken place in any battle area of the Great War.

Into all the details of that year of struggle and of carnage it is impossible in this brief narrative to go. Enough to say that by the middle of December, 1915, Italy had so established herself within Austrian borders as to make any Aus-

Stars and Stripes in Salonika. The American consulate, the busiest place in the city

CONQUERING THE ALPS. ITALIAN

ENCHMENT IN AN ALPINE RAVINE

Photo by Brown Bros.

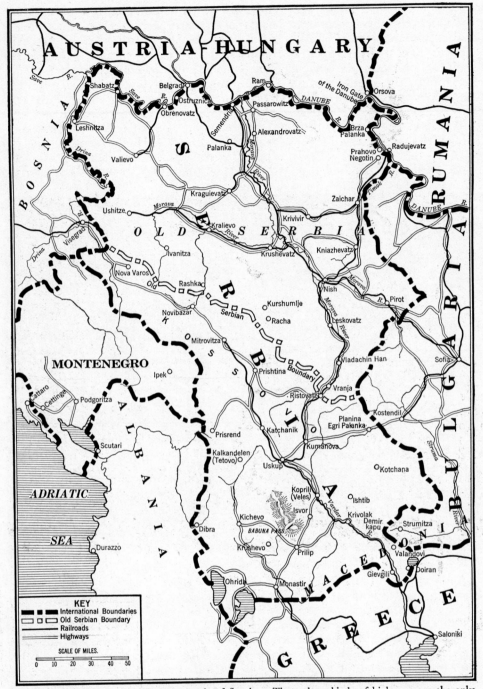

The railroads, rivers, and wagon roads of Servia. These three kinds of highways are the only practicable means of traversing this mountainous country, and their location has determined the strategy of the invasion of Servia by the Teutonic allies and the Bulgars

Gorizia had suffered heavily from the fire of General Cadorno's artillery, but though the town and its forts were in ruins the defenders still maintained what all conceded to be a hopeless resistance. But those who conceded this had little conception of how long the dogged Austrians could hold out.

The falling of winter in the narrow and precipitous defiles and towering peaks of the Dolomites ended effective operations in that section. Some fighting, indeed, progressed, and the world heard of skirmishes on skiis over snow lying seven feet deep on the level, of artillery mounted on sledges, and of hot battles fought among the avalanches. But in the main the winter passed without any material change in the positions along the Italian frontier. The Austrians were on the defensive, and every natural obstacle that the rigors of winter put in the path of the Italians was to their advantage. Nevertheless the world wondered at

trian invasion of her own territory appear improbable. The Austrian line on the Isonzo she had pierced at the centre. Tolmino, Gorizia, and Trieste were all menaced by her troops, and the occupation of any one of them meant a long step on the way to Vienna.

the slight showing made by the Italians and complaint was common in the allied press that the soldiers of Victor Emmanuel were "shirking their bit." What had really happened was that while they had crossed the frontiers at practically every point, they had been instantly checked upon coming into contact with the Austrian main lines of defence. Once so checked the Italian lines showed as little change for eight months as did the French lines in Flanders.

In May, 1916, the Austrians who had thus

portions that it had maintained in the battle-fields of France. More than 2,000 heavy guns were brought into action by the Austrians, and the weight of metal thrown is said to have been equalled only at Verdun.

The Austrian drive continued for ten days. It had been planned with the utmost skill. Many strategic points in the Trentino were recovered, and the Austrian columns penetrated far into Italian territory. At this time the Austrian War Office reported the recovery of 300 square miles of lost Austrian

French soldiers constructing barbed wire entanglements outside Saloniki

far been content with maintaining a fairly successful defensive, suddenly began an attack which in its turn threatened to overwhelm the Italian forces along the western Alpine front. It is estimated that this Austrian drive enlisted more than 700,000 men, of whom 360,000 were newly brought from the Galician front. Both in the Trentino and along the Isonzo front the Austro-Hungarians pressed the attack with such vigor that the Italians were pressed back from all the advanced positions they had won in the Austrian Tyrol, and were hard put to it to maintain their lines before Gorizia. For the first time in the eastern theatre of war the work of the artillery took on the pro-

territory, and the occupation of 300 square miles of Italian soil. The moment seemed critical for Italy, for the Austrian Tyrol penetrates so far into her territory that invading columns moving southeast from that border would not only capture Venice and Verona, but would cut off the Italian army operating along the Isonzo. Or, if the Austrians chose to coöperate with the German drive, then in progress in France, they might move westward from the Trentino salient and menace Milan and Turin, the latter a point of concentration for an attack on France's Italian frontier. Should such an attack be even threatened France would have to rush troops to the menaced front, thereby weakening her

Salonika from the sea. Salonika changed hands from Turkey to Greece in 1912

more than 60,000 men put out of action, had rallied and checked the invaders' advances. In May and June of 1916 the conditions of the same months in 1915 had been precisely reversed. At the earlier period the Italians had carried all the Austrian outposts but were checked in their career when they encountered the enemy's main line of defence. So, too, the Austrians were checked now that they had encountered the main line of the Italians. Then came the Russian diversion, and sharply upon its heels the Italians in their turn began a dashing and successful counter offensive.

defence at Verdun and in Flanders. The situation was a critical one. It found its reflection in Italian politics, for furious attacks upon the conduct of the war caused the overthrow of the ministry. But in the end Italian gallantry saved the day and wrested new victories from the very grip of defeat. It is quite true that the full measure of the new Italian successes was due to the launching in June, 1916, of the great Russian drive in Bukowina and Galicia which compelled the diversion of many of the Austrian troops to that theatre of war. But even before this the Italians, though in ten days they had lost 30,000 prisoners and 298 cannon, with

Climatic conditions compelled the Italians to force the fighting on the Isonzo line at first rather than in the Tyrol. In the towering ranges of the Dolomites the snow lies heavy until July, and after driving their foe from their own territory the Italian forces in that section rested on their arms to some extent, awaiting summer and the disappearance of the snow. But the drive on Gorizia was not delayed. The broad valley of the Isonzo is so placed that the warm winds of Italy and the Adriatic flow freely up it at all times, giving Gorizia, despite its northern latitude, some fame as a winter resort. It is indeed almost Californian in climate. The town itself lies in the centre of a ring of hills, all held by Austrian batteries. Although those immediately in front of

Only oxen are equal to Servia's muddy roads

the Italian armies were reduced by artillery or taken by trench warfare, it was futile for the assailants to occupy the town itself while it was still commanded by others on adjacent hills, and upon

Roumanian cavalry. It was the ambition of the Roumanian army to gain Transylvania

these the Italians now began a patient and persistent attack. Three hills commanded the city—Mount Sabatino, Mount San Michele, and the heights of Podgora. The last were taken by the Italians in November. The other two succumbed to Victor Emmanuel's artillery and trench warfare the last week in July. The Italians had brought to this work a prodigious equipment of new and powerful guns—1,500 were said to have been furnished the army at the beginning of its new drive in May. For two days the mountainside, which had been under heavy fire for a month or more, was subjected to such an infernal rain of shell and shrapnel that no living thing could withstand it.

Mount Sabatino had long seemed impregnable. It resisted stubbornly the fire of the terrible new guns, and was only taken by the exercise of that incredible and patient industry which characterized so many of the military operations of the war. The formation of the land in this region is of limestone, and in this the Italians had for months been hewing wide underground passageways, capable of permitting four men abreast to pass from their lines to within

twenty yards of the Austrian defences. Three such tunnels of 240 to 300 feet long were ready for use when, on August 6th, the final bombardment began. Then, after the great guns had beaten the Austrian trenches out of any semblance of form, and driven away nearly all the defenders who could escape, the Italians poured out of the exits of their tunnels and overwhelmed the amazed Austrians who remained. Mt. Sabatino thus passed into Italian hands. Mt. San Michele fell the same day. Twenty times or more it had been taken and lost, and for seven months more than half of its summit had been held by the Italians. Always domi-

Servian refugees on the road

nated by the Austrian fire from the higher Mt. Sabatino it could not be held until the latter peak had fallen. But now after sustaining attack not only from the Italian guns, but from twenty-four dirigible balloons, each carrying four tons of explosive and daringly operated, its defenders finally withdrew.

ing straw and gasoline were used at times to dislodge the defenders. For three days this sort of fighting raged, then the remnant of the Austrians fled across the bridge, blowing it up as the last company passed. Thereupon the Italians, in the face of a heavy fire, forded the stream and put the seal of completion upon their victory.

British guns to help the embattled Serbs. A part of the artillery contingent that passed through Salonika to Servia. The British expedition was small and late in arriving

Immediately upon securing the heights the Italians turned their attention to the city. It was heavily shelled to drive out the few defenders remaining. The bridge head was still held by the Austrians, and the Italians entered upon a hand-to-hand battle in the strip of territory that still separated them from it. Here there was subterranean warfare. The Austro-Hungarians had adapted for purposes of defence hundreds of caves that nature had formed in the limestone hills and crags. These they had enlarged into great halls, holding vast quantities of munitions and housing thousands of men. Burn-

Two days later the Duke of Aosta and King Victor Emmanuel rode into the conquered city. The culmination of a fourteen months' campaign had been reached. Gorizia had fallen. One great step had been taken on the way to Vienna. The Italian guns were within twelve miles of Trieste and the Austrian fleet had already been ordered to evacuate that port which had been its base and seek a new one farther down the Adriatic. A notable advance had been made in what was now obviously the allied plan of campaign—namely, to pound Austria as the weakest of the Teutonic Allies and to reduce her to impotence and perhaps complete surrender even while Germany fought gallantly on.

In all the history of the world's diplomacy there has been no more complicated or perplexing record than that of Greece during the Great War. At the end of its second year were being used to carry information of value to the Teutons. Greece yielded to this as to everything, though her pro-German King Constantine took to his bed in an illness that may well have been brought on by chagrin and pique. But the Greek Government blandly declared all this to be the part of perfect neutrality, though they confessed

Prince Andreas at the head of the Greek Army. A view of the brother of the King of Greece as he rode through Salonika at the head of a powerful army of Greek troops

the Greek Government was still nominally at peace with all the belligerents. True, an army of French, English, and Italian troops numbering more than 600,000 was encamped on Greek soil in and about Salonika, and was using that point as a base for operations against the Austrians and Bulgars in Servia. Greek ports, even Athens, were open to the vessels of the Allies bringing troops and supplies to this land of dubious neutrality. Toward the end of the second year the Allies even made a successful demand for the right to administer the Greek posts and telegraphs on the plea that they that it was a benevolent neutrality to the Allies. Some one with a taste for research in diplomatic history discovered that in 1832, after a war for independence in which she was aided by Great Britain and France, the nation of Greece was established *under the protection* of those two nations and Russia. The Convention of London, by which the Kingdom of Greece had been erected, had never been annulled, and was now in force. What more reasonable then than that the troops of the protecting nations should be hurried to Greek territory to guard it from invasion by the Bulgars and Austrians who were knocking at its northern barriers?

The plea served its purpose at any rate and saved the day for the Allies in the Balkan regions—so far at least as it had been saved to mid-summer of 1916. For the situation had for a year been most menacing to the allied interests, and only by the friendly or

peror William, whom he married in 1889. In the two Balkan wars of 1912-13 he greatly distinguished himself, and the Kaiser, anxious to tie so capable a soldier-king to his own fortunes, made him a field marshal in the German army—the only sovereign thus honored save Francis Joseph of Austria. In a speech at Berlin acknowledging this

French artillery passing a Greek cavalry regiment. The French were the first of the Allied troops to land at Salonika for the assistance of Servia when she was assailed by Germany, Austro-Hungary and Bulgaria

enforced coöperation of Greece could it have been met. That it was grave was due in part to the strong pro-German sympathies of King Constantine, and in part to the diplomatic and military mistakes of the Allies in their early dealings with the Balkan problem.

King Constantine's early military education had been at the famous French school of St. Cyr. This course completed he was sent to Berlin where he shone for some time in the uniform of the Imperial Guards, and became betrothed to the sister of Em-

honor the new Field Marshal maladroitly ascribed all his military successes to his post-graduate course in the German army. The French people blazed with resentment. Not only had their pet military academy been snubbed, but the vital fact that the armies Constantine successfully led had been trained by two successive French commissions had been ignored. Hurrying to Paris Constantine strove to dispel the hostility his speech had created. But German agents had been ahead of him, and while official Paris was most hospitable, the mob before his hotel so grossly assailed him that he said to a friend later in Athens, "As long as I live I shall never pardon the French people for

those insults." It is fair to say for Constantine that however strong his sympathy for Germany he never sought to array his people on the side of the Teutons. His constant struggle was for neutrality and peace. The earlier lethargy of the Allies in relation to things Balkan made his position easier, his plea the more plausible. Turkey was lost to them nine weeks after the war began. Servia, some part of whose territory might have been fitting reward for Greek aid, was an ally of the British. The Allies could offer no such reward, but the Germans promptly did. The expedition to the Dardanelles failed. Bulgaria went into the war on the side of the Teutons. Nowhere in the Balkan regions was there any indication that the Allies would be able to reward Greece for her adhesion, or even have power to defend her from the wrath of the embittered Teutons.

Against the strength of Constantine the king was arrayed that of Venizelos, a popular leader. Himself a Cretan, the son of a farm laborer, this man had so identified himself with the popular cause in Greece that as far back as 1906 he had been made Prime Minister at the demand of the people. His first act then was to strip the four royal princes of their military offices, putting practical soldiers in their places and calling upon France for a commission to reorganize the

Serbian refugees arriving at Salonika on Christmas morning. They had been driven from their homes by war and, with what belongings they could load on a few animals, came to ask the hospitality of foreign and neutral Greece. Many of the women and children had lost husbands and fathers in the war, and some families had been separated. Refugees poured into Salonika by the thousands every day for weeks

The British soldiers at Salonika were served with a small ration of beer twice a day, and the attendance at the function was always 100 per cent. Alcoholics are not much used in any of the armies, the use of spirits being entirely forbidden except under unusual conditions, and the amount of light wines and beer being strictly limited

Reinforcements for a hard pressed line. A detachment of troops rushed up to help their comrades hold certain trenches where an enemy assault was imminent. Note that the Servian trenches were not so deep nor so wide as those of the Western front. This is because they were hastily constructed, the army being in almost continuous retreat before a superior enemy

Servian officer's odd shelter. Headquarters of Major Merse (on platform) in command of the advanced lines at Gradek, on the Vardar River. A crude silo is shown at the right of the picture. The French and British forces proved inadequate to save Servia from her enemies

army. Yet when reorganization was complete and the Balkan war of 1912 was impending he called Constantine back to the head of the reformed army. Constantine made good. The army adored him, and its loyalty alone enabled him later to block for a time the endeavor of Venizelos to swing the nation to the Allies' side.

At the close of the second year of war Venizelos seemed to be the victor in this struggle. Though stripped of his office

Servian 3-inch gun being moved to a new emplacement

of Prime Minister he had the Greek people and a majority of the Parliament back of him. Several times he had appeared to be on the verge of triumph, but King Constantine proved an adept in diplomatic procrastination, even manifesting symptoms of the gravest illness when a decisive moment was at hand. The pressure of the Allies upon Greece continued to grow during 1916. Finally, by their insistence the king was forced to demobilize his army, the cost of maintaining which had brought Greece to the verge of bankruptcy. At this moment he sought to deliver over to the Bulgarians— led by German officers — three forts, Rupel, Spatovo, and Dragotin, facing the British position at Salonika. That proved to be an act of rashness that brought affairs to a culmination.

Copyr'ght by Underwood & Underwood

View of Sarajevo from the suburbs, showing mountainous character of the country

The populace of Athens revolted. The king fled to Larissa. The British instantly blocked all Greek ports, and the Entente Powers demanded the dismissal of the existing cabinet and the appointment of one in sympathy with their cause. All this was acceded to and, though the second year of the war ended with Greece still nominally neutral, her territory and railways were at the absolute disposal of the Allies who also assumed authority over her posts, telegraphs, and harbor authorities. Her king, stripped of all power, was an exile from his capital. Her government was administered in the interest of the Allies, and the one thing lacking to the actual participation of Greece in the war was that her armies should take the field against Bulgaria, together with the French, British, and Italians, in the autumn drive through Servia.

That culminating triumph for Venizelos or else a civil war seemed inevitable in September, 1916.

Every man must be his own tailor.   Serbians resting during a hard march

Serbian artillery retreating through the Albanian Alps

tures of the Germans for an orderly march through their country. The first step of the invader toward the boundary at Liége was met by a cannon shot.

In Greece the Prime Minister himself invited the Allies to land at Salonika. He asked of them 150,000 men to aid in guarding Servia, the ally of Greece, from Bulgarian aggression. The right of Venizelos to issue the invitation has never been questioned though the act was repudiated by King Constantine. The German troops used Belgian territory as an avenue of attack upon Belgium's friend France. The British and French troops used Greek terri-

It must, probably, go down as the verdict of history that in making Greece their base of operations against the Bulgarians and Teutons, the Allies were guilty of a violation of neutrality narrowly approaching that of the German invasion of Belgium. Technically the taunts and jeers of the partisans of Germany were justified. The rigid devotion to the rights of neutrals which led Great Britain to declare war when German guns opened upon the forts at Liége, was quite forgotten when British troops landed at Salonika.

But the two violations of neutrality, though identical in principle, differed markedly in degree. In Belgium the constitutional authorities refused the over-

A masked Italian gun bombarding an Austrian position near Lugana

Servians in the trenches

The muster before entering the trenches. A company of Serbians at Lone Tree Hill, Halinchi, near Prilip, answering roll call before entering the trenches for the last stand against the Bulgars. For many of these brave fellows it was a last roll call. In the ranks were soldiers of all ages from mere boys to grandfathers. This picture was taken within range of the Bulgar guns

tory as a base whence to give aid to Greek's ally and friend Servia.

When the Allies first sought the privilege of landing at Salonika the King himself admitted that 80 per cent. of his people favored their cause. It was evident enough that the landing of the Allied troops was approved by the Greek nation and officially authorized by the Cabinet.

There was furthermore no resistance. The "invasion," so-called, was peaceful and benevolent. There were no burned and ravaged towns, no murdered and mutilated citizens. The Parthenon did not share the fate of the great library of Louvain. If the British and French must excuse their action on the mere plea of military exigency they may at least add that they did not find military necessity compelled the burning of towns, the slaughter of babes, or the violation of women. At that point the cases of Belgium and Greece sharply cease to be parallel.

Serbian refugees bound for Corsica

CHRONOLOGY OF THE PERIOD TREATED IN CHAPTER IX

(A drive by the Teutons through Servia, Montenegro, and Albania late in the fall of 1915 brought Bulgaria into the war on the side of the Central Empires, opened a direct railroad line between Berlin and Constantinople, helped to compel the abandonment of the Gallipoli expedition by the Allies, and forced the dispatch to Salonika of a Franco-British-Servian expedition of about 700,000 and an Italian expedition to Valona with about 200,000 troops. It was expected to be the prelude to a powerful Turko-German attack upon Suez and Egypt but that did not follow. It left the Allies in August preparing for a counter-drive back through Servia and into Hungary.)

October 2, 1915. Bulgaria masses troops on Servia's eastern frontier.

October 5-7. Landing of 70,000 French and 15,000 British at Salonika.

October 9. Austro-Germans occupy Belgrade with fierce street fighting.

October 11. Bulgarians invade Servia.

Oct. 17 to November 22. Servians gradually pushed out of their country and through Montenegro and Albania to the Adriatic.

November 4. Navigation of the Danube opened to the Austrians.

November 30. First Berlin to Constantinople express via Vienna and Belgrade established.

December 8. Franco-British and Servian forces pushed back over the frontier into Greece.

January 11, 1916. Austrians capture Montenegro stronghold of Mount Loytchen.

January 12. Austrians occupy Cettinje, capital of Montenegro.

February 26. Austrians occupy Durazzo, Albania, driving out Italians who concentrate at Valona.

April 15-30. Franco-British force at Salonika reaches 550,000. Servians to the number of 150,000, refitted at Corfu with French aid, joins this force.

May 26. Bulgarians enter Greek territory and take several Greek forts with permission of that government. This brings Greek relations with the Entente Powers to a climax.

ITALY. (Italy signified disapproval of the purposes of the war by notifying Austria immediately upon the presentation of that nation's ultimatum to Servia that a war growing out of such demands would be regarded by Italy as releasing her from further association with the Triple Alliance. Thereafter, for eight months, the final position of Italy was in doubt.)

April 16, 1915. Italian mobilization results in putting 1,200,000 first-line soldiers under arms.

April 24. Rapid departure of German families from Italy.

April 29. Italy reported to have agreed with Allies as to terms upon which she will enter war.

May 19. Italy issues Green Book, claiming that Austria has broken faith.

May 20. Chamber of Deputies by a vote of 407 to 74 confers power on the government to make war. Complete overthrow of Gioletti and the pro-German party.

May 21. Senate concurs in action of the Chamber of Deputies.

May 22. General mobilization ordered.

May 23. War declared upon Austro-Hungary.

May 26. Italian forces occupy Austrian territory along the frontier from Switzerland to the Adriatic. King Victor Emmanuel assumes command and goes to the front.

May 29. Large Italian army trying to cross the Isonzo River. Italians advancing and Austrians retreating throughout the province of Trent.

June 13. Italians bombarding the fortifications of Gorizia twenty-seven miles from Trieste.

June 19. Rome reports that the Italian armies now occupy twice as much territory in the Irredenta as Austria offered Italy for remaining neutral.

June 24. Austrians heavily reënforced assume the offensive.

June 28. Italians enter territory west of Lake Garda, crossing mountains more than 8,000 feet high.

July 7. Heavy fighting at the bridge head of Gorizia.

July 16. Italians heavily fortifying all positions captured from the Austrians.

July 25. Austrian General Staff evacuates Gorizia.

July 27. The fighting along the Isonzo reported to be one of the fiercest and most sanguinary struggles of the war.

September 3. Serious Italian repulses at Tolmino.

September 22. Italians drive Austrians from the Dolomite Valley.

September 23. Austrians evacuate Monte Coston after a defence of several months.

October 23. Italians, still on the offensive, gain ground in the Carso region and the Tyrol.

October 29. Austrians still hold Gorizia bridge head against Italian attacks.

November 16. Italian bombardment of Gorizia begun, doing heavy damage.

December 5-11. Repeated unsuccessful Italian attacks on defenders of Gorizia.

December 17. Austrian defences at Gorizia in ruins but defenders still hold out.

January 16, 1916. Austrians make heavy gains near Oslavia, taking many Italian prisoners.

February 3-11. Heavy fighting around Gorizia, but winter conditions in the mountains stopped operations for some weeks.

March 14. Italians resume offensive along the Isonzo front.

April 19. Italians capture the summit of the Col di Lana, after exploding what were said to be the greatest mines used in the war.

April 26. Austrians reoccupy part of the Col di Lana—Austrian concentration seems to indicate a great offensive soon.

May 13. Austrian offensive begun southeast of Trent. Italians abandon advanced positions, losing many prisoners.

May 19. Austrians enter Italian territory.

June 5-10. Austrian offensive reaches climax with the recovery of 300 square miles of lost territory and the capture of 300 square miles of Italian territory.

June 25. Italian offensive begun with 500,000 fresh troops and 1,500 big guns.

July 1. Italians report recovery of one-third of all territory lost in the Austrian drive.

July 22. Italians successful in the northern Dolomite region with heavy captures of prisoners and guns.

ENORMOUS NEW FRENCH GUN USED IN BATTLE OF THE SOMME

Paris Zeppelin victims buried by the state. A state funeral was given the men and women who perished in the Zeppelin raid on Paris January 29, 1916. Troops lined the streets with reversed arms, and all Paris was represented, the concourse of mourners being, it is said, the largest that ever took part in a state funeral

CHAPTER X

WHEN the gray-green flood of German soldiers was pouring into France over every railroad and highway, through violated neutral lands as well as by more legitimate routes, all Paris, dazed by the inroad through Belgium and the sudden collapse of such fortresses as Liége and Namur, said hopefully, "Look at Verdun. She will hold out!"

Well. She did hold out. At the end of the second year of the war she is still holding out, drenched with blood of heroes on both sides; the ground for miles around plowed deep with shell pits and planted with the bodies of tens of thousands of the gallant dead. She holds out in grim defiance though she never really barred the way to Paris, for in those dark days of August the German army ignored the grim gray fortress hewn in the solid rock and, leaving it to one side, marched on its errand doomed to disappointment. The battle of the Marne sent the invaders flying back, but what they had done proved the worthlessness of Verdun as a fortress. As a name, however, to designate the fifty miles or more of trenches which stretch out right and left from the ancient town and

fortress in the rock, it has become symbolical of the most persistent assault and the most dogged resistance known to military history.

Fate plays curious pranks with cities as well as with men. Richmond might have gone down into history merely as the chief source of the smoker's blessings had not Jefferson Davis made it the capital of the Confederacy, and compelled General Lee to defend it even to the ultimate sacrifice of the Confederate army. Verdun, until the German Crown Prince gave it immortality by dashing his magnificent legions to pieces against its flame-tipped barriers, was famed chiefly for its manufacture of sugared almonds and other confections much esteemed at French weddings. Long after the war began and German shells were now and then dropping in the streets of the quiet town the confectioners went peacefully on with the manufacture of their "dragees," and even invented a bonboniere, like the shell of a "French 75," which on occasion would vociferously explode with a scattering hail of sugared almonds.

The old fortress of Verdun, its citadel, was built in the days before engineers understood that soft earth is a more stubborn resistant than solid rock. It was built by Vauban, most famous of military engineers, whose works have been relegated to oblivion by modern high explosives. The citadel of Verdun he hewed out of a beetling cliff, blasting out redoubts and battlements, long corridors, barracks, and assembly halls. Even an elevator was added by later engineers. But if that seemed something of an oddity in a fort its presence was atoned for by the fact that when war really befel Verdun all the guns were taken out of the old citadel. Their place was not there but far off in the trenches miles away from the city. The triumph of Vauban's engineering skill, in face of the German "Jack Johnsons" was condemned to more peaceful uses. Its impregnable galleries sheltered the wounded brought in from the real front. Its casements bricked up formed excellent ovens where bread by the thousand loaves was baked for

German forces in France and Belgium. Naturally the Germans desired to do away with this ever-present menace at Verdun. Economically Verdun was of tremendous value to the Germans, for its possession would buttress their hold upon the Basin of Briey, in which is concentrated 90 per cent. of the iron production of France. All this

General view of the Hall of Mechanics in the Grand Palace in Paris. This hall is devoted to machinery for one purpose only—the relieving of human suffering and the restoration of activity to disabled limbs. The machinery is highly ingenious, and special forms are provided for arms, hands, feet, legs, spine and in fact every part of the body.

the army. Its corridors served for offices for the administration of the town and as storage places for the munitions of war to be employed elsewhere.

Though we shall find that as the fortunes of war varied so varied the expressions of the belligerents as to the value of Verdun; it is in fact a place of great strategic importance. As a guard to Paris it, with its fifty miles of encircling forts and trenches, blocks the most direct road from Germany. As a menace to Germany it is the French post closest to Metz. The reduction of Metz would make necessary the withdrawal of all the

production has been in the possession of Germany since the first invasion of France, and German writers declare that without it the great works of Krupp at Essen could not be steadily operated. And, finally, had the Germans been able to pierce the French line at Verdun, the Battle of the Marne would have been undone, the way to Paris would again have been open, and the British in the west might have been cut off from the French line in the east. General Joffre saw the supreme importance of the Verdun position— not particularly the fort—when on the night of the Battle of the Marne he sent a telegram to General Pétain ordering that the positions on the Meuse be held at any cost and declaring that "any commander who shall give an order to retreat shall be court martialled."

Throughout the early months of the war the importance of Verdun seemed to impress the Germans hardly adequately. They had almost enveloped it in their attack from the clusive as was all the bloodshed along that long half-subterranean line that extended from the English Channel to the borders of Switzerland. The hope of the Germans was to reach and cut the one railroad line which connected Verdun with the rest of France from which new troops and supplies for the beleaguered fortress must be drawn. Though

American volunteers off to join the French Army

Copyright by Underwood & Underwood

side of the Woevre which gave them possession of St. Mihiel, their point of farthest penetration into France on the eastern front. But then, when perhaps its reduction might have been easy, they passed by and devoted their attention to other points. To keep Verdun isolated and idle rather than to capture or reduce it seemed to be the purpose of their strategy in the last months of 1914. In the Forest of Argonne on the other side of the town the Crown Prince's army kept up for a whole year the effort to cut off the town and isolate it from the rest of France, but the effort was half-hearted and without result. This fighting partook of the nature of all the trench fighting in France, and was as inconclusive

balked in this design the Germans did advance their heavy artillery to a point so near the road that it became unsafe to rely upon it alone. Then the marvelous highways of France came into play and rendered possible that amazing organization of motor transportation which will be described later.

Nor were the French much more successful in their efforts to dislodge the Germans from their positions before Verdun. In their great autumn offensive of 1915 they had launched savage attacks upon the Germans in the Argonne and Artois districts. Some ground was won, particularly in the Argonne, but the vital German position, the salient at St. Mihiel was unshaken. The British took the town of Loos with a loss of some 50,000 men, and the French gained a few yards here, and a mile or two there in the trenches of the Argonne, but that was about the net result of the Allied drive. A detailed map of the positions shows scarcely any discernible difference in the position of the belligerents before and after the effort.

It had been expected that the Allies would renew their drive in the early spring. But the Germans forestalled them by beginning a savage frontal attack on Verdun in February, 1916. It is difficult to comprehend the reasons which impelled the German General Staff to order this attack and to maintain it for months with the loss of hundreds of thousands of men. As time wore on and the chances of success grew less favorable the German press began to depreciate the importance of Verdun,

Only the soldiers laugh in France. The civil population is staid and sedate under the shadow of the national calamity, but the soldiers, constantly in danger of death, are as jolly as Frenchmen are wont to be

Big shells for Verdun. One of the many ammunition depots in the rear of the French lines at Verdun

and declare that continuance of the attack was dictated only by consideration of the moral effect its abandonment might have upon public sentiment in other lands. Military authorities in France, too, underestimated the worth of Verdun and seriously contemplated ordering its evacuation. But in time it became a symbol. The German people had been educated to believe that its capture was the certain assurance of victory, and the army dared not abandon the attack. To France the holding of Verdun was the army's supreme test and the army would not shirk it.

Whatever their motives the Germans launched their historic attack upon the Verdun positions on the 21st of February, 1916. The Crown Prince was himself in nominal command. Though there was growing doubt as to the military capacity of this eldest son of the

Kaiser, political considerations made it imperative that to him should fall the honor of some great victory —and no German then doubted that Verdun was to be the scene of a great national triumph. There was every reason for Germany to anticipate success. The winter had checked operations in the Russian and Balkan theatres of war, and the veteran troops from those regions were hurriedly brought to join with troops from Ypres, the Somme, and the Aisne. Great guns in tremendous numbers, more than 3,000 according to report, and appalling calibres had been concentrated as early as December, and great piles of shells and bombs were stored at every place along the point where they would be needed. The concentration of the men began in January and for a month or more they were held out of action, abundantly fed and equipped in

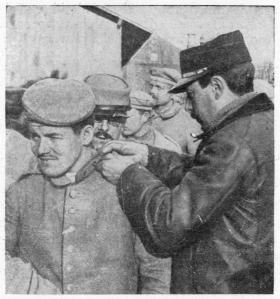

No more fighting for them. German prisoners being inspected by French officers

Copyright by Underwood & Underwood

A French reconnoitring machine with two machine guns joined together on a turret behind the pilot

every way for the triumphant attack which their general confidently expected. An order of the day issued by General von Daimling, found on a German prisoner, announced to his men that the decisive day had come at last, and that their irresistible attack on Verdun would put an immediate end to the war. The plan for the attack which was to produce this tremendous result was that which has become typical in this war—a racking and crushing artillery attack, followed by an assault by infantry. With the French front once broken the Germans expected to close in on Verdun from behind, cutting off the French retreat and annihilating the French army. Had the latter end been attained it would indeed have been a great step toward the conclusion of the war.

Perhaps the French gave no thought to retreat. Nevertheless, the question of how to get their army away should disaster befall, and how to feed it and furnish it with fresh munitions and reënforcements was one of the utmost importance. At the outset there were about 550,000 men in the French army about Verdun, this number rising at times to as many as 750,000. To supply this enormous force there was but one railroad available, and that one at points exposed to the fire of the enemy. The Germans anticipated that the defenders would

there is lacking to the city any railroad. In September, 1914, the Germans took St. Mihiel and cut the railway coming north along the Meuse. On their retreat from the Marne the soldiers of the Crown Prince halted at Montfaucon and Varennes, and their cannon have commanded the Paris-Verdun-Metz Railroad ever since. Save for a crazy, narrow-gauge line wandering along the hill slopes, climbing by impossible grades, Verdun is without rail communication.

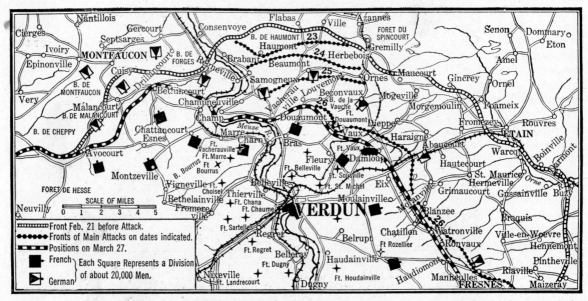

The attack on Verdun.   The German assaults, which began against Verdun on February 21st, continued with fury through the spring and summer unabated

be severely handicapped by this inadequacy of railroad transportation. So they would have been had not the French General Staff recognized the situation and met it by using the marvelous French highways, level and solid as a floor, for the organization of a system of transportation by motor trucks that, by its perfection and efficiency, aroused the admiration of all military critics. The transport service of an army is as important as its strategy or its spirit. In fact, neither can be maintained if there is failure or delay in bringing up reënforcements or munitions. At Verdun the French solved the problem conclusively. Mr. Frank H. Simonds, editor of the New York *Tribune*, who visited Verdun in the midst of the siege, thus describes with convincing vividness the nature and appearance of this transport service·

"To understand the real problem of the defence of Verdun you must realize that

"It was this that made the defence of the town next to impossible. Partially to remedy the defect the French had reconstructed a local highway running from St. Dizier by Bar-le-Duc to Verdun beyond the reach of German artillery. To-day an army of a quarter of a million of men, the enormous parks of heavy artillery, and field guns—everything is supplied by this one road and by motor transport.

"Coming north from St. Dizier we entered this vast procession. Mile after mile the caravan stretched on, fifty miles with hardly a break of a hundred feet between trucks. Paris 'buses, turned into vehicles to bear fresh meat; new motor trucks built to carry thirty-five men and traveling in companies, regiments, brigades; wagons from the hood of which soldiers, bound to replace the killed and wounded of yesterday, looked down upon you, calmly but unsmilingly. From St.

Dizier to Verdun the impression was of that of the machinery by which logs are carried to the saw in a mill. You felt unconsciously, yet unmistakably, that you were looking, not upon automobiles, not upon separate trucks, but upon some vast and intricate system of belts and benches that were steadily, swiftly, surely carrying all this vast material, carrying men and munitions and supplies, everything human and inanimate, to that vast, grinding mill which was beyond the hills, the crushing machine which worked with equal remorselessness upon men and upon things.

"Now and again, too, over the hills came the Red Cross ambulances; they passed you returning from the front and bringing within their carefully closed walls the finished product, the fruits of the

A characteristic snapshot of the Kaiser

"Night came down upon us along the road and brought a new impression. Mile on mile over the hills and round the curves, disappearing in the woods, reappearing on the distant summits of the hills, each showing a rear light that wagged crazily on the horizon, this huge caravan flowed onward, while in the villages and on the hillsides campfires flashed up and the faces or the figures of the soldiers could be seen now clearly and now dimly. But all else was subordinated to the line of moving transports. Somewhere far off at one end of the procession there was battle; somewhere down below at the other end there was peace. There all the resources, the life blood, the treasure in men and in riches of France were concentrating and collect-

day's grinding, or a fraction thereof. And about the whole thing there was a sense of the mechanical rather than the human, something that suggested an automatic, a machine-driven, movement; it was as if an unseen system of belts and engines and levers guided, moved, propelled this long procession upward and ever toward the mysterious front where the knives or the axes or the grinding stones did their work.

ing, were being fed into this motor fleet, which like baskets on ropes was carrying it forward to the end of the line and then bringing back what remained, or for the most part coming back empty, for more—for more lives and more treasure.

"It was full night when our car came down the curved grades into Bar-le-Duc, halted at the corner, where soldiers performed the work of traffic policemen and steadily guided

Colored troops fight for France. Part of a regiment from Tunis, on the march in the Argonne, are on their way to reënforce the defenders of Verdun

the caravan toward the road marked by a canvas sign lighted within by a single candle and bearing the one word, 'Verdun.' All night, too, the rumble of the passing transport filled the air and the little hotel shook with the jar of the heavy trucks, for neither by day nor by night is there a halt in the motor transport, and the sound of this grinding is never low.

"It was little more than daylight when we took the road again, with a thirty-mile drive to Verdun before us. Almost immediately we turned into the Verdun route we met again the caravan of automobiles, of *camions*, as the French say. It still flowed on without break. Now, too, we entered the main road, the one road to Verdun, the road that had been built by the French army against just such an attack as was now in progress. The road was as wide as Fifth Avenue, as smooth as asphalt—a road that, when peace comes, if it ever does, will delight the motorist. Despite the traffic it had to bear, it was in perfect repair, and soldiers in uniform sat by the side breaking stone and preparing metal to keep it so."

Verdun, built on a hill on the bank of the River Meuse, which at this point flows nearly north and south, was surrounded by a circle of higher hills. On the crests of these are perched twenty-four permanent forts, mak-

The rolling kitchen stops for lunch. At the end of a long, hard march hot coffee and hot soup are ready for the men and do much to keep up their morale

A halt in front of Hartmansweilerkopf. A company of the Foreign Legion in Alsace. The high hill in the background is Hartmansweilerkopf, about which the battle has raged at intervals for two years

ing a circle with a five-mile radius and the city for the centre. But it was not about these forts, with one or two exceptions, that the battle raged. By this period of the war it had been too thoroughly demonstrated that fixed fortifications were of but little value, and that a defence only five or six miles from the citadel was no defence whatsoever. Accordingly the true French defence was in three lines of earthworks, with the usual wire entanglements, thrown out eight or ten miles beyond the ring of fixed forts and forming a bow nearly seventy-five miles long from Bourelles, west of Verdun, to Combres far to the southeast. A multitude of little villages were included in this line, and back of it were the twenty-four forts so that the detailed story of the battle, which at the end of eight months is still in progress, is filled with confusing names of localities most of which may well be omitted here. Indeed no detailed nor technical report of that titanic contest is possible. It was a war rather than a battle. In it were involved from first to last not less than 2,000,000 soldiers with such an equipment for war as the world had never before known. At the moment of writing these lines it is still in progress—though momentarily with less activity on the part of the Germans—having lasted eight months without interruption. When the Battle of the

Fourth of July party at the front. Some of the American members of the Legion waiting for their train near Rheims

A view near Verdun. These guns of 240 millimetre calibre are mounted on specially constructed steel cars from which they are fired. Note the curious, mottled way in which they are painted. This is to render them less visible to aerial scouts

Aisne was fought steadily for twenty-two days in 1914 the world wondered, and pointed to it as the longest sustained conflict of modern history—Mukden which determined the issue of the Russo-Japanese War having lasted twenty days, and Gettysburg which saved the Union but three. The Aisne was a drawn battle. Verdun was fought to bar further progress of the Germans toward Paris. So long as that barrier is effective, as it is to-day, it is no drawn battle but a French victory.

The first German attack was directed against the sector dominated by Fort Douaumont. That fort itself, though giving its name to the seven and a half miles of front of

which it was the centre, had been dismantled and its guns mounted in the neighboring trenches. The attack begun soon after sunrise of a bitter winter's morning with a furious fire from the closely packed German batteries. French aviators flying over the enemy's lines declared that it was impossible to note the position of the different batteries, the cannon stood almost wheel to wheel in one continuous line. The shells flying up into the air looked like a salvo of thousands of rockets in some great celebration. But their fall released stifling gases, or the strange fumes that brought floods of tears to the eyes of all who came in contact with them, or liquid fire that burned

A big gun that will never fire a shot. A genius in the French army conceived the idea of building a dummy gun out of papers sent to the soldiers at the front, and the result is shown in the photograph. It looks like a 240 millimetre gun, and concealed in a wood, will be spotted by enemy aviators and will draw many shells from their big guns. But no one will be hurt

and seared every object within reach and refused to be extinguished by any ordinary means. Only the more commonplace shells scattered shrapnel by the thousand or jagged pieces of metal to rend and slay their victims. Over the line of batteries floated a number of captive balloons from which observers telephoned to gunners below directions for the rectification of their aim. No safe post this, for the French gunners and the French aircraft made the balloons their target with frequent fatal effects. "Our first lines were almost levelled by this avalanche of steel" writes one of the French officers. "Trenches, parapets, shelters, no matter how well made, were utterly destroyed."

This end attained, the infantry attack followed. First reconnoitring groups of about fifteen men each, then larger detachments armed with hand grenades, and after them the solid masses of the unapproachable German infantry. In the face of this assault the defenders stood firm. In the crushed and shattered remnants of their trenches, in the craters made by the great shells, they crouched low, working their rifles and their machine guns. Death stalked through both lines. A French soldier in the trenches at Douaumont wrote for the Paris Figaro a description of the fighting that smells of the very explosives and the blood itself. It is violently French, of course, and full of defiance and contempt for the enemy, but as a battle picture it has life and undoubtedly truth:

"Despite the horror of it, despite the

AUX MORTS DE LA GRANDE GUERRE

A LA MEMOIRE
DE
PEUGEOT JULES ANDRÉ
CAPORAL AU 44e RÉGIMENT D'INFANTERIE
MORT POUR LA FRANCE
Le 2 Août 1914
HOMMAGE DE LA NATION

LA PATRIE RECONNAISSANTE

The French government presents a commemorative diploma to the families of French citizens killed in the war. This is a reproduction of the parchment issued in memory of the first Frenchman who fell in the Great War

ceaseless flow of blood, one wants to see. One's soul wants to feed on the sight of the brute Boches falling. I stopped on the ground for hours, and when I closed my eyes I saw the whole picture again. The guns are firing at 200 and 300 yards, and shrapnel is exploding with a crash, scything them down. Our men hold their ground; our machine guns keep to their work, and yet they advance.

"Near me, as I lie in the mud, there is a giant wrapped in one of our uniforms with a steel helmet on his head. He seems to be dead, he is so absolutely still. At a given moment the Boches are quite close to us. Despite the noise of the guns one can hear their oaths and their shouts as they strike. Then the giant next to me jumps up, and with a voice like a stentor shouts "Hier da! Hier da!" Mechanically some of us get up. (My wound, which had been dressed, left me free and I had forgotten.) I was unarmed, and so I struck him with my steel helmet and he dropped, with his head broken. An officer who was passing sees the incident and takes off the man's coat. Below is a German uniform. Where had the spy come from and how had he got there?"

Early in the battle the French were driven from their first line of defence. Their own writers insist that this was the plan of strategy previously determined upon. They compare it to the retreat from Mons and the ultimate halt to win a victory upon the Marne. The theory sounds like an afterthought,

One of the villages on the environs of Verdun showing a parade of newly arrived French troops prior to relieving their comrades on the outskirts of the village

and it is vastly more probable that the first four days at Verdun were in fact a series of well-earned victories for the Germans. At any rate, in that period they had driven the defenders from their first line, had taken the villages of Haumont, Brabant, and La Wavrille. Every foot of their advance was savagely contested, for the French were fighting to hold the foe back until their own reserves could come up.

Douaumont, the immediate German objective—village and fort both—had been pounded out of any semblance of form. It was no longer a fortress, but a mass of shattered masonry. It was no longer a little typical French village, with its streets of closely built stone houses, its church, public square, and cheerful cafés. It was a wilderness, a ghastly skeleton of a town peopled only by corpses. Yet such as it was the Germans coveted it —or rather were impelled with a fierce purpose to make that the point of piercing the French

Thousands of cases of 75 mm. shells are stored here, but not for long for ammunition at Verdun disappears as rapidly as snow and rain

A laden ambulance passing through Verdun on the way to the base hospital

lines. Saturday and Sunday, the 25th and 26th, the struggle around this point became more violent and sanguinary. "The enemy no longer count their sacrifices," said one of the French reports of the day, chronicling a commonplace, for at no time during the war did the Germans count the price in human life they paid for a position they were determined to take. And as a result a party of Brandenburgers did cut their way into the ruins of the old fort and the word went out from the General Staff to all the world that "the armored fort of Douaumont, the cornerstone o' the French defence of Verdun, has been carried by a Brandenburg regiment." But the triumph was for but a little while. Sweeping

back into action the French captured the village and enveloped the Bavarians helplessly imprisoned in a useless fort. For the next week the tide of battle swept back and forth with now the Germans, then the French, in possession of the group of ruins

French infantrymen spending the night round a fire in a roofless church in the environs of Verdun

Dismounted German Hussars hold the first line trenches

intermissions the fighting went on unabated until June 7th when, after a particularly savage attack, and a bombardment of almost incredible ferocity, the fort fell. A document found on a German prisoner showed that General Falkenhayn (then chief of the German General Staff) had ordered that the fort must be taken at whatever hazard and however great the cost. Every engine of warfare—gas, liquid fire, and lachrymal bombs—was employed, and the assailants came on in rows to be laid on the field like swathes from the scythe of the reaper. So gallant was the defence made by Major Raynal, its leader, that in the midst of it

called Douaumont. Month succeeded month, and as late as August the armies were still fighting savagely over the scene of desolation and death.

Somewhat east of Douaumont lay the fort and village of Vaux. Not as powerful a fortress as the former, even in the days when both were formidable, this post early attracted the German attacks. Success and failure alternated for several days. Tens of thousands of lives on either side were sacrificed for what was in effect but a single link in an armor of defence. With occasional

he was made a commander of the Legion of Honor. But the next day the fort fell for lack of food and water, and the gallant Major was sent to a German internment camp. It is pleasant to learn that the Crown Prince himself was so impressed by the heroism of the defence that he gave orders that Major Raynal's sword should not be taken from him.

Photo by Paul Thompson

A Red Cross depot in ruins

An inconclusive battle lasting eight months, and in which
more than 500,000 men have
been sacrificed, is unique in
the history of warfare. But
that, in a phrase, is the story
of the Battle of Verdun. During the first two weeks the
Germans seemed to be carrying all before them, but the
fact was that the French were
retiring from weak positions
to stronger ones, and when
confronted by the latter the
Germans stopped. Only the
capture of Vaux was added to
their earlier laurels as the
months rolled by.

Undoubtedly the salvation
of Verdun was largely due to
the perfection of the new
"French 75s" a type of artil-
lery hardly known at the beginning of the
war when the big "Busy Berthas" of Krupp
and the great Austrian howitzers held first
place as engines of death. A correspondent
of the London *Times* visiting the field at
Verdun gives this lively description of a battery of these guns in action:

"When I asked the General to be shown a
battery of 75s every face in the group of

A street in Verdun after six months' bombardment

officers beamed. Winding through the woods
was a tiny trail, and this we followed until we
emerged into a little clearing. A look dis-
closed the hiding place of a battery. I was
escorted by the young Captain in charge into
the nest of one of these guns. Squatted com-
placently on its haunches, its alert little
nose peered expectantly out of a curtain
of brush. If there ever was a weapon which

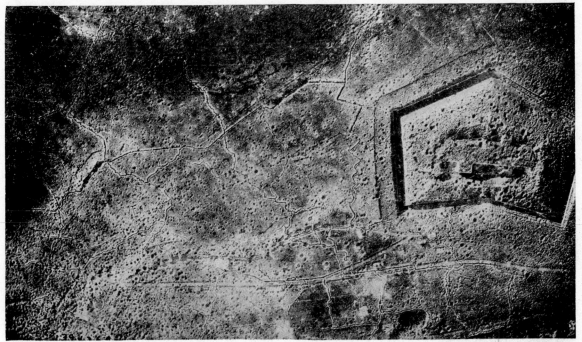

Douaumount village photographed from a French aeroplane flying at a great altitude

What a soldier sees through a trench periscope

"With a speed of fire of thirty shells to the minute and with a well-trained crew serving it with clockwork regularity, it resembles a machine gun rather than a field piece in action. So exquisite is the adjustment of the recoil that a coin or even a glass of water can be placed on the wheel while in action without being jarred off.

"In one of the Russian battles one of their batteries fired 525 rounds to the gun in a single day, which seemed to me at that time an extraordinary rate of fire. When I mentioned this to the Captain, he laughingly replied, 'I have fired from this (four-gun) battery 3,100 rounds of shells in forty-five minutes.' I listened to him in amazement. 'How long do your guns last at that rate?' I asked him, for the theory before the war was that a field piece did not have a life exceeding 8,000 to 10,000 rounds of fire. The officer placed his hand affectionately on the gun that we were inspecting. 'This is a brand-new gun which I have just received,' he said. 'The one whose place it has taken had fired more than 30,000 shells and still was not entirely finished.' Then he added, 'You are surprised at my speed of fire, but there have been 75s in this war that have fired 1,600 rounds in a single day.' From the guns he took me to his magazine and showed me tier upon tier of brightly polished, high-explosive, and shrapnel shells lying ready for use."

had a personality it is surely this gun. Other field guns seem to me to be cynical and sinister, but this gun, like the French themselves, has nothing malevolent or morose about it. It is serious, to be sure, but its whole atmosphere is one of cheerful readiness to serve. Its killing is a part of its impersonal duty, as indeed one feels to be the case with the clean, gentlemanly soldiers of France. They kill to save France, not because they have the lust of slaughter.

A French device for breaking through wire entanglements

As the weeks wore on the determination to hold Verdun to the end became a fixed thought in the mind of the French people. Whatever of value it had had at first as a strategic point was now discounted by line after line of new defences constructed in the rear by the French to receive their troops and beat back the enemy in case the main Verdun line should be carried. But the French were obsessed by the idea that that line never should be carried. It was a dead town. Its homes and shops were mere masses of ruins. Its Place d'Armes was desolate and abandoned though little scarred by shell fire. It was there that the Crown Prince was to have received the surrender of the town at the hands of the defeated French general. There the Kaiser was to stand and decorate once again his favorite son. The square is there but neither Kaiser nor Crown Prince has yet visited it, and over it the tricolor still waves defiantly.

Another view through the trench periscope

For the last two months of the Battle of Verdun the persistence of the German attacks in the face of their tremendous losses perplexed the military world. To strategists it seemed that whatever value the spot had ever possessed was gone, with the time during which the French had been permitted to prepare new lines of defence should these be broken. Yet day after day and week after week the solid ranks of German infantry were hurled against such points as Dead Man's Hill (L'Homme Mort) or the Wood of the Crows, or Fort Vaux. They changed their attack to the opposite side of the Meuse, but found, there, too, that the French had erected such works that no military power could possibly dislodge them. By the 9th of April the regularity with which the French repelled every attack had convinced all the world outside of Germany that Verdun would never be taken. From that time on the operations, except for the storming of

"One of Krupp's"

VERDUN IN RUINS PHOTOGRAF

The portion of Verdun around the little open square, where

YPRES, PHOTOGRAPHED FROM A FRENCH AEROPLANE

The Grande Place, where only a ring of shrubbery is seen, has suffered most from German shells

A big grenade of the rocket type

Fort Vaux, took on the character of a siege, with only occasional attacks. Reluctantly the German war authorities were compelled to inform the people that the Verdun attack which had been expected to end the war had ended only in failure. Perhaps it was to defer or to minimize the effect of this confession that a pretence of activity against the French lines was kept up until long after the war entered upon its third year.

The French had one great incentive to the desperate defence of Verdun of which the non-military world had no knowledge. The war had now been in progress for eighteen months or more, and the greatest flaw in the strategy of the Allies had been the failure of systematic coöperation. The Allies' fronts were far separated, one from the other, without those close communications such as would make complete unity of action possible. The Teutons were surrounded—a situation which has its terrors to the non-military mind, but is not without its advantages. The belligerent thus situated has shorter lines of communication than its foes, and, unless attacked simultaneously on all sides can shift its troops from a front not menaced

The defense against modern "stink-pots." The purpose of modern German asphyxiating gas and medieval Chinese stink-pots is the same—to confuse and overpower the enemy so that an attack can be made upon him before he recovers

to one which the enemy is assaulting. This Germany had done systematically since the beginning of the war. Her legions were rushed from France to save East Prussia in 1914. They were hurried from East Prussia after Hindenburg's victory down into Galicia to rescue Austro-Hungary from the Russian drive. They sped back to Flanders to check the French effort to flank Von Kluck's right wing and cut his communications. Outnumbered as a whole by their enemies, the Teutons by virtue of their shorter lines were usually able to outnumber them at any particular point of attack.

Late in the winter of 1916 a conference of the Allied leaders undertook to provide for more perfect coöperation between their armies. Great drives were planned for the spring by the French, Italian, and Russian armies each in its own field of operation, and all to be conducted simultaneously. This menacing program Germany thought might be headed off by a brilliant success at Verdun. Even if complete success could not be won, a continuance of the savage attacks there would tie up so great a part of the French army as to compel the abandonment of the

A German setting a "star light" for use at night

The revival of the steel helmet. French soldiers wearing head armor of a pattern almost identical with that of helmets worn in England after the Norman conquest. They are highly efficient in deflecting rifle bullets and shrapnel bullets

Photo by Paul Thompson

The shattered town of Verdun, photographed from the ruins of the Bishop's Palace

drive planned for the more western battle area, or at least cut down the number of the men whom the French could safely devote to that purpose. If this were indeed the reason for the pertinacity of the German attack at Verdun those who accepted it were misled. Even while the fighting at that point was at its fiercest the Anglo-French offensive was launched July 1, 1916. It was at first directed against the German lines on both sides of the Somme opposite Péronne. At that moment the Russians had just taken Czernowitz and were resistlessly rolling on toward Lemberg. Farther south the Italians were pushing into the Trentino and their guns were thundering down upon Gorizia, destined soon to fall. In the Balkans the British, French, Italians, and Serbians were massing at Salonika preparatory to a drive northward through Servia to the Austrian line. On no single frontier could the Teuton armies gain any rest. From no line or sector could the Kaiser withdraw any troops to succor a spot more menaced, for every foot of the

German fire rockets illuminating an enemy position

View of Verdun showing the bridge over the Meuse

long Teutonic line needed all the force that could be exerted there to withstand the pressure of the enemy. At no time during the war did the outlook for the Central Powers seem so desperate. It had its result in the determination of Roumania to join the Allied cause, and the virtual surrender of the Greek government to Allied influence to which the people of that kingdom had already given their active sympathy.

Nevertheless the Germans continued their bloody and seemingly suicidal assaults at Verdun until the historian is tempted to say, as General Bosquet said of the Charge of the Light Brigade, "It is magnificent, but it is not war."

It is proper, however, to say here that the Germans had not, up to August, 1916, conceded that the capture of Verdun was impossible. They not only hoped for ultimate success, but insisted that the French were losing more in the defence than they in the attack, and finally that the continuance of the battle was worth all it cost them by diverting the French attention from other fronts.

The French nation, however,

never felt any apprehension of the fall of Verdun after the middle of May, 1916. The

The German "flammen-werfer" utilizes exactly the same ingredients as the Greek used in "Greek Fire" in the defence of Constantinople in 1453

Swiss troops guarding their frontier against transgression by belligerents

stern defiance "They shall not pass," which the army had adopted as a watchword in the early days of the assault, was accepted thereafter as the mere statement of a truism, abundantly demonstrated and easily maintained.

The Allied drive of the Franco-British forces in Picardy, which began July 1st, did not for a time produce the effective results which the nations involved had hoped for. Great Britain had at last proclaimed herself fully prepared. To the volunteer force

French took up the line near Montauban, and extended it to the southward across a similar country, intersected by the River Somme, which their armies had to span. The whole country was dotted with little villages whose stone walls and houses made favorable defences against the attacking forces. The names of the hapless hamlets still exist, but they themselves are now but mere heaps of ruins. French they were, but French shells had to rend them out of all

Verdun aviation camp as seen from a French aeroplane

raised by Lord Derby were added the conscripts recruited and trained by Earl Kitchener. For the first time the store of munitions was plenteous, a tribute to the efficiency of Lloyd George. Sir Douglas Haig led the British forces, General Foch the French, while supreme command over both was exercised by General Joffre. The line on which the British operated may be called the Bapaume line, after the little town of that name. It was about eleven and a half miles long, extending over a slightly rolling country, plentifully sprinkled with villages and orchards. When the armies first settled upon it like a blight the land was covered with wheat fields, poppies, and beets. The

semblance of form that the Germans who tenanted them might be driven out.

At the beginning the British carried all before them. Pozieres, Contralmaison, and Longueval fell to their advancing hosts. The Germans were strong in their defence. In clumps of woodland, in ruined houses, and stone barns they hid machine guns and trench mortars. But this resistance was beaten down by the cannonade. Germans were buried alive, in their dugouts and cellars, by the explosion of the monster shells which made a mountain where there had been a cellar, or a crater where there had been a hill. At Montauban the Teutons had such a network of trenches, traverses, redoubts, and communications, all guarded by barbed wire, that no infantry could have assaulted it and lived. What the British shells did to it is vividly described by Philip Gibbs, a war correspondent:

"It was the most frightful convulsion of the earth that the eyes of man could see. The bombardment of the British guns tossed

must lie buried there. But some had been left in spite of the upheaval of the earth around them, and into some of these I crept down, impelled by the strong, grim spell of those little dark rooms below where German soldiers lived only a few days ago.

"The little square rooms were fitted up with relics of German officers and men. Tables were strewn with papers. On wooden

Brave firemen fighting a fire lighted by incendiary shells in Verdun

all these earthworks into vast rubbish heaps and made this ground a vast series of shell craters so deep and so broad that it is like a field of extinct volcanoes. The ground rose and fell in enormous waves of brown earth, so that standing above one crater I saw before me these solid billows with thirty feet of slopes stretching away like a sea frozen after a great storm.

"The British must have hurled hundreds if not thousands of shells from their heaviest howitzers and long-range guns into this stretch of fields. Even many of the dugouts going thirty feet below the earth and strongly timbered and cemented had been choked with the masses of earth so that many dead bodies

bedsteads lay blue-gray overcoats. Wine bottles, photograph albums, furry haversacks, boots, belts, and kits of every kind all had been tumbled together by the British soldiers who had come here after the first rush to the German trenches and searched for men in hiding. In one of the dugouts I stumbled against something and fumbled for my matches. When I struck a light I saw in a corner of the room a German who lay curled up with his head on his arms as though asleep. I did not stay to look at his face, but went up quickly, and yet I went down into the others and lingered in one where no corpse lay, because of the tragic spirit that dwelt there and put its spell on me.

"An incident was told me by a kilted Sergeant as he lay wounded. From one of the dugouts came a German officer. He had a wild light in his eyes, and carried a great axe.

"'I surrender,' he said in good English, and in broad Scotch the Sergeant told him if he had an idea of surrendering it would be a good and wise thing to drop his chopper first; but the German officer swung it high, no more swish of bullets, but only a rising of smoke clouds and black dust.

"Longueval was a heap of charred bricks above the ground, but there was still trouble below ground before it was firmly taken. There are many cellars in which the Germans fought like wolves at bay, and down in the darkness of these places men fought savagely, seeing only the glint of each other's eyes and

Photo by Paul Thompson

The village of Vaux after a terrific battle

and it came like a flash past the Sergeant's head. Like a flash also the bayonet did its work.

"While the men were cleaning up the dugouts in the first-line trenches other men pressed on and stormed into Longueval village. The great fires there which I had seen in the darkness died down, and there was only a glow and smoulder of them in the ruins; but the machine guns were still chattering

"In one broken building there were six of them firing through holes in the walls. It was a strong redoubt, sweeping the ground which had once been a roadway and now was a shambles Scottish soldiers rushed the place and flung bombs into it until there was

feeling for each other's throats, unless there were bombs still handy to make a quicker ending.

"It was primitive warfare; cavemen fought like that in such darkness, though not with bombs, which belong to our age."

The French, meantime, fighting farther to the eastward, were meeting with similar successes. Hardecourt, Curlu, Compierre, and Becquincourt fell to their arms. After three days of fighting they held as trophies ten batteries of heavy artillery, many machine guns, and nearly 10,000 prisoners. The British by that time had 6,000 prisoners, and the captive host increased rapidly day by

Collecting the booty left behind by the Russians in trenches captured from them by the Germans

day. A correspondent who visited the French lines July 9th gives this description of its advanced position near Peronne:

"As far as the eye can see the view is utterly the same: utterly monotonous, nothing but desolate slopes that once were a

The skeleton work of an underground bomb-proof shelter

thickly populated French countryside. The complete inhumanity of outlook strikes one tremendously. Here two great armies are at death grips, yet apart from the incessant tumult of cannonade and the never-ending rows of little smoke clouds—new ones forming before the preceding ones have time to melt—one might be thousands of miles from civilization. Our maps are of little assistance. Here should be Feuillers, there Flaucourt, farther on Assevilliers, but one can distinguish nothing save heaps of blackened stones that appear through the glasses. Even the roads have been swept away by the bombardment. Nothing but ditch-like trench lines mark the presence of humans.

"Suddenly voices cried: 'Look over there, you can see soldiers.' About half a mile before us one sees groups of men like ants working busily on the hillside. Through the glasses one sees that they are sheltering themselves with extraordinary care. Some have strange oblong shields like the ancient Roman legionaries. Others are grouped under a kind of casemate on wheels whose roof touches the ground in front rising in a curve behind to give room for the workers. Still others hide behind a ripple of ground or hillocks.

"All are working furiously with picks and shovels. I have been told that the British losses have been heightened by an utter disregard of danger. Even when not engaged in attacks our Allies seem still not to realize

Officers' quarters in an underground bomb-proof dugout

the necessity of unremitting caution. But the French have learned the lesson that Verdun hammered home—that the best soldier is he who regards his life as belonging to France, something precious, never to be risked save when sheer necessity demands it. That, combined with the magnificent artillery service, is the reason why the French losses in this battle have been less than half—I speak from intimate knowledge—those in any previous French offensive in proportion to the number of troops engaged."

It must not be thought that the Germans failed in any degree to oppose the Anglo-French advance with equal gallantry. The assailants won not a foot of ground without paying the price. After the first successful rush of the British, continuing for five days, further advance on that section of the line was checked and the Germans took the counter offensive. They did not, however, regain any of the lost territory, nor were they able to check the French who advanced steadily though slowly in the direction of Peronne. But the stubborn German resistance had compelled a deadlock on all but four and one-half out of the twenty and one-half miles of battlefront. By the 1st of August German writers were declaring that the Battle of the Somme, as this whole operation had come to be known, was a failure, and had degenerated into mere trench warfare. At the moment their contention was well founded, but

later activity, in August and September, of which this volume cannot treat in detail, carried the tricolor again triumphantly forward. But even at that the announcement of the German military authorities that they had prepared new defensive positions back of, and quite as strong as, their main line, gave

A busy scene in a trench dugout before Verdun

French soldiers engage in field sports behind lines after fighting in two great Verdun battles

little promise that the Allied drive would result in the early expulsion from France of the invaders. Indeed the determination of the Teutons to hold their ground, not for weeks only but indefinitely, impressed every observer. A correspondent of the New York *Times*, Mr. Cyril Brown, writes from the field on this subject thus:

"It is worthy of notice that Germany's defensive fight against England, the 'hunger war,' is being carried right up the trenches. Every arable square inch in this part of France in German hands which I have seen is under cultivation, and promises a bumper crop of rye, oats, wheat, and barley, little damaged by the Battle of the Somme except immediately back of the trenches and about the villages which are under heavy fire. French civilians were already busy getting in the harvest, ably assisted by the German reserves,

and it was a paradoxical sight to pass for miles American harvesters, reapers, and binders, and motor threshing machines, working peacefully within the roar and range of the guns.

"Still another phase of the food war is to be seen here at the front. The aristocratic old Colonel showed me part of his regimental piggeries, ten very fat grunting hogs, so busy eating that they paid no attention to the correspondents or the French shells howling overhead. The titled swineherd told me that each German company at the front now has a troop of ten hogs to eat up its food scraps. Efficiency could go no further.

"The penultimate front and its immediate rear are in general more important than the first-line trenches for sizing up the present condition and the prospects of the modern battle. Here the most significant fact was the right of the 'shiller' divisions be-

Observation post on the first line at L'Homme Mort (Dead Man's Hill)

Photo by Paul Thompson

All that is left of a trench after the "curtain of fire" has descended upon it

hind the front—the uniformed laborers engaged in laying line after line of field fortifications, digging and delving as if against time. For the Germans, while not admitting the necessity, are, nevertheless, preparing to defend every foot of French soil by a stand every few hundred yards or so.

"I walked down a narrow, winding pathway through a jungle of underbrush full of infantry reserves. It was the strangest gypsy colony I had seen on any front. The men were living in galvanized zinc sheds, semi-cylinders about ten feet in diameter, easily transportable, quickly set up, absolutely rainproof, and resembling miniature models of the Zeppelin hangars. Eight men could sleep beneath each zinc dome.

"At first blush there seems to be little to choose between the locked foes. A longer study of the great battle front from all angles tends to correct this impression, and warrants

Photo by Paul Thompson
Monument to those who fell in 1870 at Verdun, in the garden of the Bishops Palace at Verdun

the opinion that the margin of Teuton supremacy on the ground is small, but adequate for all practical purposes, while in the air it is still smaller, but enough to turn the very slow scales of battles. If the Teutons can maintain this margin of safety—and I saw no reason here for believing they could not —they have ultimate victory in the Battle of the Somme clinched."

When the second year of the war closed the Battle of the Somme was still raging and bade fair to equal the Battle of Verdun in its duration and the sacrifice of human life. Like that contest it promised nothing decisive for the year 1916.

Horrifying though the sacrifice of human life has been it is only too evident that many more years of war must be fought before either belligerent will be crushed by loss of life alone. Signs of suffering are many, of exhaustion few. The Austrians, it is true, have manifested

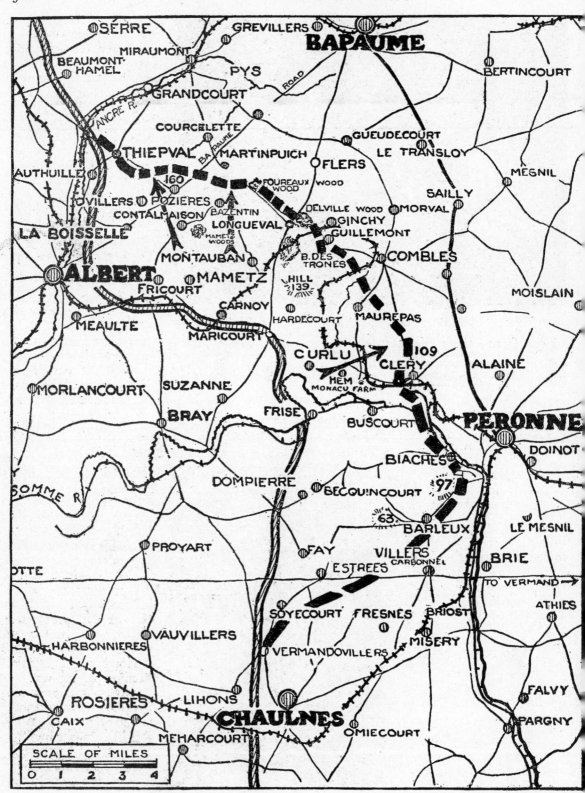

Progress made by Anglo-French forces in the Battle of the Somme after six weeks' fighting shown by broken line

How the French artillery batteries before Verdun devastate Hun columns

the Allies' effective forces, the Teutonic losses are estimated at about 1,750,-000 of which 1,000,000 are chargeable against the army rolls of the Germans alone. Though relatively less than the losses of the Allies, this loss, in proportion to the total strength of the two belligerents, is actually greater. Competent statisticians estimate the Teutonic loss as 10 per cent. of their total fighting force, and that of the Allies as about 7 per cent. For the whole war from its beginning to September, 1916, the Allies are believed to have lost 10,000,000 and the Germans 8,000,000 men, not all permanently, as about 50 per cent. of those wounded or missing are returned to the ranks.

weakness by calling boys below and men above normal military age to the colors. But the prodigious slaughter in the German and French lines does not seem to have checked the steady oncoming of new fighting forces. The Germans declare that the French are "bled white," that the nation is obliterated, but France neither admits it nor manifests the irreparable loss to the most observant visitor. Conservative estimates put the losses of the Allies in the period including the operations around Verdun and the Battle of the Somme at about these figures:

French	400,000
British	400,000
Italians	200,000
Russians	1,000,000

With approximately 2,000,000 thus struck from

Restoring a maimed foot to usefulness. France has taken over for military uses the magnificent Grand Palais, in Paris, where so many exhibitions have been held, and the upper floors are devoted entirely to hospital treatment for convalescent soldiers

French poilus eating behind the lines at Verdun

CHRONOLOGY OF PERIOD TREATED IN CHAPTER X

(The German attack upon Verdun, beginning February 21, 1916, was still in progress at the close of the second year of the war, August 1, 1916. At the latter date it appeared that success could not possibly crown the German efforts. In all probably 750,000 men were put out of action in this prodigious conflict. Begun originally by Germany to assure her control of the iron mines of Lorraine, and to capture a French railroad, the attack came ultimately to be pressed mainly in order to give the Crown Prince a chance to win a great triumph. Verdun was defended by the French less for its strategic value than because its abandonment would be heralded throughout the world as a crushing defeat to the Allied cause.)

February 21. After three days' bombardment 300,000 Germans under the Crown Prince attack French trenches west of the Meuse.

February 25. Germans advance over a twenty-mile front on both sides of the Meuse where they capture part of Fort de Douaumont and then lose it.

March 30. Germans capture Malancourt.

March 31. German night attack completes capture of village of Vaux, which, on March 11th, had been announced as the capture of the Fort de Vaux.

April 3. French in counter-attack retake part of Vaux village.

April 5. Germans capture Haucort, west of the Meuse.

April 8. French withdraw from Bethincourt, west of the Meuse.

April 9. Germans make a general attack over twenty-mile front on both sides of the river.

April 30. Germans make fierce but unsuccessful assault against Dead Man's Hill, west of the Meuse.

May 5 and 6. Fierce bombardment and capture of French trenches on north side of Hill 304, west of the Meuse.

May 8. French lose more trenches at Hill 304, and 1,300 prisoners.

May 21. French recover Haudromont quarries, east of Meuse.

May 22. French recapture part of Fort Douaumont.

May 24. Germans take Cumières, west of Meuse, and again occupy Fort Douaumont.

June 2. Germans begin a general assault on Fort de Vaux, five miles northeast of Verdun City.

June 6. Germans occupy Fort de Vaux, but take few unwounded prisoners.

June 12. Germans penetrate advance positions on Hill 321, four miles from Verdun.

June 15. French win at Le Mort Homme and Caillette Wood.

June 22. French recover ground between Fumin and Chenois Woods and Germans are repulsed at Hill 321.

July 1-29. Germans gain footing at Thiaumont work, Damloup redoubt, and Hills 304, 295, Le Mort Homme, and 265, only to be excluded by the French with great slaughter. Germans remove 300,000 men for service on the Somme and the great Verdun offensive comes to a deadlock, temporary or final.

(The Franco-British offensive, which began July 1, 1916, north and south of the Somme, is directed against German railway communications. Its ultimate purpose is to force the retirement of the Germans from France. As late as September it was still in progress and almost uniformly successful along its line. At that time more than 150 square miles of French territory had been redeemed.)

July 1. Franco-British offensive begins north and south of the Somme after a bombardment by the British of the whole front from Ypres to the Somme for five days, interspersed by night raids with the taking of prisoners.

July 2-10. British take Fricourt, Ovillers, and La Boisselle, and reach Contalmaison; the French capture five towns on the way to Péronne, cut the railway to Chaulnes, and take Hill 97 overlooking Péronne.

July 11-12. British and French casualties placed at 3,000; Germans at 150,000. British advance through Trones Wood, leveling all defences, and cover a twelve-mile front to a depth of five miles. The French penetrate on a front of six miles to a depth of six miles. German reënforcements arrive from before Verdun.

July 21-29. The British storm and level Delville Wood and take Contalmaison and Pozières and push on over the Albert-Bapaume Road northeast and occupy all of Longueval. The French meet German counter-attacks south of the Somme, establish a new line south of Soyecourt, and bombard Péronne.

INDIAN FIGHTERS WITH THE BRITISH AT THE FRONT

A Red Cross section advancing under fire to aid the wounded

CHAPTER XI

WAR'S ECHOES IN ASIA AND AFRICA—LOYALTY OF BRITISH COLONIES—REBEL-
LION IN IRELAND—THE AERIAL WAR—CASE OF MISS CAVELL—COST OF THE WAR

SCARCELY was war declared when the thunder of the German guns at Liége was echoed from every one of the four quarters of the globe. Peoples that scarcely knew whether Servia was in Europe or Asia rushed to arms as the result of the assassination of Austria's Arch Duke. Men to whom Belgium meant no more than Ooonalaska tore at each other's throats on the banks of the Yellow Sea or in the depths of the

Indian soldier in France

amerunian forests. Guns ared at Tsing-tau because oliticians at Westminster Wilhelmstrasse pulled e strings.

This fighting in far-dis- nt lands was uniformly nfavorable to Germany ainly because it was war- re in which naval force as the decisive factor, and e British navy was all owerful. But these scat- red operations were prac- ally without any effect hatsoever on the final out- me of the war. Indeed it is been suggested that it ight have been better had reat Britain, instead of ex-

pending her energies in China, Mesopotamia, and Africa concentrated all her forces upon the fighting in France where the outcome of the gigantic struggle must ulti- mately be determined. But the criticism hardly holds. The campaigns in Mesopo- tamia were needful for the protection of the East Indian frontier, and the British armies in Palestine were sent thither to guard the Suez Canal. On the China coast most of the fighting was left to the Japanese, who had a very immediate interest there, while the invasion and subjection of the German col- onies in Africa was necessary in order to furnish the Allies with captured territory to use as a set-off to the German conquests when the peace conference with its bartering should begin.

How considerable were these conquered German colonies may be judged by a state- ment made in the House of Commons by A. Bonar Law, British Colonial Sec- retary, that at that time, July 14, 1915, the Allies occupied German colonial possessions amounting to 450,000 square miles. Most of this land was in South Africa where at the beginning of the war Germany held more than a million square miles in the regions of Togoland, Kamerun, Southwest Africa, and East Africa. Wild, indeed, and with but a sparse settling of Euro- peans along the coast and the rivers, is this territory, but it is nevertheless an em- pire in the making, worth struggling for. Should the determined drives of the Allies on the plains of Flanders and the hills of Champagne be unavailing

Mr. Asquith, Prime Minister of Great Britain, photographed with his small son in his garden by Mr. Hare

Canadians crossing a newly constructed pontoon bridge at a Canadian training camp

The Annanite Troops on their way to Camp Gallieni, near Versailles

to drive the Teutons from their positions in Belgium and France, then these broad expanses of African plains and forests will in the final settlement be offered as part payment for the German surrender of their fruits of conquest. On the other hand, should the Allies clear France and Belgium by force of arms this mighty sub-tropical empire will be theirs. This is one reason why talk of peace at the end of the second year of war was discouraged in the chancelleries of the Allies.

It is impossible to describe the campaigns by which the Germans were utterly stripped of their colonial possessions. The blows of the Allies fell fast, and were of irresistible force. The colonies to go first were the insular possessions in the Pacific which were speedily taken by the colonial troops of Australia and New Zealand—destined later, in connection with the Canadians, to win fame for their prowess at Gallipoli and in Flanders under the nickname of "The Anzacs." Japan aided in stripping Germany of her Asiatic insular possessions most of which were turned over to Australia, though some naval bases, like Tsing-tau were held by the subjects of the Mikado. British and French troops together took Togoland on the north shore of the Gulf of Guinea.

A street scene in Jericho, which has changed but little in four thousand years

Southwest Africa was overrun by the Boers under General Botha, who sixteen years before had headed the Boer rebellion against British suzereignty. Kamerum—larger than France and Germany combined—and German East Africa were better prepared for defence than any other outlying station of German Imperial power. They were heavily garrisoned by both German and native troops amply equipped, and were in communication with Germany by many wireless stations. In Kamerum the campaign for subjection was conducted by the British and French in unison. Complete success was attained by the surrender of the last German post, Mora, February 18, 1916. It is believed that the captured territory will be divided equally between the victors. In German East Africa the defenders had established fortified posts all over the country defended by about 50,000 native troops with German officers. The rugged character of the terrain, the dense jungles, the narrow trails through the impermeable undergrowth held easily by a single machine gun against all comers, gave the defence a notable advantage. The attack was left to Boer troops, led by General Smuts, who, like General Botha, had been a revolutionist during the Boer War. Late in the struggle

An ancient and beautiful arch over one of Jerusalem's streets

Some of the men who conquered the Germans in Africa

Belgian and Portuguese colonies from their contiguous territory joined in the invasion. In August, 1916, southeast Africa was not entirely subdued, but the military situation there left no doubt that German authority would be obliterated by the end of the year.

But while the Germans had been losing colonies, they had been taking and holding great expanses of territory belonging to the powers with whom they were at war. The balance sheet of lost and won was not so unequal as the paragraphs on the colonial warfare would indicate. At the end of the second year of war the belligerent powers were in possession of the following extents of territories not previously classified as theirs:

The Canadian contingent was completely equipped by the Dominion government and sailed for England with horses, field guns, small arms, hospital corps, commissary equipment, ammunition and every detail ready for active service. Even a motorcycle corps for dispatch riding was included

	AREA SQUARE MILES	NORMAL POPULATION
Great Britain	2,510,000	22,000,000
Russia	412,000	5,350,000
Germany (Including Belgium, part of France, and a great area in Russian Poland)	127,000	29,000,000
France	112,600	1,800,000
Austria	31,500	3,400,000
Bulgaria	17,000	2,270,000

The patriotic enthusiasm and zeal of the Boers, who had so lately been in active war upon Great Britain, was one of a series of important incidents which united to demonstrate the great power and cohesiveness of the British Empire and the loyalty of even the most distant colonies to the mother country. Prior to this war not only did Britain's enemies hope, but her friends gravely feared, that any serious danger to her far-flung empire would be at once attended by the revolt of some of its colonies seeking independence. Such an event was confidently looked for by the Teutonic powers, and they employed every possible method of intrigue to arouse rebellion in such colonies as seemed promising for that end. Brief rebellion was indeed stirred up in British South Africa among a few of the Boers still nursing the grievance of their defeat sixteen years earlier. But it enlisted the support of but few, even of that people,

Algerians in street fight

French poilus behind Verdun, waiting to go into action

and was in fact put down by Boer troops and Boer generals. Like efforts to incite rebellion in Egypt proved utterly futile. While it is known that the Teutons relied greatly upon arousing revolution in India, and indeed planned their southern drive in Asia Minor with this end in view, no serious outbreak ever became known to the world. At the height of the German advance southward there was apparent a certain degree of nervousness in British comments on the Indian situation. But this wholly disappeared as the year wore on.

The record of Australia, New Zealand, and Canada in the war was one of unqualified loyalty, enthusiasm, and sacrifice. The

Anzacs, as the soldiers of these colonies were called, set the high-water mark for bravery and efficiency in the British lines. Volunteers all—for the conscription in England did not extend to the colonies—they came in ever increasing numbers and won the highest plaudits for their soldierly qualities.

The most serious break in the record of British loyalty occurred in Ireland. The Irish question is one that Great Britain has ever with her and that many hold will not be settled except by granting complete independence to the Irish, a majority of whom are intolerant of British dominion. At the moment war broke out Parliament had passed an Iri

The end of the charge. Bomb throwers who headed a rush on the German trenches. To do this is almost certain death, and yet there are always plenty of volunteers when the call comes

South African volunteers arriving at Cape Town

home rule bill; the Protestants of Ulster had armed themselves and threatened to resist its enforcement by arms; some British officers in high command had laid down their swords rather than coerce the Ulsterites, and many others had threatened to do likewise should the moment of action arrive. The homerulers outside of Ulster, taking the cue of their adversaries, also armed and drilled for action. The outbreak of war, August 1, 1914, stopped for the moment this threatened civil war.

The discontent of Ireland, however, was not allayed. Though a great majority of the Irish people sympathized with the Allies the irreconcilable faction led by the Sinn

A little corner of a trench showing the sand bags and steel shields used to guard against grenades, and the barbed wire entanglements that keep off infantry attacks

Fein Society, who believe that Ireland should be free and independent, seized upon the moment to plot a secession from Britain. Undoubtedly both moral and material aid was given by Germany. A picturesque figure in the revolutionary movements was Sir Roger Casement, an Irishman who had achieved prominence in the British consular service, and had been rewarded for his especial efficiency by a pension and a title. Despite these honors Casement held himself an Irishman rather than an Englishman. The war had hardly begun before he visited the United States trying to raise fund for an Irish revolutionary movement. Thence he went to

British and Germans fighting in Africa. A desperate fight in the vicinity of Mount Kilimanjaro in British East Africa

Germany where he worked in the prison camps trying to induce Irish prisoners to relinquish their allegiance and enlist in organizations to fight the Allies. He had practically no success whatsoever, and then turned to trying to stir up sedition in Ireland itself. Though

Indian soldiers on the way to the front in France

he always denied receiving monetary aid from Germany, he certainly had the assistance of her authorities in his work in the prison camps, and at the climax of his career was furnished with a German submarine to take him to Ireland, and an auxiliary cruiser laden with arms which he hoped to land. But fate was against him. He was captured in the very act of landing, April 24, 1916, and the cruiser with its cargo was sunk.

What Casement was planning was made clear when the news of his capture reached Dublin. Instantly the city was at war. Members of the Sinn Fein Society seized the General Post Office and tried to cut off all telegraphic communication with England. Armed bands seized other buildings capable of defence and soon made them into

Copyright by Underwood & Underwood
French soldiers bringing in their wounded Corporal

true forts. Streets were closed by barricades and many passersby were shot. Dublin Castle was attacked, but the rebels were beaten off. Meantime they had erected a Provisional Government, proclaimed the Irish Republic, and established a newspaper to defend their cause.

But that cause was hopeless. In a short week the Republic was snuffed out and the gallant, if misguided, men who planned it had paid for their act with their lives. A British gunboat in the Liffey shelled the republicans' fortified positions, and a large force of troops under General Sir John Maxwell cleared the streets of Dublin of the rioters. On Saturday the provisional government ordered the republican forces to lay down their arms.

In the moment of victory the British government was merciless. Fourteen republican leaders were immediately executed, seventy-three sent into penal servitude, and 1,706 deported. Roger Casement, stripped of his title, was tried for high treason and

Rookies getting down to the real
business of war

hanged in Pentonville yard. There was a wide-spread feeling that the British authorities had been wiser had they been more merciful. Certainly they left the Irish question, that has plagued them for centuries, more bitter than ever. Casement showed so many evidences of an unbalanced mind that to spare him would have seemed only an act of ordinary humanity, and the high personal character of those ordered to summary execution, without trial, certainly would have justified clemency. A certain degree of resentment was aroused in other lands and a great meeting in New York thanked "the Government of Germany for extending to Ireland as fast as the present military situation will permit the same kind of aid as was rendered to the infant American Republic by France."

French troops practicing with the rifle behind the firing line

It was but seldom, however, that the charge of deliberate inhumanity was brought against either the French or British authorities. When such a charge was made against any of the belligerents the one accused gave evidence of the potency of public opinion by the earnestness of its endeavors to disprove the charge. The case of the Red Cross nurse, Edith Cavell, put to death hurriedly and almost secretly by the German authorities in Brussels stirred the whole civilized world.

Miss Cavell, a woman of English birth, was serving as a nurse in one of the Red Cross hospitals in Brussels during the German occupation of that city. In October, 1915, she was arrested, charged with having helped many English and some Belgian soldiers to cross the line into Holland, whence some of them were able to get back to England. The offence was clearly a crime under German military law, and was admitted by Miss Cavell. But the Germans not only inflicted

Boy scout pointing through a ruined window of Whitby Abbey to the sea whence the German raiders fired

upon her the extreme penalty of death, but conducted her trial and execution in a way that shocked humanity and aroused bitter resentment in England and the United States as well. Toward the United States Minister to Brussels, Brand Whitlock, who appealed for a commutation of sentence, or at least a delay in executing it, the Germans took an attitude at once arrogant and deceptive. They concealed as long as possible the fact that sentence had been passed, and did all in their power to have the execution over before the United States Minister should know of it. Sentenced at five o'clock in the afternoon

Miss Cavell was shot dead at two the next morning. She was denied prior to the trial the opportunity to consult with her counsel —who had been designated for her by those intent upon her death—and prior to her execution she was refused a consultation with her own clergyman. Her foes provided both her legal and her spiritual advisers. In the brief space between the sentence and execution Minister Whitlock made an earnest appeal for clemency basing his right to speak upon the fact that at the moment the United States Ambassadors in London, Paris, and St. Petersburg were protecting German interests and succoring German citizens in those lands. Moreover, even then, the United States was one of the greatest forces in the work of feeding devastated Belgium—a task which by all the dictates of humanity should have been performed by Germany. None the less Mr. Whitlock's appeal was ignored and the sen-

General Ferdinand Foch, Commander of the French armies on the Somme

The Allies shipped Serbian refugees by the thousands to Corsica, where arrangements were made to shelter and feed them.   Many others were sent to Italy and some to France

tence executed without an instant's delay. In a war which has cost its millions of lives and in which innumerable women have met fates more inhuman and more frightful than that of Miss Cavell, this incident caused an expression of world-wide public condemnation vastly more vigorous than its seeming importance warranted. In the United States especially the callous indifference to the appeals of our Minister caused bitter feeling against German militarism.

There is much reason to believe that certain incidents of her submarine and aircraft warfare cost Germany more by awaking the hostility of neutrals than she gained in military advantage.   It

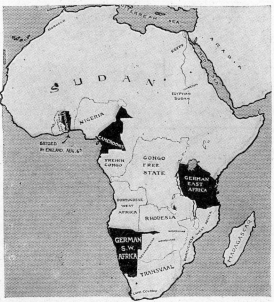

The map shows German possessions in Africa before the war.   The area of Togoland is 33,000 square miles.   Germany's other African possessions were the Cameroon Protectorate, 191,000 square miles; German Southwest Africa, 322,000 square miles, and German East Africa, 384,000 square miles.   Germany has lost practically all this territory in the war.   As the chief economic force pressing Germany into the war was the need for colonies to provide for a rapidly increasing population, the loss of this great African field will be a serious blow

was apparent enough as the months passed by that German official opinion had come to regard the sinking of the *Lusitania* as a blunder. It did not check for an hour the service of passenger ships between the United States and belligerent ports; it did not delay or reduce the shipments of munitions of war, but it did bring the United States to the verge of entrance upon the war, and build up a body of anti-German sentiment in this country that was for a time menacing. It may be noted in passing that Great Britain later by vexatious, arrogant, hurtful, and unwarrantable interference with our foreign trade and our mails did much to neutralize this senti-

M. Raymond Poincaré, President of France

Moving reënforcements toward the French trenches

ment by creating an anti-British sentiment almost as strong. Indeed while the first year of the war closed with the United States and Germany on the verge of a serious break, the second year had hardly ended when Congress, by formal legislation, authorized the

President to employ the armed forces of the nation to compel Great Britain to respect the sanctity of our mails, and cease unwarrantable interference with American commerce on the high seas.

The German use of Zeppelins, or dirigible

French reserves on the way to the trenches

General H. Joseph Jacques Césaire Joffre, who prepared the French army to meet what he considered the inevitable conflict, and is now directing the machine he created

Training Kitchener's "mob" to rush the Germans, a lesson that soon proved useful

balloons, also created a certain hostile sentiment to that nation among neutral peoples. In one respect the use of aircraft almost revolutionized strategy in this war. The aeroplanes, with which in differing types all the belligerents, after the earliest days, were about equally provided, put an end to secrecy in warfare. Scouting above the enemies' lines they detected masked batteries, noted the movement of troops, checked surprises, made cavalry scouts practically useless. No nation will ever hereafter fail to include a great fleet of flyers of the aeroplane type in its military establishment.

But the dirigibles which the Germans had brought to the point of greatest perfection in their Zeppelins have not yet proved their worth. Marvelous machines as they are, and likely to be adapted to peaceful uses after the war, they have as yet made no record of notable military achievement. It is quite true that as the Zeppelins were exclusively in German hands, and most of the avenues of publicity controlled by the Allies, a great veil of silence has been flung about some of the rumored exploits of the Zeppelins. There is no authenticated case of a Zeppelin successfully attacking a trench, a fort, or inflicting serious damage upon a battleship. Though repeated raids have been made upon England no great military base has suffered from Zeppelin bombs. Civilian property employed for peaceful uses, and civilian lives, often those of women and

Searchlight crew that helped to shoot down a Zeppelin

A caisson of high explosive shells struck, yet there was no explosion

served no imaginable military purpose, unless it has been to impress the German people that the horrors of war were being brought home to the English. As against this has been the fact that in neutral lands the Zeppelin raids have spread the idea that to Germans dropping bombs on a hospital, or killing women and children in a theatre, is worthy of national applause.

Who can estimate the cost of the War of the Nations? With precision indeed we children, have been the main victims. Along the crowded battlelines of Flanders, Picardy, Champagne, and the Verdun region the "Zeps" have done nothing. They even, for some unexplained reason, abandoned attacks upon Paris after the first months of the war. Their repeated raids upon England have can set down the amount the warring governments have borrowed, the ships they have lost, the number of square miles of territory they have ravaged, the number of human lives they have sacrificed, the number of the lame, the halt, and the blind their infernal machines of mutilation and death have

Taking captured ammunition to a place of safety

turned out to make a
miserable way through
such years of life as
are left them. But
there is no way
of estimating its
material cost in
the almost com-
plete interrup-
tion of useful
industry and
industrial prog-
ress for years,
or its æsthetic
cost in the de-
struction of the
beautiful cities
of Flanders with
their irreplace-
able monuments
of Gothic art like the
Cathedral at Rheims,
the Cloth Hall at
Ypres, the library at
Louvain, and the
Town Hall at Furnes.
The obliteration by

French poilus hastily constructing a trench

Russians and Germans, at one for once in
the devilish work of destruction, of the quaint
and picturesque towns of Poland inflicted,
too, a loss to which mere figures furnish no
adequate index. But above all the im-
measureable losses is the spiritual loss to all
mankind by the substitution of international
hatred, individual callousness to other's
agony, rough and brutal irresponsibility,
contempt for property, for beauty, for human
rights, and for human life for the kindly ideals
of peace. The virtues of war are often close
parallels to the vices of peace, while as to the
vices of war they find no parallel outside hell.

This little pile of guns represents about 200 killed and wounded

The strong man of Great Britain, David Lloyd George, Minister of Munitions in the British cabinet, is the man to whom the nation has turned in its difficulties

There are observers of the years of war in Europe who hold that their material effect is not wholly hurtful. They point to the blow struck to the liquor traffic by the stringent police measures made necessary by regard to the social welfare. Russia, by employing to the fullest its autocratic power, abolished the sale of vodka. In a report printed in the summer of 1916, M. Bark, the Russian Finance Minister, declared that everywhere in the Empire the efficiency of labor had increased, and the development of trade and industry had been unprecedented. The money formerly spent for vodka was being used for clothing and household necessities, with the result that legitimate trade was greatly stimulated, or was being saved as the sudden jump in savings deposits proved. Before the overthrow of vodka the net deposits in the national savings banks, says the Minister of Finance, amounted to from 50,000,000 to 70,000,000 roubles *annually;* after that epoch-marking order they reached the amount of 150,000,000 roubles *monthly.* The story could not be better told. On every side it is agreed that Russia will emerge from the war a strengthened nation both morally and intellectually.

In England the effort to grapple with the

Explosion of a German "Jack Johnson"

liquor question was complicated by politics, and its results, therefore, less successful. The utmost that could be effected was a material reduction in the hours during which the public houses could be opened. To the amazement of observers, however, this reduction in the hours of selling was not accompanied by any decrease in the quantity of liquor sold. It is probable that the chief material good that will be derived by England from the necessities of the war will be the extension of the field of women's work, and the greater efficiency that will spring from the systematic organization of industry. Mor-

British and French shoulder to shoulder

ally there will come to the nation, too, a certain advantage from the heavy taxation that has been levied upon large incomes. The English leisure class was undoubtedly a beautiful picture of social life, and perhaps a refining social influence. Existing, however, side by side with the squalor and abject poverty of Whitechapel and Seven Dials it was not a healthy nor a hopeful symptom. The imposition of an income tax, reaching 50 per cent. of exceedingly large incomes, will put an end to much parasitic idleness and aristocratic snobbery which had become a menace to the nation.

Scotch soldiers making barb-wire entanglements

In considering at this early date, with the end of the war not yet in sight, its cost in various ways the reader must bear in mind that the tables herewith presented are in the main estimates. No government has issued an official statement of its precise losses or expenditures during the first two years of the war. On the contrary, each one is endeavoring to minimize the degree to

Peaceful use for a rifle. At the front, where commissary arrangements are sometimes interrupted, soldiers prepare their own food. This one is grinding coffee with the butt of his rifle

which it has suffered, and to magnify the sacrifices of its enemies. But the following tables, prepared in every case by an expert student of the subject, are approximately correct—probably as nearly accurate as will be possible for some years after the war has ended:

CASUALTIES FOR TWO YEARS OF THE EUROPEAN WAR ESTIMATED AT 13,557,627

	KILLED	WOUNDED OR MISSING	TOTAL CASUALTIES
Germany	907,327	2,255,300	3,162,627
Austria-Hungary	500,000	1,500,000	2,000,000
Turkey	60,000	240,000	300,000
Bulgaria	40,000	110,000	150,000
France	800,000	1,200,000	2,000,000
Great Britain	150,000	470,000	620,000
Russia	1,000,000	4,000,000	5,000,000
Italy	35,000	140,000	175,000
Belgium	30,000	120,000	150,000
Total	3,522,327	10,035,300	13,557,627

The casualties for the first year were 8,673,805.

In the London *Economist* a writer endeavored to translate this vast expenditure of "human capital," as he called it, into terms of money. Estimating the value of each man killed at six years' purchase of his average productive value, by which process the slain Briton was valued at $3,000, the Frenchman at $2,500, and the German at $2,250, he fixed the total sacrifice of human capital for the two years of war at $7,925,000,000—and this with no allowance for sorrow, tears, and human agony which baffle the most versatile of statisticians.

Nor is the tale of sacrifice yet complete. Military authorities agree that the war is almost certain to continue for yet another year, and the statisticians fix the number of

men *and boys*, now available for
what the Germans have long
with brutal frankness called
"cannon fodder," as follows:

PRESENT EFFECTIVES

	MEN
Russia	9,000,000
France	6,000,000
Great Britain	5,000,000
Italy	3,000,000
Serbia and Belgium	300,000
Allies' total	23,300,000

	MEN
Germany	7,000,000
Austria	3,000,000
Turkey	300,000
Bulgaria	300,000
Teutonic total	10,600,000

New clothes for the fighting line

General Francis V. Greene in
an address at West Point in the
latter part of 1915 made some
striking comparisons between the
figures of this war and of earlier
conflicts in Europe and our own
country:

"The fabled stories," said General Greene,
"of the countless hordes who crossed the
Hellespont with Xerxes and Alexander have
been far surpassed by the actual numbers of
the forces engaged in the present conflict.
The figures are certainly startling. In Europe 78 per cent. of the population at war;
in all the world 56 per cent. of the population
involved in the conflict; 13,000,000 men
actually under arms; 2,000,000 killed, nearly
4,000,000 wounded, more than 2,000,000
prisoners. We cannot grasp these figures,
but we can get some idea of what they mean
by comparing them with the results of previous wars. We were accustomed to speak of
our Civil War as the greatest conflict of modern times, but apparently it was only one-
tenth the magnitude of the present conflict.

"At no time did the number of men actually under arms, north and south, exceed
1,300,000, and the total number of those
killed in battle
and died of
wounds on the
northern side
was 110,070, and
on the southern
side probably
not more than
80,000; so that
in four years of
war then the de-
struction of life
was less than
one-tenth of the
destruction of
life during a
little more than
one year at the
present time. In
the Napoleonic
wars from 1796
to 1815, the
largest army
ever assembled

French gunners and their "75." The French 75 millimetre field piece is a national pet

Thirty-two shots in two minutes is the record of this gun, one of the French 75's

WAR LOAN OF BELLIGERENTS $40,000,000,000 SINCE WAR BEGAN	
ENTENTE	
Great Britain	11,000,000,000
France	8,622,000,000
Russia	5,853,000,000
Italy	1,385,000,000
Belgium	100,000,000
Japan	28,000,000
Serbia	18,000,000
	$26,996,000,000
CENTRAL POWERS	
Germany	$9,288,000,000
Austria-Hungary	3,596,000,000
Turkey	220,000,000
	$13,104,000,000

These figures do not include extensive war credits. Estimate of expenditures of five of the Powers from the beginning of the war until January 1, 1916, are as follows:

England	$14,000,000,000
France	7,500,000,000
Germany	8,000,000,000
Austria	5,550,000,000
Italy	4,500,000,000
Total	$39,550,000,000

was that which Napoleon led into Russia in 1812, and this numbered somewhat in excess of 500,000. The German armies fighting to-day in Russia on the east and in France on the west are more than six times as large."

What the embattled nations spent in money may be partly estimated by what they had to borrow. Exact and official as these figures are in respect to the loans negotiated, they are insufficient to the total expenditures. All the countries had their "war chests" to draw upon at the outset—Germany a prodigious one which she supplemented by liberal taxes and penalties imposed upon the unfortunate towns of Belgium and France that came under German domination. But while the record of loans is not an adequate record of war expenditures it does accurately represent the burden of debt:

To these figures must be added at least $10,000,000,000 which the nations actually at war expended from their annual revenues or by their creation of paper money. Moreover, the neutral nations, forced through motives of self-preservation to mobilize their armies, have had to borrow nearly half a billion of dollars and have expended, so it is estimated, about as much more from their current exchequer. The war to-day is costing approximately $100,000,000 daily. The borrowing still continues. Such a burden of interest-bearing securities is be-

The elephant of the clouds. One of the French balloons making its descent in the air as the gas was escaping

citizen taking an intelligent interest in his country's welfare. But, important as it is, it must for the moment be regarded merely

The army passes General French in review

ing rolled up for future generations in Europe to bear upon their shoulders as the mind can hardly grasp. In the countries involved now in this terrible conflict the burden of taxation in future years merely to meet the interest account will be so heavy that it hardly seems possible for them to tax further for public improvements or purposes of general welfare. The sins of the fathers, whoever they may have been, who plunged Europe into the war will bear heavily upon the children for many generations yet to come.

At this moment it is idle to attempt to determine the ultimate influence of this war upon society, industry, and commerce in either our own country or any other in the days after the declaration of peace. That speculation should be today the subject which most engrosses the mind of the statesman or the

as speculative. Too many factors of prodigious operative force enter into the problem to make any forecast of its solution possible.

In the United States the most immediate effect of the cessation of the war is likely to be manifested in the labor market. That will be wholly disorganized. There will be a superfluity of labor in occupations of one kind, a grave stringency in another. The end of the war will mean the closing of our munitions factories, which for two years have been employing hundreds of thousands of skilled workmen, and probably the decided restriction of output in factories of another class whose products, though not technically munitions, have been demanded in illimitable quantities by the nations at war.

Prior to the war the United States had for some years demanded and assimilated

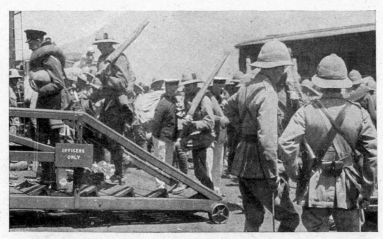

Field artillery embarking. In the South African forces Boers and British, who were a few years ago engaged in a desperate war with each other, are now fighting side by side for the British Empire

yearly a body of immigrants varying from 900,000 to 1,200,000. The latter figure was that of the year the war began. The year following the number dropped to 326,000. It is improbable that for many years to come this flood of labor will attain its former high water mark.

Upon these immigrants the United States has been almost wholly dependent for labor for its mines and upon its great outdoor construction work. They lay the roadways of our railroads and keep them in repair. They construct our great public works, irrigation systems, roads, and canals. They have been drawn largely from nations devastated

Troop trains at the dock. The South African passenger cars are on the European style

by this war, or who have taken a costly part in it. Austria-Hungary in 1914 sent us 278,000 laborers. In the year following she sent 18,000. The rest were not engaged in constructive work, but in destructive activities on the battlefield. Italy and Russia were the next largest sources of supply for our common labor market. They can be so no more, at least for many years to come. It is only reasonable to apprehend that these nations which have given so heavily of their industrious manhood to the remorseless machinery of war will after the war is ended keep the remnant of their citizens at home to take up the work of reconstruction.

The shell that killed him dug his grave. The dead man was once a German grocer in New York

The Cloth Hall at Ypres before the war. It was reputed to be one of the most beautiful buildings in Europe

The governments of Europe are not going to lose anything of their autocratic powers as a result of years of military rule. They will control absolutely the lives of their citizens after peace as they do now. Already in England, Germany, and France industry is rapidly being organized on a semimilitary basis, and not merely the remuneration and the hours of labor of the workmen are determined by the government, but even their freedom of choice of an occupation and their right to shift from one calling to another is subject to governmental regulation.

These governments are certain to prohibit their ablebodied working-men from leaving their territory during the two or three decades when the

services of every productive laborer will be essential for the rebuilding of the devastated communities. Announcement has been made in England that the emigration of men even to the British colonies will be, at least, discouraged, while the emigration to independent nations will most certainly be prohibited. Mr. A. Bonar Law, the British Colonial Secretary, said in an official address, "Whatever emigration does take place shall be within the limits of the British Empire and shall not lessen the strength of the empire as a whole." And he went on to declare that the government would

After the first bombardment. This took place early in November, 1914, and the historic structure was badly damaged by shells and fire

probably prohibit emigration to lands without the far-reaching borders of the British Empire.

It is not probable that the skilled labor of our factories which may be displaced by the end of the war demand, will be either willing or able to take the place of the unskilled day laborer whom we have been drawing from southeastern Europe. The managers of great constructive enterprises have long complained that the so-called American labor will not do this work and is indeed physically unfit for it. Huns, Magyars, Czechs, Sicilians, Sardinians and other south Italian peoples have long been doing

The second bombardment, on November 22, 1914, battered parts of the walls to pieces and fire swept the structure from end to end removing the roof

Ruined town hall at Ypres

Here are the gun and gunners that destroyed the Zeppelin L 77 with a lucky shot. The gun is a "soixante-quinze" mounted on a motor truck. The first shot hit the Zeppelin and the sixth brought it down. As the Zeppelin, all ablaze, was falling one of the crew crawled down a rope, dangling from the car, but fell when 1,000 feet above the earth. All of the crew perished

the heavy work in our mines and on our railroads. There is already a serious pinch in this labor market which has resulted in a temporary cessation of railroad building and in increased cost of production in other industries. The heads of these great enterprises are seriously disquieted over the outlook for the future and it is not improbable that demand may be made for the admission of Asiatic coolies to do the work which has heretofore been done by the European laborers who will be held at home.

Indeed there is some apprehension, based to some extent on formal reports gathered by railroad and immigration bureaus, that the insufficient supply of labor of this character that we now have may be still further reduced by the return of tens of thousands of these workers to their native countries when it shall be safe for them so to do.

Next to the labor situation the industrial community in the United States regards with the greatest apprehension the possi-

German infantryman leaving his billet for the front

The soldiers' farewell on leaving their billet

bility that the war in Europe may be followed by a trade war in which neutrals shall be even more hardly treated than they have been in the clash of armies and navies. Already a formal conference of representa-

Fort on the Bosphorous near Constantinople

tives of the Allied nations has been held in Paris at which the delegates pledged their respective countries to mutual coöperation against the Teutonic countries when peace shall have been declared and the struggle for trenches shall give way to the struggle for trade. This end it is declared is to be attained by discriminatory tariffs against foes and necessarily also against neutrals, by the abolition of the "most favored nation" clause in their treaties, by the interchange of capital, the amicable partition of trade territory and other devices which may accomplish a complete coöperation between

Sleeping under a rain of shrapnel

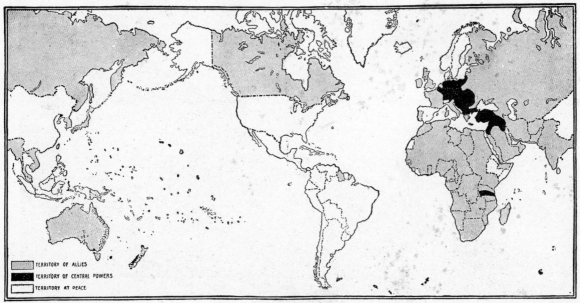

The world at the end of the second year of war. All of the German colonies have been conquered except a narrowing strip in the middle of German East Africa. The black area is that now held by the Central Powers; the shaded belongs to the Entente Allies; neutral countries are white

TERRITORY OF ALLIES
TERRITORY OF CENTRAL POWERS
TERRITORY AT PEACE

one set of nations for their advantage and for the undoing of all outside their combination. Opinions differ as to the extent to which such combinations can be made permanently effective. Natural law tends to break them down. Business competition is hard to control by combinations made wholly for the general good. Nevertheless the menace is sufficiently serious to the United States to have led Congress to take

Giant tractor used by the English in Greece to transport heavy guns and supplies

The great British armored tank or caterpillar. Much of the reported success of the Allies on the western front is attributed to the "Tanks" of this type. This steel-protected monster crosses streams, climbs hills, veritably spans chasms. On each side of the gigantic armored machine are batteries of rapid-fire guns. There also are loopholes fore and aft through which machine-gun fire is literally poured in the path of the land battleship. Two wheels in front have no connection with the "tank"

certain preliminary steps for meeting it, and to have caused both the State and the Treasury Departments to discuss it seriously from the standpoint of international law and obligations, and that of the power to restrict or encourage trade by tariff legislation.

But even if the attempt to bolster up at American expense the industry and trade of the belligerent nations by methods of governmental regulation should fail the

getting a longer work day by setting the clocks ahead one hour has been successfully tried. In the field of distribution municipal market places, the regulation of prices, the careful control by the government of supplies and distribution have been adopted in every country. The minimum wage and other social legislation which prior to the war was looked upon as rank socialism have all found place on the statute books as matters of military necessity.

The *U*-53 as she appeared at Newport when she stopped here on Saturday, October 7, 1916. Members of the crew can be seen on the deck of the submarine

new conditions of industry in countries like France, Great Britain, and Germany are such as to threaten the United States with extremely effective competition. To support the war it has been necessary in all these countries to put industry on almost a military basis. All have found it essential to get out of every workman his utmost productive capacity; out of every shilling, franc, or mark its highest return as productive capital. We have seen England reduce the drink evil to a minimum, Russia and France as well. The hours of labor in France, Germany, and England have practically been put under government control, and in the latter country the drastic regulation for

Accordingly the nations with whom we must compete when peace comes are as ready for that competition as Germany was for the stern struggle of war when she first moved upon stricken Belgium and half-prepared France. With them efficiency has been the rule for three years of struggle. With us the happy rule has been the long-accustomed go-as-you-please system of American industry. Perhaps more than military preparedness this question of industrial and commercial preparedness for the war for markets and trade supremacy should engage the attention of American thinkers to-day.

No writer upon the war can be justified at the present moment in predicting its outcome. The strength of Germany has been and still is amazing. It is obvious that but for her marvelous military and material resources the whole fabric of the Teutonic alliance would have long ago gone to pieces before the assaults of its enemies. How long Germany can carry tottering Austria-Hungary and bankrupt Bulgaria and Turkey it is impossible to conjecture. Enough at this moment to say that as the first year of the war ended with virtually all its victories to be credited to the German arms and with the Teutons everywhere conducting a spirited offensive against the Allies who were fighting for time, the end of its second year presented the situation absolutely reversed. To-day confidence rests with the Allies. Their troops have become superior in number and equipment. They are everywhere attacking the Teutons who in their turn are wholly on the defensive. If, as Napoleon cynically said, "God is on the side of the heaviest battalions," the issue of the war cannot much longer remain in doubt.

THE END

THE COUNTRY LIFE PRESS, GARDEN CITY, N. Y.